**KNOWSLEY LIBRARY SERVICE**

Please return this book on or before the date shown below

2 2 AUG 2008

- 1 OCT 2010

WITHDRAWN

MR HARDIE

MR HARDIE

Henry Archer

The Book Guild Ltd
Sussex, England

Knowsley Library Service	
3 804326733664	
Askews	18-Dec-2003
347.401409	
1262818	

First published in Great Britain in 2003 by
The Book Guild Ltd
25 High Street
Lewes, East Sussex
BN7 2LU

Copyright © Henry Archer 2003

The right of Henry Archer to be identified as the author of this work has been asserted by him in accordance with the Copyright, Designs and Patents Act 1988.

All rights reserved. No part of this publication may be reproduced, transmitted, or stored in a retrieval system, in any form or by any means, without permission in writing from the publisher, nor be otherwise circulated in any form of binding or cover other than that in which it is published and without a similar condition being imposed on the subsequent purchaser.

The publishers acknowledge the kind permission of Sybille Bedford to use parts of the account – the sole extant account it is believed – of Mr Hardie's second tangled weave in her novel *Jigsaw*.

Typesetting in Times by
Keyboard Services, Luton, Bedfordshire

Printed in Great Britain by
Antony Rowe Ltd, Chippenham, Wiltshire

A catalogue record for this book is available from
The British Library

ISBN 1 85776 752 7

*'Oh! What a tangled web we weave
When first we practise to deceive.'*

Marmion, Sir Walter Scott

PREFACE

There should perhaps be some explanation of why I have decided, so long after his death in 1993, to publish my husband's book, which he was still working on two days before he died. The book had taken some years in the writing and was virtually finished, apart from the manuscript being in a state of chaos and with four different endings to choose from.

I took it out of his desk several times and always put it away again, not wanting to meddle with his story. Then two years ago I began reading it again, and when I had finished I knew I must get it into print. It was so obvious that he wanted that more than anything, and I had, after all, 'researched' some of the material and knew the story backwards. So much about the private life of Henry McCardie had been destroyed when he died, and given the great distance in time, few of those who would have known him were around any more. But a great deal did come to light – much of it from the McCardie family, and from many other sources. The story inevitably is incomplete and some tantalising questions about Henry McCardie's life remain unanswered. Nevertheless, my husband told his story as fully as he could. By any standards it is a remarkable and interesting story, and also historically significant. It is a tribute to his personal qualities that my husband emerged with such integrity and distinction, and with such a joyous attitude to life.

I would particularly like to thank Sybille Bedford for her help, and for her encouragement when it was most needed.

I would also like to thank Conrad Dehn for reading the manuscript, and for his helpful comments.

Elizabeth Archer 2003

FOREWORD

In the garden of a holiday bungalow my mother and Mr Hardie are sitting in deck chairs. It must be the nineteen twenties. Tea is over: its remains lie on a low table between them, patrolled by a solitary wasp. The afternoon seems endless – it tastes of seed-cake. There is a vague smell of Virginia stock and tobacco; the drowsy chitter of sparrows; in the distance the clang of a tram. Sprawled on my back I stare up at the sky, lacing and unlacing my fingers to make a pattern against its untroubled blue. Sunlight winces and sparkles through the shivery leaves of the poplars which line one side of the garden. Their shadow is beginning to creep over the grass: already it is faintly damp. My golliwog lies flopped beside me. I pick him up and hurl him across the lawn, angry with him because I am angry with Mr Hardie. Mr Hardie is my father, but I don't know that. I know that I don't see him often and I am jealous of the attention he is giving to my mother. 'Poor Golly,' she murmurs. I don't trouble to respond. She is only trying to curry favour, she doesn't care twopence about Golly, or about me.

Mr Hardie goes on smoking his cigarette. The smoke curls up in the still air and then mysteriously slips away. The afternoon, which seemed to promise so much, is slipping away too. A sad procession of empty afternoons stretches ahead. I long to do something violent, but I can't think what. Why do they go on talking, talking? What on earth can they find to talk about? What *do* they do with themselves?

How the bruises still ache, how many hopes have been deceived! A scar on my knee, a bit of old circuitry in my skull, is all that's left of that skinny, sulky, solitary little boy, but I still trail his ghost about with me. He'll have no dwelling place when I'm gone too, unless I tell his story; and, more important, the story of my father entwined with it. My father was a remarkable man, full of surprises, and he left so suddenly. I owe him a special duty of remembrance.

Going back into the past, it is sometimes difficult to resist the temptation to interfere, warning and scolding the shadowy actors. They in their turn look askance at us. My father left no papers, I kept no diaries, and people, now dead, whom I could have consulted had I been less inhibited, might well have gainsaid some of the things that I think I remember. When we know what happened afterwards, we can't hope to recapture experience exactly as it was. But I've tried to be as truthful as I can.

I
BAR SINISTER

'Vous êtes nègre?'
'Oui, mon Général.'
'Alors, continuez, mon enfant.'

One

I was conceived towards the end of May, 1918. Not, alas, under its darling buds, but in Queen Anne's Mansions, a large apartment block, since demolished, which overlooked St James's Park. My father had a bachelor flat there. He had leased another for my mother. He was forty-eight years old and had been appointed a Judge of the High Court some eighteen months before. She was thirty-one, the only daughter and fourth child of a railway porter. They never married.

Failure to honour this customary rite might not be of much consequence today, when the unmarried mother is almost regarded as virtuous, a paragon of the welfare state. But it certainly mattered then, at any rate where I was; appearances still had to be kept up – men didn't like to be seen in public without their hats. I suspect it still matters more than is commonly supposed. During my early life I was deeply ashamed of it; and what agonies of shame a child can experience!

No-one ever told me I was illegitimate, but I was soon aware that all was not normal. Although there were boys at my school whose mothers were war widows and in that sense fatherless, they'd had a father, but lost him, whereas I apparently had no father at all. I was a parent short. We all have some need to put on an act, small boys most of all, and here was I for a start with only half the props that other boys had. I didn't ask anyone to explain this deficiency. You would think I'd have asked my mother, but no. I took it for granted, as little children do; and when I got bigger and could take it for granted no longer, it seemed a bit late to bring the matter up. I was left to nurse a recurring fear that I shouldn't be on the stage at all, that I was an extra, unwanted; or caught in the first-class with a third-class ticket. I've never quite managed to shake the feeling off.

The syndrome is common enough and it would be wrong to make too much of it. Life went on, and was often very funny; and mostly I forgot about it among the play of everyday sensations and ideas. But it was always there; and in adolescence, when the sense of identity is dislocated anyway, I became piercingly conscious of the gap between what was expected of me and who I was, ambushed sometimes in long lonely summer evenings by a meaningless despair. Winter, paradoxically, was more supportable because I seemed to be missing less. I suppose a black man in a white world may experience something of the same discomfort.

Launched at a different time or into a different class, I might not have been ashamed to be a bastard. After all –

> No sickly fruit of faint compliance he,
> But stamp in Nature's mint of extasy!

Thus Dr Johnson's friend, Richard Savage, who was one. I doubt if he was quite as chuffed as he pretends – he lays it on suspiciously thick. There could be consolation in being a 'love child', but most such children are accidental, not desired. I almost certainly was. Possibly for this reason – and the fact that the best kind of father may be the one who's rarely there – I've never experienced the slightest oedipal twinge. It brought another advantage, too. Many children dream that their real parents must be much more splendid than the awful ones they're saddled with. In my case, the dream became half true. This didn't do away with my sense of separateness, but made it more tolerable.

Savage dedicated his poem 'with all due reverence' to his mother, Mrs Brett. Whether Mrs Brett found it reassuring, I don't know. Perhaps she didn't need reassurance; they took these matters more robustly in the eighteenth century. But my mother, Mayna, lived in a more prudish age. She was ashamed, not of me, but of her predicament. She didn't, I'm sure, feel that what she'd done was wrong – she was not religious, she had no sense of sin. She never blamed my father; she never ceased to love him; she would not hear anything against him, except when she laughed at him herself, which she often did. She was profoundly conscious, however, of having offended against society at the point where its pretensions are most tender – the bottom of the lower middle class. In London it was different; no-one knew her there. But when she came back to Norfolk with her baby she felt ostracised. And ostracised she certainly was (and so was I) by my father's family when, later on, they learned of our existence. As the years went by, she retreated into herself until, towards the end of her life when her sight was failing, she became almost a recluse. Even then, under a rather formidable *tenue*, her gay young self still bubbled away. But it was a buried talent.

She might have been consoled to know that another unmarried mother, Rebecca West, had lived a few streets away and given birth there to Anthony, the son of H.G. Wells, on the day the Great War broke out. Anthony West, sent away to school even earlier than I was and born of parents so deplorably articulate, not surprisingly had an even larger chip on his shoulder.

Two

I don't know how my mother came to be called Mayna. Perhaps it was a pet name my father invented (it was certainly a blessing for she was christened Mabel Maud). Nor do I know when they first met – some years at least before that fateful spring embrace in Queen Anne's Mansions; it wasn't a single wayward womb-shot that brought me down. I still have some books of verse inscribed by my father: *'To M.M.A., February 1915'*. This doesn't suggest great intimacy at the time, but in the matter of personal disclosure he was a cautious man, though wildly reckless, as it turned out, in other ways. He was cautious about me, too. When I first lisped his name, it came out as 'Mr Hardie' and he was happy to assume this alibi.

Mayna was Norfolk-born. Her mother kept a boarding house in the infant seaside resort of New Hunstanton. My father, then a highly successful barrister overloaded with briefs, had formed the habit of coming down to Hunstanton for the week-end. Convenient through trains ran from London; he liked the quietness and the keen east coast air; and he played golf at the local club, which he joined in 1908, or at Brancaster. He found it convenient to take a week-end flat in Seagate, the road where Mayna's mother had her boarding house. Later he was to move to the Sandringham Hotel, more consonant with his increasingly prodigal life style.

His first encounter with my mother may well have been – unromantic thought – on the station platform, a bleak expanse where gales whistled off the sea. There is a story that on his first visit to Hunstanton he asked a porter where he might stay. The porter was Mayna's father and suggested his wife's place.

However they met, Mayna was the sort of girl to take the eye, slim, dark-haired, wilful, almost beautiful, with high cheek bones and long hair like a docile tide. My father, a stocky, vigorous man, moody sometimes but of great charm and strong temper, was easily susceptible: he liked women, but on his own terms, shying away from any formal commitment. He liked extremely what he saw of Mayna and his liking was returned. Soon she was passionately in love. In what fashion their affair proceeded I have no knowledge. I didn't ask and Mayna never told. The flat in Seagate offered distinct possibilities; but severe logistical problems must have stood in the way of intimacy, no doubt giving their love-making an added piquancy. Their association would not have gone unnoticed; Hunstanton was a small town where gossip thrived. No-one could have supposed that he intended to marry her; the society of the time was nothing if not profoundly snobbish, and his family, to whom he was a nonpareil, would have had a fit! Her parents were humble, to say the least; embarrassingly so. Somehow they'd managed to send her to a local private school, where her Norfolk accent had been sponged away and she had learned to play the piano and acquired an elegant cursive hand. But her education was limited and her knowledge of the world even more so. He was over fifteen years older, talented, successful, sophisticated, used to rubbing shoulders with the wealthy and influential, a bachelor ripe for the plucking in the discreet orchards of the better class.

Forbidden fruit in Seagate, though, and out of reach. The old jingle comes to mind: 'She was poor, but she was honest, victim of a rich man's crime.' It wasn't like that at all; I suspect it rarely is. It was a willing, happy seduction based on a strong mutual attraction and full of tenderness and warmth. Mayna was certainly not his only conquest, nor his first, nor perhaps the one closest to his heart, and I have sometimes wondered whether their relationship would have persisted had I not arrived upon the scene. Who knows? Arrive I did, and the tenderness and warmth continued until his death: I can testify to it. Mayna, of course, was dazzled, enraptured. For him the attraction was primarily sexual – which is not to disparage it. But it was more than that. She was game and innocent, naked to life, emotionally ardent though perhaps sensually less so. Proud, too. Untutored and without the slightest interest in ideas, she was intelligent and quick to see the funny side. He needed someone to confide in. With a multitude of acquaintances, he had no close friends. Mayna provided him with sympathy and intuitive understanding, even if half the time she didn't really understand. He liked singing and they sang together. She adored the luxury he was able to give her: she scarcely did a hand's turn all her life. She gave him a simple, uncritical love – something he had not received from his mother, a woman of great strength of character, ambitious for her children and difficult to live up to. Mayna made no demands. Her lips were soft (I remember how soft they were); the sunsets burned on the water; the gulls rode on the wind; the gold sovereign was solid in the pocket; the bustle of London and the Courts miles away. The Great War had not yet dug its terrible ditch...

So Mayna became, in the parlance of the time, his mistress. The term 'mistress' sounds misleading, for she was in most ways very conventional and as far removed from the accepted idea of a mistress, just as he, having prospered in one of the most conventional of professions, was in fact very unconventional. The Italians have a better word to describe her status – *mantenuta*. She was *una mantenuta* – a position which, until the day of his death, she was content to retain.

The war when it came doesn't seem to have touched them much. He brought her up to London and installed her in a flat near his own in Queen Anne's Mansions. She had her hair bobbed. She would go to him at the end of the day. He bought her evening dresses and handbags and jewellery and she wore them when she went to him; but he never took her out to dinner or the theatre, presumably lest he might meet acquaintances or friends and have to account for her. Often he dined out, generally he would be away for the week-end. She led an isolated life – she told me how she would sit alone in St James's Park on winter afternoons wrapped in a cloak to hide the swell of her pregnancy – but she seems not to have wanted or expected more from him. Which was perhaps as well. À propos his recent appointment as a Judge, he remembered, a little tactlessly in the circumstances, that he was 'bored stiff by having nothing to do in the evenings'.

What were her feelings when she became pregnant? Again, I never asked her, and no letters survive. All her letters to my father were destroyed when he died; and she kept only one of his letters to her, and that by chance – ironically it was a request for money! (She didn't keep any of the hundreds of letters I wrote to her, either; she cut us both down to size.) So I can only speculate. Was she appalled, or did she secretly welcome the planting of the seed? Was she tempted, did she try, to get rid of the child, or was she determined to have it? I saw Queen Anne's Mansions only from the outside, and it looked a gloomy place to ponder a nativity. As likely as not she was pressed by my father to seek an abortion. This was a matter on which he held firm opinions which he expounded with increasing vigour and which he must then have felt to be only too well-founded. It was lamentably easy to foresee the complications that would arise when this embryo got to its legs and started asking questions. My race for existence could well have been a close-run thing: I'm glad I made it in the end.

At this critical moment, Mayna later told me, my father offered to marry her. She refused him. Common sense told her that he would have been no good as a husband; he wasn't cut out for the long haul of marriage; he wouldn't have 'weathered' properly, any more than he did as a Judge, for all his gifts. She was also deeply conscious of her own deficiencies and she hadn't met a single one of his friends, let alone his family. She might know little of the world she would have had to move into, but she knew enough to realise how that world would treat her. To be exposed to the quiet cruelty of a rigid class system, to be ignorant of so many topics of social discourse at functions and dinner parties to which she would be invited, would have been a harsh and lonely ordeal for an unsophisticated working-class girl already with child, much worse for her than for him, as he must have realised. Though she was well-spoken and could have had a better stab at it than she supposed, she knew she would have been found wanting in the end and her loving relationship with him destroyed. He would never have forgiven her. Whether either of them gave any thought to my own future view of the matter, I doubt. It might console them to know that I back her decision to the hilt. Marriage would have been a disaster and I should have been left clinging to the wreckage. I do sometimes reflect, though, how different my life would have been if the decision had gone the other way.

So Mayna departed, without the comfort or constriction of a wedding ring, to Bournemouth to have her baby. It seems a strange place to choose – that piney haunt of bath chairs and tea-shops. But there she went, and there I was born under the watery sign of Pisces at No. 2 Wellington Road on Friday 28 February, 1919. (My father, strange to say, was also born in a road of the same name.) Appropriately, the weather was dull, showery and cold.

The papers still carried lists, only short ones now, of those who had been killed in action or died of wounds. Although the Courts were sitting, my father was not in his place. Presumably he was also in Bournemouth. When, however, Mayna went to report my arrival to the local Registrar on 2 April, the spaces in his register for the name and rank or profession of father were left blank. How deafeningly those blanks banged off whenever I was called on to submit my birth certificate!

Three

I remember being wheeled in my pushchair down a tree-lined lane. Above my head leaves twinkled in the sun. I can still picture that lane. It has gone now, replaced by a tarmac road. Where was it? In Hunstanton, I'm afraid, for Mayna returned with me from Bournemouth to live with her parents. Now, however, it was in a different house. The boarding house in Seagate was abandoned and, with my father's aid, we were ensconced in a corner property at the top of Westgate, formerly Shinglepit Road. Called for some reason 'Stratton House' – which, like the name Westgate, made the place seem much more distinguished than it really was – it had been built in 1894 out of a local brown stone known as carstone. Either the stone was porous or the house was badly made, for it was always damp.

A little further down on one side stood the local council school, the old 'board school', with its asphalt playground. Beyond that was the police station. Opposite was a large convalescent home for children. Every afternoon the street would echo with their cries, reinforced in term time by yells from the council school. Across the way on Westgate was a garage, where my father arranged to install in one of their private lock-ups a two-seater Wolseley car in which Mayna used to drive him about. There was no driving test in those days, and no synchromesh, and a drive with Mayna was a hair-raising as well as an ear-splitting experience. Private cars were then relatively rare on country roads, with only an occasional Clyno or bull-nosed Morris to be seen; traffic consisted mainly of milk carts and farm wagons and an infrequent lorry or bus. At one point there was a spate of Trojan vans which were chain-driven and made a distinctive, tinny noise. Mayna must have been one of the earliest members of the AA and, perched up in the dicky at the back, I used to take as a personal tribute the salute we got when we passed an AA scout on his yellow motor-bike. My father never touched the wheel and showed remarkable courage as a passenger. But I'm jumping ahead. All this didn't happen until some years later – about 1925, I suppose.

Our household consisted of my grandfather and grandmother, Mayna and myself. A plump girl named Eva, who smelt vaguely of Hudson's soap, came in to clean three mornings a week. My grandmother did the cooking – a solid, suety old-fashioned diet which, according to modern theories, should have been a disaster. But my grandparents, like other Victorians, seemed to thrive on it. My grandfather smoked like a chimney as well. Mayna took care of me, and developed a passion for doling out, on top of all the other food, a sticky malt extract called Virol, which I absorbed in quantities that must have done me lasting harm. She was not demonstrative and rarely hugged me, so lack of physical contact may have harmed me more than the Virol. But I remember sometimes being taken into her bed and snuggling up to her huge, comforting body: warm hills and valleys under the satin nightdress.

Until I went away to school, this made up my human world apart from regular visits from Mr Hardie – whom I regarded as an immensely benevolent stranger – and rare short visits from Mayna's three brothers, Ernest, Fred and George, and even rarer and shorter ones from their wives and children or, in George's case, his consort, Queenie, and her children, of whom only some, if any, were his. There may have been – there must have been – more distant Norfolk relatives living not far away. If so, I can't (with one exception) recall any. The other set of relations I would otherwise have seen, my father's, were notably absent. But, since I had no inkling of their existence, I didn't miss them.

Mr Hardie excepted, my early experiences were therefore limited to the Archer family, whose name I took. A good English soubriquet, though sullied since by being attached to an interminable radio serial and some very bad novels. However, I did share my father's first name, Henry. My grandfather was also named Henry. When I knew him, he was in his seventies. The son of a farm bailiff, he had earned his living first as a labourer and latterly, as I've mentioned, a railway porter. He must have been one of the early employees on the line between King's Lynn and Hunstanton (which we pronounced Huns'ton). This line, now torn up, had been constructed at the beginning of the eighteen sixties and was one of the cheapest ever built, costing only £3,000 a mile. It ran along the edge of the Wash over flat infertile heath all the way: heather and then marsh stretched gloomily towards the sea. For someone of my grandfather's placid temperament it provided an ideal setting, in which an overturned milk churn or a lost valise constituted an emergency. The train stopped at every station, including Wolferton, the royal station for Sandringham, where the stop was presumably a gesture of obeisance since nobody ever appeared to get on or off. The journey from Lynn seemed interminable. How Mr Hardie managed to stand it week-end after week-end is astonishing. The only flicker of pleasure it ever generated in me was the arrival on the homeward run at Heacham, the last station before Huns'ton, at night in the war in winter. A porter would hurry up and down the platform with a lantern shouting: 'Change hair for Dockin', Burnham and Wells,' the engine hissed, steam curled into the frosty air from the hoses between the carriages and, when I lowered the window and leaned out, I could hear the distant breathing of the sea and sniff its briny, twiny smell tinged with engine smoke.

Mayna's three brothers all worked for the railway – the old

LNER – but it was Uncle George who took the palm. He was an engine driver. Think of that! Whenever I went by train I used to run up to see the engine before the journey started in the hope he would be there, my hero on the footplate, wiping his hands nonchalantly with an oily rag. And when I got the chance I would hang over the railway bridge waiting for a train to roar underneath, its carriages trailing after it like a string of scraggy cows behind a bellowing bull, and engulf me in a gritty cloud of smoke and steam. But I never caught sight of Uncle George. I would have adored to climb up on the engine with him. If I hadn't been sent away to school so early, I might have managed it; but every school holiday I had to start again from scratch and my pleas were always ignored. I knew why. George drank. He became unmanageable on Saturday nights. Once he had struck my grandfather. My grandfather had forgiven him, but my grandmother had not. George fornicated as well. This was a less heinous offence; he was nevertheless judged in the matter much more severely than my father, who was a gentleman and knew no better. George wasn't a gentleman and should have done. Above all, George had been a favourite son who'd let his mother down. She kept a picture of him in the parlour, painted when he was a young man by some visiting artist. It was a striking portrait: bold brown eyes, sensuous curling mouth, coal-black hair. The loss of such an insolent and gipsy charm must have been hard to bear – he became puffed and portly and somewhat sly, and he suffered from bronchitis made worse by his habit of going off with his spaniel to shoot duck in winter on the marshes. She didn't think George was fit company for me; and she disliked Queenie, whom she regarded as a tart. Mayna backed her up. Mayna was very prim about George, although the high moral line she took hardly became her. But I never travelled with him on the footplate and he died from his bronchitis one November when I was away at school.

My grandfather was entirely governed by his wife. She was

very fond of him – she couldn't help it, he was a lovable man – but he also infuriated her because, by lying low, he escaped her. He passed no judgements, had no ambition and seemed to have no worries. 'Hurry' was a word unknown to him; there was about him a sense of total placidity. He wore a beard like Edward VII's, grey and faintly stained with nicotine. I can't recall his voice, perhaps because he said so little, giving me affection untrammelled by advice. He had a little white dog who seemed more ancient than he was. The two of them sat for hours together by the fire in the parlour, a small room off the kitchen, the dog breathing heavily and my grandfather smoking his pipe. Periodically they would both lie back and drop off. On the mantelpiece, beside the tobacco jar and the candlesticks, stood a black marble clock which had been presented to him when he retired with the rank of foreman porter from the railway service.

When I was still very small he fixed to the wall by the fire a wooden box from which he hung the round lid of a tin of St Julien's Mixture, the tobacco he commonly smoked. We used to pretend that this was a telephone or a wireless set – a crystal set in those days – and that we talked to each other through it. My cousin Gil, who was a year or two older than I was and clever with his hands, had made a real crystal and, when he came down soon afterwards, he taunted me about my wooden box and pulled it off the wall. My grandfather was angry and rebuked him. Later he put the box back, but our talks through the tin lid of St Julien were never quite the same again.

Not that we said much. I had a limited vocabulary and my grandfather was not a loquacious man. He wasn't much of a reader, either. His only serious reading was the *Daily Mail*, and *The People* on Sundays. He read these slowly, for he had received virtually no education. In fact he taught himself to read. There had been no compulsory schooling in his day and boys from the labouring classes were expected to start earning when they were five or six years old. At that age he was sent to earn a few pence bird-scaring – an isolated, monotonous job. Thomas Hardy's Jude had also been put to it at the age of six, scaring rooks from Farmer Troutham's land; and there is a fine Victorian picture by Sir George Clausen called *The Bird Scarer* which conveys something of what it must have meant for a young boy to be sent out by himself into the frozen fields from dawn to dusk. One afternoon my grandfather came home early because there was a partial eclipse of the sun and he thought it was evening. For this he was beaten. It was the one experience in an unfair world which still rankled with him. Otherwise he accepted life's buffets with equanimity and, by lying low, avoided most of them. But not all. For instance, he was allergic to mussels, which he loved to eat. And when his old dog had to be put down, he wept. And so did I.

He was responsible for the garden around Stratton House. For a short while he kept hens on a bald patch of wired-in earth in front of the coal shed – I have a vague memory of seeing them scratching about. Their clucking was a restful sound. I don't know whether they were felt to be inconsistent with the dignity of our transition from Seagate to Westgate, but they didn't last long. My grandfather planted loganberries and an apple tree instead and grew flowers – wallflowers and sweet peas and lupins and night-scented stock. The stock seemed to smell more fragrant and the loganberries to taste sweeter than they do now.

But the allotment was where he liked to be. He had his own hut there which he'd knocked up from driftwood and orange boxes and old railway sleepers. At one time he reared a pig. He and his mates, who were gathered round him in similar huts, practised recycling and ecology long before these words were invented. In summer when the weather was kind they sat outside their huts in clapped-out armchairs and surveyed their runner beans.

The allotment was about half a mile away, where the Lynn road broke free of the town and began to dip down Redgate Hill, near one of the two brick water towers with which the town was then endowed. One tower was square and crenellated like a castle, the other round with a bulge at the top like an erect phallus. Why two towers? Why were they shaped like this? I never found out. The tower by the allotment was the one of lesser interest, the square one. It dominated the skyline and, when the wind was right, you could hear the water gurgling about inside. It seemed to exert a malign influence and made the allotment, from which we had a full-frontal view of the gas works, seem on certain days peculiarly bleak. Nevertheless I liked to go up there with my grandfather and his dog. Sometimes, when he wasn't carrying up supplies or household compost, I was allowed to ride in his barrow. He didn't say much, but I felt the warmth of his companionship. This meant more to me than I realised for I was a lonely little boy.

After he died and my grandmother went permanently into black, this loneliness became more acute. It did not present itself as loneliness, but rather as a kind of grief which flooded in upon me from the outside world so that I felt totally lost. I had no name for it; it was too deep for tears, it was just the way things were, to be accepted without question. But it had a voice. Its voice was the wail of the wind in the telephone wires at the top of Redgate Hill on a February day. I can hear that sound still. It told of some irreparable absence; but what, I did not know.

Four

If I'd been able to frame words for the desolation that regularly swept over me and summoned up courage to blurt them out, my grandmother would have given me short shrift. She had few orthodox grandmotherly qualities. Physical pain and discomfort she could accept, but she had no patience with complaints of a more esoteric kind, like being unhappy. If you were unhappy it was your duty to make the best of it and turn your mind to something useful instead. In the hard school she'd been brought up in, people didn't worry about happiness, but about survival. Grub first, dreams after.

She was born in January 1854, the year the battle of Balaclava was fought. She was small and very determined. All her life she got up early and worked hard. Her habit of industry was invincible – a habit which her husband and her daughter wisely never acquired. Her father, John Large, was a farm labourer, probably illiterate. Her mother, Jemima, certainly was and signed with a cross when she registered the birth. They made their home at Titchwell, near Brancaster (where my father later played golf), some three hours' walk along the coast from what was to become New Hunstanton, past the end of the Peddar's Way, the old green road to Norfolk. The nearest town of any size was Lynn, with a population of some 15,000. On the map it's called King's Lynn, but no Norfolk man worth his salt ever put the word 'King's' in front of it. A visit to the annual Lynn Mart – a springtime fair of national importance in the Middle Ages – was the highlight of the year. It was quite a journey from Titchwell. The railway wasn't extended from Lynn to Hunstanton till my grandmother was seven. Most people walked, along roads full of dust in summer and mud-sodden in winter. Walking was the ordinary way of getting about, unless you were lucky enough to have your own pony trap or could hitch a lift on a wagon or the carrier's cart. Heavy traffic went by sea. Small villages along the coast, like Blakeney and Wells, now the haunt of old salts from Solihull and other week-end sailors, were thriving ports which handled not only fishing boats but sailing ships of thirty to forty tons, of about the same capacity as large lorries today, bringing in cargoes of coal, timber, manufactured goods and the like and taking out agricultural produce.

The Larges brought up their family in circumstances that no-one would be prepared to put up with now. Only by endless drudgery could Jemima feed and clothe her children and raise them in fair decency. Their tied cottage would have no sewage or piped water; gas and electricity were unheard of; kitchen utensils were made of iron. Wages for men were pitifully low and their working hours intolerably long. Husbandry was still traditional. With the exception of the threshing machine, the tools employed were little different from those of 1764; the reaping machine 'with its splendidly painted sails' only came into widespread use some years later. Wives and children had to help on the land, too. Besides bird scaring, there was stone clearing after the ploughing, 'charlocking' (weeding) when the crops began to grow, planting and picking potatoes, gleaning after the harvest. Back-breaking work. And, as their lives came towards the end, many of the poor were haunted by fear of the Relieving Officer and the workhouse, a great square brick building, grim as a prison, at Docking, where in their last days husband and wife were cruelly separated.

It would be wrong, though, to paint too dark a picture. The eighteen fifties and sixties were a golden age of English agriculture, before cheap grain began to pour in from North America. The immemorial rhythms of the natural world, the teams of horses in the fields, the changing seasons, the self-sufficient community of the village, provided deep if limited satisfactions for farm workers and their families. Life was centred round a few familiar fields and hamlets. Most had a piece of ground for their own use and some access to common land. The pleasures of life, being rarer, were sharper. There was plenty of laughter about. I think of my grandmother as old and bad-tempered; but she was once a girl and danced in muslin.

I wish I had written down what she told me about her childhood. She spoke out of the lost hours of the day, seldom recorded; and she spoke about a past seen, not from the top or the middle, as it usually is, but from the bottom. She taught me respect for the men and women engaged in apparently unskilled labour in their homes and in the fields. They may not have been readers of books, but they weren't fools. Class distinctions were courteously observed, but with a healthy scepticism. If they doffed their caps, they did so in the way a soldier salutes an officer – deference paid to rank, not to the individual unless he deserved it, and not because they believed he was inherently superior. They didn't want or expect much, they didn't *get* much; but, since it is wants and expectations that above all create a sense of poverty, they were not discontented; and the surroundings of natural beauty they lived among kindled a steady glow of consolation through the eye. They knew how to endure, and how to enjoy themselves. Two generations later I learned the value of these virtues: I've tried to stick things out and done my best to muster up a fair imitation of having a good time. But I haven't made much of a fist at it, perhaps because I got off to an uneasy start.

Although they were married and buried according to the rites of the Church of England, religion played little part in my grandparents' lives – or in Mayna's. (Or, for that matter, in my father's, except for a persistent hostility to the Roman Church, which was heartily reciprocated.) Respectability was a different matter, of course, and it seems strange that my grandmother, as a shrewd and prudent woman, didn't take steps to warn her daughter against my father. Perhaps she did – too late. At first there probably seemed no need. He was a barrister and therefore honourable. That he should be taken with her pretty daughter, that her daughter's face should light up at the sight of him, was understandable: these things were common enough. They are likely to have met secretly and, once their relationship became serious, it was too much to expect her mother to warn him off, whatever strict morality might require. No doubt she, too, was captivated by him and a little intimidated; she may even have persuaded herself that the bond might be legitimised. My grandfather could be expected to take his usual indolent line. Whatever arguments and heart-searching took place in the boarding house in Seagate, they were resolved without an open break. Evidently my father wasn't going to desert Mayna. He was charming and reasonable, free-spending, unfailingly generous; and it was a relief after all for any woman to have such a benefactor to support her, even if he was not her husband. By the time I was old enough to sit up and take notice, a fait accompli in grey flannel shorts, my grandmother was as deferential to 'Mr Hardie' as if he'd done her family a favour. Which, since all her life she had been ill-rewarded, in some respects he had.

Five

When she was sixteen my grandmother went up to London to wait on the wife of Dr Brett, a master at the Bluecoat school. She was happy there, but in November, 1873, when she was nineteen, she left his household to get married. She and her new husband, who was twenty-six and had taken temporary work as a corn porter in Long Acre, then came back to Norfolk – no doubt with relief, for much of Victorian London was a noisome place in every sense. Men had to shout to make themselves heard above the grinding of iron tyres over granite sets. The streets were filthy, jammed with horse-drawn traffic and permeated by an urban stench compounded of dung, effluent from drains and the reek of cabbage and mutton from kitchens ventilating into front areas. Each winter morning, as the fires were lit, a pall of smoke spread over the city, the tainted air below it full of smuts and often yellow with fog.

Norfolk must have seemed a sweet and wholesome place to return to. They decided to settle at New Hunstanton, where jobs were going on the railway. It was called New Hunstanton because in the eighteen sixties a new town was being built at the end of the line by Hamon L'Estrange, the local bigwig. The L'Estranges, so the rumour ran, had come over at the Conquest (unlike the Archers, who were presumably already here). Hamon, however, wasn't strictly a L'Estrange. He came from a family called Styleman and had taken over the name, along with the Gilbertian title of Lord High Admiral of the Wash. He had a keen commercial eye and his plans for developing the new town were well founded. Cliffs rising to some seventy feet, showing a layer of red chalk sandwiched between sandstone and white chalk and topped by a wide swathe of open grassland with a lighthouse and a cluster of coastguard cottages at one end, formed a charming background. On a clear day the tower of Boston parish church, 'Boston Stump', can be seen on the other side of the Wash. As a result of the slow erosion of waves and frost, large sandstone rocks, soon surrounded by weed-fringed pools, had spilled down on the beach, which, pebbly at first and then patterned by little streams and deltas from the rock pools, spread out to the sea at low tide in an immense expanse of damp, bare, ribbed sand.

Where the edge of the chalk escarpment dips under the glacial sands and clays, the new hotels and terraces were grouped round a green slope running down to the sea. They were built mainly of carstone in a restrained neo-Tudor style popular at the time. It gave the town in its early days the quality of a sepia photograph. An elegant cast-iron pier was constructed by a Mr Simpson in 1871 and its long spidery silhouette reached out each evening towards the sunset. A church was built and named after St Edmund, a local martyr 'spreadeagled' by the Vikings when he refused to give up his faith. A bandstand was erected, public gardens made and tamarisks planted, and three rather gloomy shelters, like miniature pagodas, were set up at intervals beside the chalk path along the cliffs. A golf course was laid out among the dunes at Old Hunstanton in 1891 and may have lured Mr Hardie down. On the beach of the new town there were bathing machines and boats for hire and deck chairs and donkey rides and a Punch and Judy man, and stalls on the esplanade sold buckets and spades and shrimping nets and all the paraphernalia of a seaside holiday, including 'jumping poles' with which to vault from rock to rock over the pools.

It was the ideal watering place for large Victorian families. No wonder that the young Mr Archer and his wife had been attracted by its opportunities, he to work on the station, she (fortified by the skills she'd learned in service) to let summer rooms. Houses were cheap to lease: L'Estrange was anxious to fill them. The population of the two Hunstantons trebled in twenty years and by 1892 they had acquired a town hall and the dignity of an urban district. By that time also my grandparents had acquired four children – first Ernest, then Frederick John, then George and finally Mabel Maud (alias Mayna). It was a good place to bring up children. My grandparents weren't the only people to think so. The same families came for holidays year after year and no less than four private schools were set up in the town: three preparatory schools for boys and a girls' school, Rhianva College. A sign of something special, surely, if only the quality of the air, so clear that in winter, when the wind came out of the east, the sound of a bicycle bell would pierce like a knife. The Archer boys went to the board school, of course – a penny a week each for their schooling, not a trivial sum in those days. Mayna was specially favoured and sent to Rhianva – an extra cost that must have represented a considerable burden: there was no Mr Hardie money then. Without this touch of privilege, I probably wouldn't exist.

It is sometimes hard to believe that I wasn't there whilst all this was going on. I wish I had been, for the Hunstanton I remember was much larger and uglier, tarnished by a fun-fair and a cinema like a large ugly box. New suburban houses had infiltrated the cliffs and fields. Day trippers poured in torrents from the station on summer week-ends and displaced, as grey squirrels had the red ones on Ringstead Downs, the more genteel visitors, who moved further along the coast, where they felt less spiritually threatened.

But then, for years I didn't see Hunstanton as a town at all. It was a collection of streets and smells and puffs of wind, of holes and corners, unformed thoughts, the sound of a barrel-organ in the distance, girls leaning on a wall, receding trap-doors of memory and sensation: a curious, lost, disquieting world. When I think about it, what I feel is emptiness: a tide of emptiness laps round my childhood days and secretly pervades them. Maybe this is a part of the melancholy that lurks behind the jaunty facade of all small seaside towns out of season. The sea halves their circumference and imposes on their inhabitants an implacable itinerary – along the beach and back, along the cliffs and back, along the front and back, past the shingle-strewn bandstand and the shuttered shrimp stalls with their peeling paint, past the net curtains and their dangling signs 'Vacancies', 'Vacancies'. Nothing happens. The same people exchange the same banalities; the same wind tugs at their hats; the same torn posters flap on the billboards; the same mongrel dogs with ruffled fur lope sideways through deserted streets. Yet I must often have been happy and, after the trailing age, I ran more often than I walked.

Six

The predominant colour inside Stratton House was brown. Varnish was a favourite covering of the time because it lasted well and didn't show the dirt. The doors and skirting boards were grained in light brown, the furniture stained in dark brown. The walls were papered in floral designs, with a decorative frieze just below the picture rails from which cheap black and white reproductions, some of them very big and framed in mahogany, hung from brass hooks. Later on, in the drawing room, there appeared a number of small Victorian water-colour paintings from my father's collection, which had become so extensive that it filled every wall of his flat in Queen Anne's Mansions, including the bathroom and lavatory, so that he had been obliged to weed some of them out. I still have two of these water-colours. As a boy, I thought them frightfully boring. Nearly all the other pictures in the house, apart from George's portrait in the parlour, I found meaningless, if not revolting.

But two tiny coloured oleographs did move me. They were in my grandparents' bedroom, on each side of the window in gilded oval frames. One showed a robin in the spring, on tiptoe among green leaves, singing his heart out; the other showed him in the winter lying on his back, his red breast like blood against the snow, his little feet sticking up into the air. When I felt specially unhappy I would go upstairs to look at these pictures. They made me want to cry. They also made me feel unaccountably better. They provided my first aesthetic experience and sweetened the rather austere atmosphere of my favourite refuge – the underside of the dining room table. Here

I was securely overarched by the hidden struts and small blocks of unstained wood that strengthened its thick barley sugar legs; and there was an iron crank, source of magical power to those in the know, though ostensibly put there to allow another leaf to be inserted in the top should need arise. Need never did arise. The table was only used when Mr Hardie came to tea. Nobody ever came to dinner. Visiting relations, rare creatures anyway, always ate with us in the parlour.

The games I played under the table – in the company of a large brass housefly whose wings lifted up to exhale a glum odour of futility and metal polish – also embraced the chairs. They had barley sugar legs, too, but thinner. A whole family of legs sprang up around me out of the blue-patterned carpet, including four spindly ones, slightly bowed, that belonged to a high stand near the window bearing an aspidistra in a green pot; and four very short, fat ones with castors on the end that supported a vast easy chair. This chair had a prickly, dusty smell and, when I put my eyes close to it, I could see a forest of little velvety hairs which opened and sprang back when I ran a finger through them. Once I found half-a-crown down the side of the cushion; it must have fallen out of Mr Hardie's pocket. I took it in triumph to Mayna, who kept it, and I never saw it again. I decided there and then that, if ever I found another, I wouldn't tell anyone. This decision was never put to the test for I found nothing more interesting afterwards than a button, which proved on examination to be one of my own flies. There were no zips in those days.

Having surveyed Stratton House from under tables and chairs and crawled around its expanses of carpet and linoleum, I can testify that, however modest it might appear on the outside, it was a pretty large place. At night in winter it became enormous, full of dark pools where faceless things lay in wait for me. The curtains bulged and swayed with their presence; they tiptoed behind me and gently touched the nape of my neck. When I was taken up to bed hanging on to Mayna's hand, their existence only added excitement to the journey. The time came, however, when I was expected to go up to bed by myself, to fly solo, as it were, into the cold, gaslit darkness. Nowadays electricity has driven ghosts and demons out of their old haunts – one click of a switch and they're gone, or nearly gone. But electricity didn't come to Hunstanton until the late twenties. The house of my childhood was lit by candles and by coal gas, which had a living and sinister quality of its own. The mantles hissed and purred. You had to go into the darkness first to light them with a match. On the landing a fish-tail gas jet, flecked with green and yellow, cast a dancing five-fingered shadow on the walls.

When bed-time came, Mayna went up to put the light on in my bedroom and a waterbottle in the bed. Then it was my turn. I would hang around the fire in the parlour framing excuses for putting off the ordeal. It never occurred to me to explain why I didn't want to go. It would have been useless anyway. To be told 'Don't be silly, there's nothing there' wouldn't have helped at all. Adults had no cause to fear: it was me 'they' were after.

The worst bit was when I started to climb the stairs. The gas in the hall wasn't lit, unless it was one of Mr Hardie's visiting days, and I was cut off from the consoling gleam that shone under the parlour door. Above lay the landing where the fish-tail flickered and a menacing shaft of light from my bedroom slanted across the wall. All I could do was to count out loud the number of banisters and touch each one in turn as I went up. Once in the bathroom, I was safe; I had the geyser to protect me, a squat, powerful copper god, dangerous but friendly. Under its guardianship I made a few ritual gestures of washing and cleaning my teeth, undressed as fast as I could and, clutching my clothes and shoes, made a dash for bed. In bed I was safe so long as no finger or toe protruded. 'They' couldn't touch me there. The sheets were like ice, but the waterbottle, with my pyjamas on top, created a little nest of warmth. I put my pyjamas on in bed – a bit of a struggle, but it was important not to venture beyond the palisade. I said my prayers in bed as well: to a Deity in whom, even then, I did not really believe. I certainly put no trust in Him. It wasn't easy to put trust in Someone who afforded me less protection than the geyser. But I assumed that He existed on the other side of the sky in much the same way as Australia existed upside down on the other side of the earth, though what either of them were doing in these remote places I couldn't conceive. One of the things I was told He was doing was keeping an eye on me, and a none too friendly eye at that.

When all my tasks had been completed, I would call out to Mayna and she would come and say goodnight. First she would read to me a little. My favourite characters were Little Black Sambo and Mr Jeremy Fisher. Both had been badly frightened and got away with it, so that I could identify with them. The best picture in all the books was one of a snarling tiger with Little Black Sambo's shoes draped over his ears. I would ask to see this picture again in order to savour its full horror. After that I could snuggle down in peace.

When Mr Hardie was there, he came upstairs to say goodnight instead of Mayna. He smelt of tobacco: he was a heavy smoker of Ardath cigarettes, a brand that offered coupons, which he kept for us so that we could exchange them for items in a catalogue. He didn't read to me; he stroked my head and told me stories, which I liked better. Sometimes, though, he hadn't done his homework and was stumped for a theme. I used to feel quite anxious for him while he was casting about for something to say and occasionally he would ramble on about activities like pig-sticking that were completely over my head. Over his, too, I shouldn't wonder. But it didn't matter what he said, it was enough for me to have him all to myself. His best stories concerned Richardson, a man of fantastic bravery and immense modesty, rather like Jack Martin in *Coral Island*, who was one of my later heroes. What

Richardson was brave about I can't remember. But I loved to hear about him. My father must have been heartily sick of the man.

When he had kissed me goodnight, my father went down to the drawing room to join Mayna until his departure. He never stayed the night. I would wonder from time to time what the two of them did down there after I'd gone to bed. I could hear them laughing. I knew that occasionally they sang, for I heard the sound of the piano and Mr Hardie singing. He liked to sing popular ballads – *I did but see her passing by* and the like. He had a pleasant baritone voice and he had bought Mayna a piano so that she could accompany him. He had also bought her expensive editions of the English classics so that she could improve her mind. These books were all lined up in glass-fronted book cases along the drawing room walls. The firelight danced on the glass when he came. I don't think Mayna ever read the books. The ones she read came out of Boot's Library and could not in any way be described as classics. Nor did she play the piano again after my father died.

The powers of darkness were much less in evidence on the nights when he was there. His presence seemed to disperse them. Besides, gaslights were turned on all over the place then, including the hall. The other nights when I didn't mind going up to bed were bath nights, though the geyser had to be reckoned with – friendly, but baleful and threatening like Uncle George after the pubs closed on Saturday. The apparatus was aroused by applying a match to a brass jet which swivelled back into its body. After an awful pause there was a tremendous roar and a ring of flame bellowed into life. Then water could be heard approaching and a thin, brown, scaly stream would emerge from the spout and trickle into the bath. As the bath filled with water, the bathroom filled with fumes and steam, but without becoming warmer, so that on winter nights it turned into a kind of frigid inferno. The geyser shook and rumbled, biding its time. (The time came on a famous night in the thirties – not long before the airship R101 crashed at Beauvais – when the stream of water failed, and it blew itself up.) The bath, being made of cast iron, remained ice cold and never warmed up enough to sit comfortably in until it was time to get out. I had to shelter in a layer of brown water that was too hot, sandwiched between a cold iron base and the even colder foggy air round about. This created a disturbing, perhaps premonitory, sense of physical luxury being always just out of reach.

Bath over, I rejoined my golliwog. Golliwogs aren't much to be seen nowadays because, like Little Black Sambo, they are alleged by foolish busybodies to be racially offensive: we are as much obsessed by race as the Victorians were by sex. (Indeed we've gone one better and contrived to be obsessed by both race and sex at the same time.) Golly was a good friend, prepared to take some hard knocks if need be. But he was of no help against the dark – perhaps because of his colour – and we weren't especially intimate. We rubbed along well enough, without much close rapport. Eventually I lost touch with him. I learned instead to cope with loneliness by splitting myself into the observed and the observer. Generally the observer was the dominant partner, a sort of guardian angel; but sometimes he would stand aside in admiration while the observed me (whom, though subordinate, I regarded as the 'real' me) was transformed into Sexton Blake or Beau Geste or Jack Martin. He has stood me in good stead throughout life. In the war he proved invaluable. And afterwards, too. During strenuous walks in the Welsh hills, for instance, he would put me through a little drill if nobody was looking, and an elderly gentleman wandering in a faded anorak down the Watkin Path could be seen to turn about, mark time, then turn about again before going on his way. I don't know what I would have done without him.

II
SNAKE BELTS AND BAT OIL

When Berenson fell ill with neurasthenia, Mary, his wife, said, 'He needs something else. I don't know what – a different childhood, I imagine.'

Seven

In 1923 my father decided that I should be sent as a boarder to Lynfield, one of the three boys' preparatory schools in the town. Arrangements were made for me to start in the autumn term. The main thing was to avoid contamination by the children who shouted in the playground of the nearby council school, where I would otherwise have been compulsorily enrolled at the age of five under the regimen of Mr Smith. Mr Smith was a savage disciplinarian. Sometimes he passed our back gate, a small ferocious man with a peaky nose. He would give me a sharp glance as he went by, no doubt marking me down as future prey. It put the wind up me just to see him.

The decision to pack me off to Lynfield was a sentence of banishment. It made no difference that the place of banishment was only a short walk from home; if anything, I felt even more cruelly bereft. Had I been a mature four and a half it would have been bad enough, but I was young even for my age. I'd never been away before. I'd never been invited out. I led a solitary life in a kind of closed community of three adults, two of whom were over seventy. I had no idea how to cope with other boys. It took me long enough just to wash. It took ages to do up my woolly combinations, to button my shirt, to tie my tie, to fasten my flies, to lace up my boots. This multitude of tasks was beyond my capacity to perform on a winter morning between the rising bell and breakfast. I was always late and invariably scruffy. Sometimes I would miss out a button hole and the whole apparatus would be weirdly skewed. On Sundays we had to wear Eton collars, with studs back and front, which presented problems of even more frightening complexity. The benefits of gaslight and coal fires only extended to the ground and first floors of the school, so that I had to struggle through this daily humiliation by candle light in an unheated attic dormitory, having sobbed half the night away with homesickness, and to the mockery or indifference of my companions before they disappeared downstairs, leaving me alone with my innumerable buttons and my twisted tie. By the time I turned up, breakfast was half over. One morning I felt sick as well, but I dared not tell anyone. Finally, as I tried to eat some lukewarm porridge, I attempted to tell Watson, the boy beside me. In the telling, I vomited over him. He was extremely good about it and afterwards I spoke of him to others as my friend, the first I ever made. He wasn't really my friend, for he was much older than I was; but he was a kindly boy and took me under his wing.

It wasn't merely a matter of my being late and scruffy. When Mayna had taken me to buy my uniform at Catleugh's of Lynn (a local emporium whose proprietor had a son at the school), they held no stocks of a size to fit a boy as small as me and she had been talked into buying a size too large, to allow, as the salesman said, for 'spreeding'. The result was to make me even more conspicuous. Racked by despair, draped in clothes too big for me, always struggling to keep up, I had no-one to turn to. Even Mayna had let me down. When she'd asked me whether I wanted to go to school, I'd said yes because she told me I would like it, that I would have other boys to play with. Although a doubt had crossed my mind at the thought of my cousin Gil and his crystal set, I put the doubt from me. I was persuaded that school was a kind of gift parcel which every little boy was eager to open. But on that blowy late September afternoon in 1923 when she took me to the school door and left me there, I suddenly realised she had been lying. The gift parcel was a booby trap. I sobbed and screamed as I was torn away from her and led into the darkening corridor by a firm and alien hand.

Lynfield was the smallest of Hunstanton's three boarding schools for boys. The other two, Lydgate House and Glebe House, with whom we played football and cricket, were larger and turned out different products, at any rate in our eyes. The boys of Lydgate were pleasant, the boys of Glebe were not; it may have had to do with the character of their headmasters.

Lynfield didn't have a headmaster, but a headmistress. Except for the games master, a willowy and (to me) unbelievably tall man by the name of Wilson, the school was staffed wholly by women, led by a formidable triumvirate: the Misses Worthington, Cross and Porter. Miss Worthington was the Head, Miss Cross ran the commissariat and Miss Porter supplied the brains. Miss Worthington and Miss Porter slept in the same room. I remember them both with respect and affection; Miss Cross, who slept alone, less so. However primitive our living conditions, the quality of teaching was remarkably high; there was a marked change for the worse when I got to my next school. Nor was there any bullying. The women of Lynfield did not see it as their duty to desensitise the boys in their charge, but to do the reverse. They must have been aware, of course, that the East Anglian climate, tempered by minimal heating, did most of their work for them, providing on its own a scale of austerity which scarcely required further intervention by the staff. On nights of fierce frost, when the stars burned in the sky, the dormitory water jugs would freeze over in the annex, where there was no bathroom and tin basins were provided to wash in.

I have one clear recollection of the rigours of the climate. On 20 November, 1925, Queen Alexandra, former consort of Edward VII, died at Sandringham. Her body was to be taken the next day to the royal station at Wolferton, thence to lie in state in Westminster Hall prior to burial at Windsor. It was thought proper that the boys of Lynfield should line up along the route and doff their caps as the cortège went by. Black arm bands were issued. All this meant little to a boy of six, although a vague romantic notion about the passing of a Queen had been instilled. The day was bitterly cold: there may be some kind of land mass between Wolferton and the North Pole, but it wasn't evident. We arrived early and the cortège was late – appropriately so, for Queen Alexandra's beauty (long since gone, of course, with 'all her lovely airs, her little graces') had been matched by her unpunctuality and her penchant for driving very slowly so as 'not to run over a dog'. None of us, least of all the little ones, were equipped to stand still for hours in the cold, as the solemnity of the occasion required. Soon our hands and feet were numb, except for the ache of chilblains. We were transfixed in a dull misery. By the time the procession had gone by, we could scarcely climb into the bus that came to take us back to the school. There, in front of the fire, we began to thaw out: a knot of small boys weeping and moaning, some literally wringing their hands. Queen Alexandra, a kindly woman who loved children as well as dogs, would have been appalled if she could have seen us. But the pain passed, we were given a special lunch; and I have developed a soft spot for her since I learned that, when she was a young bride and Tennyson read out an *Ode of Welcome* he had written for her wedding, she could not stifle her laughter, which proved so infectious that he was soon laughing helplessly as well and was unable to continue.

By now, tucked under the wing of Watson, I was beginning to make friends at Lynfield and know my way about. The building consisted of a large house with an annex and a big extension at the back. A disproportionate area was allocated to the staff. In this respect it resembled a small man o' war, the mistresses, like officers, being spaciously accommodated; the boys, like pressed men, cooped up in quarters both cramped and bleak. The main staircases, the best rooms – all, as far as I could glimpse them, heavily appointed in a Victorian style – were out of bounds. In our part of the school it was linoleum and bare boards. There was a big schoolroom, with a raised dais at one end which was also used as a stage. Classes were held there in the day, and in the evening, after supper, it served as a common room where we played cards and chess and Dover Patrol and the like. It was there, sitting on a bench and reading *The Wizard*, that I was bitten by Bunn, a long, lank boy who came from Diss: I don't recall why. The sanitary arrangements were meagre in the extreme. We used to have a bath once a week, taking it in turns to get in. The water was changed or partly changed from time to time, but its texture remained routinely soupy, like that of communal rugger baths later on. One night, when Miss Cork, the Senior Mistress, was on duty, Runciman, who was exceptionally well endowed, got into the bath ahead of me, and promptly had an erection. We wondered what Miss Cork would do. We did not have long to wait. She took a large wooden spoon from a shelf above the bath and banged it hard down. Runciman gave a sharp cry and, either out of agony or bravado, emitted a colossal fart which boiled to the surface as his crimson penis sank down again beneath the water. Nothing was said. The smell hung about in the air like a puff of malodorous smoke from some conjuring trick. The spoon was replaced on the shelf.

Our main dormitories were lit by candles and there were chamber pots under the beds. One boy, whose father was a retail chemist, used to bring back samples of Gibb's toothpaste and eat them: every night he would froth at the mouth. Those who had no Gibbs learned to chew candle grease. Talking was permitted after the candles were blown out so long as we were reasonably quiet and, when I became a senior boy, one or two of us used to tell stories, patched up no doubt from books or magazines we'd read. I invented a character called 'The Turbanned Terror', who went down very well, particularly on winter nights when the wind was up and pale shafts of light from the gas lamps in the road outside created a spooky criss-cross pattern on the wooden ceiling. During one summer term while I was still innocent I slept alongside a boy whose name I have forgotten and we would take turns to tickle each other's arms in the long twilight before we went to sleep; there was no sexuality in it, just mutual pleasure.

I was granted a special concession on Sundays – I was allowed to go home after Morning Service until 5 o'clock. This was initially a recognition of my age on entry. In fact it made things worse by re-opening the wound of separation once a week instead of allowing it to scab over. When the wound had healed, I would still rather not have gone. For one thing, Sunday lunch was the best school meal of the week – cold roast beef, salad and fried potatoes – and I missed it. For another, Sunday afternoon was free time at school and I missed the mucking about. It was understood that, whilst *I* could go home, it was not in order to invite anyone to go with me. Not that I wanted to, because I was ashamed of my circumstances. Mr Hardie's presence might have redeemed the situation, but he always departed for London on Sunday. Otherwise I could offer nothing of interest. Conversation at home wasn't exactly animated. It was a foretaste of the torpor of the holidays. There was no time to do much more than mooch around after a heavy meal until I had to go back.

My weekly spell of home leave fitted neatly into the school's religious timetable. On Sunday morning it was the custom for us to walk to Matins at St Mary's, Old Hunstanton. Older boys were taken on Sunday evening to Evensong at St Edmunds, New Hunstanton. I dropped off the long school crocodile on its way back from St Mary's and, when I was old enough, returned in time to join the short one headed for St Edmunds. Thus there was no interference with my attendance at both services. I did not mind this. I was addicted to sermons from an early age, and moved especially by Evensong, that peaceful service created by Thomas Cranmer, which combined the old monastic offices of Vespers or Compline. The cool patternings and immemorial words (in the old prayer-book) used to console me. There were other consolations – watching adults trill and bellow, for example, making the contents of some hymns, already odd, seem odder still; and the pleasure to be got from the difference, which I sensed but didn't understand, between low church at St Mary's and high church at St Edmunds, where incense hung in the air and there were little red lamps.

Despite their periods of boredom, these Sunday services enriched my life to an extent which I only now appreciate. Although I rarely go today, I still have a deep affection for the Church of England, rooted mainly in its language. In its Englishness, too. To be an Anglican is often thought to smack of credulity, whereas to be a Roman Catholic is supposed to confer a kind of intellectual panache. The credulity is no less and no more in the latter case; the fact that the Roman Church is buttressed by a more austere dogma has little relevance to the strength of its foundations. Like my father, I have always been repelled by dogma, which is a form of bullying.

On our walk to Old Hunstanton we were often accompanied by the village idiot, a round-shouldered, bandy, grinning youth who would caper about on the other side of the road, much to the silent indignation of Miss Worthington, who led us from the back. We nicknamed him 'the Scorcher' because of his habit of sprinting first ahead of us and then behind. He did not come to church, but waited near Periwinkle Wood for our return journey. He is linked in my mind with early summer. In those pre-herbicidal days the ripening barley, swept by long shadows like watered silk, was flecked by poppies; and the hedgerows were full of dog-roses and wild honeysuckle and the flicker of butterflies. The clear, bright light from the sea washed over us. I took it all for granted then. But it comes back to me now with a new freshness, like a cleaned picture.

Sunday walks were not the only ones; we had Saturday walks, too. Indeed, with games every week-day afternoon – and dancing lessons at the town hall as an unpopular extra for those who paid – we were well exercised. On Saturday afternoons we commonly walked to the Downs at Ringstead in winter and to the beach at Old Hunstanton in the summer – long walks for a small boy. The road we took to the Downs was little more than a farm track wandering through fields, muddy in the wet, crackling with ice on cold days when we would all be scarfed up, corners tucked in. It foreshadowed the emptiness of inland Norfolk – the sad cry of peewits, the huge bare fields with starlings spraying across the sky and gulls wheeling and calling, and now and then a great pile of swedes. Near a path through the woods which led to Hunstanton Hall there was a fence strung with small corpses – moles, stoats, weasels, jays. They swayed in the wind until fur, flesh and feather fell away and there was only bone, the little grinning skulls of stoats and weasels sinister to the last. These tiny gibbets had about them something primitive and magical; they brought me the first whiff of mortality. The gamekeeper who put them there took death for granted as a necessary thing, as in due course I would come to do. But not yet. The bang of a gun in the woods, the hurtle of a pheasant through the trees emitting its strange wild cry, were just things I saw and heard, part of the endless bombardment of sensations which had to be sorted out.

Another turn of the track brought us to the Downs, a small green valley guarded by an untidy farmhouse where a corroded pipe, stained deep orange, discharged a trickle of water into a cressy pool, at about the same rate as the geyser at Stratton house. This was the Iron Spring, famous for its therapeutic properties. We fanned out then, the older boys splitting into gangs, some of whom – out of sight of Miss Worthington – would engage in stone-throwing contests, which have left me with considerable sympathy for riot police. The younger boys would just run about. One alarming pleasure was to link arms and run down the steep slopes faster and faster until, legs unable to keep up, we keeled over and rolled down to the bottom.

Finally the whistle blew and we headed home. Sometimes on our way back in the early dusk of a winter's day, when the puddles, touched into crimson by sunset, were starting to freeze at the edges we would meet a pair of horses, as tired as we were, returning from work in the fields, steam blowing from their wide, velvet nostrils, huge friendly creatures jingling and creaking, with the ploughman wrapped in a sack, perched side-saddle on one of them. And when we got to the main road, waiting to cross, I would seize the chance to press my ear against a telephone pole and hear that faint twanging buzz – the sound, I thought, of crowds of strangers talking. By this means I would try to give some sort of human voice to the terrifying wail of the wind in the wires overhead.

In summer there were the bathing trips to Old Hunstanton, where we had two school huts – part of a small colony which straggled along the beach among the dunes at the end of the cliffs. In the smaller hut the staff changed for the sea and, later on, a picnic was prepared, announced by the welcome hiss of a Primus. Supplies of fish-paste sandwiches, sausage rolls, hard-boiled eggs, etc., had been laid in earlier. The mistresses when they emerged in their swimming costumes were not erotic figures, save for Miss de Groot, a South African, whose svelte, elegant body Runciman frequently eulogised. Miss de Groot, accustomed to warmer water, did not stay long in the sea, unlike Miss Cork, who, short and corpulent as her name implied, could stay in for hours and was to be seen bobbing around in the middle distance long after everyone else had come out. Miss Cork taught me to swim. The process took time because I felt the cold so acutely. But she was a determined woman and in the end I was pushed out on my own in a flurry of foam from under the jut of that enormous bosom, like a weakling whale-calf shouldered from its dam.

We changed in the larger hut. I remember the hollow, tarry, seaweedy smell inside, the shouts and the bumping of bodies, the sandy wooden boards; the rush for the sea, bare feet sinking deep into the dry sand at the start, over the shelly tide mark on to the ridged damp sand which hurt your insteps, then on to the wet sand near the water's edge, which squidged up between your toes and blanched as if in pain when your weight pressed the water out of it; and at last into the sea, plunging straight in even though it was shallow so as to avoid the agony of a slow immersion, gasping and yelling with the shock of it. And afterwards running back over the different surfaces in reverse order, shivering, teeth chattering, hair dripping, balls shrivelled up, the hard rough towels getting sticky with salt as we rubbed the wetness off and put the heat back. Then out again into the warm sun with dry shorts on and the Primus hissing and a hunger on us as if we hadn't eaten for days.

After the picnic, chewing an apple, we would roll over in the sun, full tummy pressed against the warm abrasion of the sand, chin deep in the sparkling granules so close to our eyes that they grew as big as rocks and one could imagine oneself a tiny insect toiling among them. We built long sand bridges and tunnels down the slope of beach below the hut, burrowing through the dry surface to the secret layer of moist sand underneath. When the roadways were complete, with walls and forts added, we would roll down Sorbo balls and watch them swoop and climb and swerve to the terminus at the bottom. Soon the moist sand would dry out and start to crumble as in a desert wind; like the slow erosion of history being speeded up. Even then we couldn't wait. As if by prearrangement we would suddenly jump on the tunnels and bridges of our little Babylon in a fury of destruction and smash them to bits.

Usually, of course, it wasn't hot. There would be a brisk wind off the sea, and sometimes rain, which spotted the sand and pocked on the felt roofs of the huts and pricked the sea with little holes like a pincushion. Days for rounders or beach cricket; anything to get the circulation going again after the compulsory dip, this time in a grey-green sea with spume blowing off the wave tops and scudding across the beach. The wind would harass us. Whirligigs of sand sting our bare legs. And, hot day or cold, there was always the long walk back along the cliff top, clutching our damp rolled-up bathing togs, the smaller boys straggling behind and chivvied along by Miss Cork, refreshed by her long immersion, until the road was reached again and the Lynfield crocodile re-formed to march in good order to school.

Tuesday was also a special day of the week for me, because I then enjoyed, thanks to Mr Hardie, an afternoon off to go riding. I was put into the hands of Howling, a small, 'nutty' groom with a weather-beaten face and twinkling eyes who could do anything with horses – and with me. I can still hear him hissing happily away as he saddled up a pony in the yard, with its smell of dung and leather and the sound of horses shifting from one hoof to the other in their stalls. When our two hours were over he would put me on the bus back to home or school or, if the bus wasn't due for a bit, he would flag down a passing car: 'Perhaps you could give this young gentleman a lift to Huns'ton.' Howling was invariably well turned out, and he expected me to be too. There was no slouching about. Under his tuition I graduated from a nervous little boy on a leading rein to a bigger boy just as nervous but hardened by the usual quota of falls. He taught me to 'gather' a horse – something which helped me in a curious way when I came to fly aeroplanes. One of my proudest days was when he entrusted to my care a little shivery mare called Cigarette who pirouetted and danced about sideways like the thoroughbred she was. I used to love riding her and Howling would try to make sure I did. It was more important for me to be in Howling's good books than in anyone else's, which showed that I'd acquired an appreciation of quality in one respect at least.

In the winter before my father's death, again no doubt at his instigation and on the sound principle that a day's hunting would teach me a lot more than a day at school, Howling took me out with the West Norfolks, having picked out two or three suitable 'near' meets. We had to ride some way to get there in the chilly morning air, through unfamiliar country. I was more than usually conscious of his friendly but critical gaze: I was his 'young gentleman' for real this time, and he expected me to live up to it. Needless to say, I was also wide-eyed with apprehension, a small stranger in a strange world, surrounded suddenly by large hearty people on large animals, most of them slightly windy too (though it never occurred to me that they might be), waiting restlessly to move off. But once the horn was blowing and the hounds were yelping and streaming across the fields, I found myself breathlessly carried along, spattered by the riders in front, and clearing a low hedge before I had time to think about it. I began to feel wildly exhilarated. When the man in front went over a fence, I went over it after him – or rather my horse did, for the horse was in charge, not me. When he went over a bigger one, I did the same; but this time the horse didn't. I picked myself up on the other side, unhurt but deeply chagrined. Howling, relieved that nothing worse had happened, tore me off a strip for bad horsemanship; but I got a feeling that he was secretly quite proud of me – a feeling which I soon began to share myself.

At the second meet, after finding myself apparently alone in a field, I managed under Howling's unobtrusive guidance to keep up with the pack and be in at the kill where, to his great pleasure, I was duly 'blooded'. I was bemused when the warm blood was rubbed on my cheeks and forehead, and too shy to say anything when people came up and congratulated me. A barbarous ritual, and callous. But anyone who has seen what a fox can do in a hen run must accept the need to keep their numbers down. Hunting at least gives the fox a chance. And scruples are soon swept aside by the high note of the horn and the sound of the hounds in a tall wood, like the echo of organ music in a church, and the blood-tingling gallop across the stubble, with your horse going flat and smooth under you, as excited as you are.

Perhaps the best moment of all is the return home, bone weary, ambling through the darkening leaf-strewn glades or clattering through the villages with smoke rising from the chimneys and the lights coming on and mist curling up from the fields, home to the bellowing geyser and boiled eggs for tea. This experience has been described all too often, but its enchantment remains. The only comparison I can make is the return in the dawn after a night bombing raid.

Alas, my riding career ended when my father died. No more money. But I continued to think of life as a series of fences to be cleared.

Eight

About the middle of my school career I caught measles. The symptoms came on a Sunday, so I was kept at home. My eyes were badly affected and the local doctor, Dr Bull, was summoned. Small, self-satisfied and natty, he tut-tutted vigorously and pronounced against any reading. I was installed in Mayna's room and the blinds were drawn as if in anticipation of death. Though I felt burning hot, a fire was lit and a paraffin heater brought in which gave off a metallic fumy smell and projected a curious circular pattern among the reflections which played on the ceiling.

Not long after I had got over measles and returned to Lynfield I turned bright yellow and went down with jaundice. I was put to bed in a small dressing room which led off the room where Miss Worthington and Miss Porter slept. I was a favourite of theirs then (before I blotted my copybook by writing a cloacal rhyme on a paper dart which swerved on to Miss Porter's desk and by exhibiting an overweening self-importance after playing the part of Toad in a school production of *Toad of Toad Hall*). They used to come and see me in their dressing gowns, with curlers in their hair. I could hear them talking, even giggling, in their room and I realised for the first time that schoolmistresses led lives of their own outside their hours with us. They lent me a candlestick with a big brass reflector and I loved its soft buttery light. I was reading *Prester John* and shorter editions of *Ivanhoe* and *The Talisman*. I could hear the distant sounds of school life and see boys playing cricket on the playing field on the far side of the road. It was a strange, empty time. Dr Bull, who was also the school doctor, came to see me again. He called me 'young man', which I thought patronising. Mayna didn't come. She knew I wasn't seriously ill, I suppose, and for her my sick-room was, as it were, in ticklish territory.

I have mentioned the quality of teaching and, if that is the main criterion by which a school should be judged, Lynfield emerged with flying colours. Today I suppose the teaching would be regarded as old-fashioned; and no doubt it was – when I was born the Victorian age was still only eighteen years away. There were no concessions to creativity or self-expression. In one of my essays I referred to 'the bending ice'. The word 'bending' was struck out in red and a sharp exclamation mark inserted in the margin. I protested that ice did bend: like light, I might have added, if I'd been an Einstein. I knew it bent, because I'd pressed on it and made it bend – and watched it blanch and split into stars – in the shallow puddles on the lane to Ringstead Downs. I was told not to be foolish. Nor did we have such imaginative aids as plasticine and poster paints. There was little music, though we had singing lessons once a week from a dear old man named Roden Hilder, who couldn't keep order. We learned our tables by rote and we learned poetry by heart, reams of it. We had to learn the Collect every Sunday. We learned history by memorising dates and geography by memorising maps. The atmosphere was unfailingly competitive. The youngest boys were taught in a small upstairs room with a coke fire round which we sat. It was like a miniature RAF hut. I enjoyed it because I had a good memory; that was half the battle.

Higher up the school, when the solving of problems partly replaced the injection of facts, repetition remained a feature of the system. And we still went on learning poetry, including quite long pieces like Macaulay's *Lays of Ancient Rome* – splendid stuff! – and Tennyson's ballad *The Revenge*. Miss Worthington would go round the class calling for a verse in turn. I was often stirred; and it has left me with a love of language which I've never lost.

Eventually I joined a very small class at the top of the school, including two identical twins, Basil and Gordon, who looked the same to other people but quite different to us, and a charming freckled boy called Vincent who was extremely bright. We did relatively difficult work; the maths were more advanced than any I've done since. It was a period of intellectual expansion. The other boys took scholarships to public schools. For some reason I didn't; probably I wasn't good enough. I took Common Entrance instead.

Mayna went back to Lynfield only once after that traumatic afternoon when she left me at the door. Whether she ever met Miss Worthington, who could be a pretty stiff character, I can't say; I suspect it was all done by correspondence, with my father as ghost writer. She didn't visit my next school at all. It meant that only once during my school days, whether at school functions or sports days or at week-ends, did a parent or relative come to see me. Admittedly other boys didn't seem very proud of their parents unless they had a large car or could produce a pretty sister; indeed, they generally had to make excuses for them, not least for the hats their mothers wore. But they did have visitors to make excuses for. I can't quite forgive Mayna for not having made an effort to come and see me more than once, though at least I didn't have to worry about her hats. In fairness it must be said that my father never came at all; but there were perhaps more compelling reasons in his case.

Nine

Once I had settled down at Lynfield, I was happier there than at home. In the holidays I missed the camaraderie of school and the romping about. That's not to say I didn't look forward to the end of term and the expectation of freedom ahead. But expectation soon turned to disillusion. What was freedom for? I have never been able to find a satisfactory answer. It creates one kind of discomfort by its absence and another kind by its presence; the only time it gives unadulterated pleasure is at the point of change.

Of course there were many compensations: above all, the relief of being alone. Maybe I had grown accustomed to loneliness and missed at school the very thing I seemed to be most afraid of at home. At school there was no escape from other people; holidays at least conferred the privilege of solitude. But, as soon as I put my head inside the door of Stratton House, I knew the privilege was worthless. All at once the weeks stretched before me like a desert to be crossed – and to what purpose, except to go back to school again at the end? The same old rooms, oppressed by the dusty, wasted hours piled up inside them; the same lack of understanding by Mayna (or so I thought) of what I had been doing or might be going to do. She couldn't put herself in my place, or I in hers – naturally reserved, unacceptable socially in a dull town. My grandmother was too old; my grandfather was soon to die. We were a melancholy quartet.

What did I do all day? I have forgotten, though two days in the week had a special quality of their own – Tuesday, when I went riding, and the Saturdays when Mr Hardie came. For the rest, most of the things which happened to me happened inside my head, as they do to any small boy who has to spend long periods by himself. After the age of toys had passed, the age of Meccano duly succeeded. I played quite a lot of 'dab-cricket', with squared paper dotted with numbers (for runs) and methods of dismissal, I took care that my cricketing heroes – Hobbs, Fender, Hammond – got satisfactory scores. But neither Meccano nor dab-cricket can provide much food for the imagination, whereas books can. So I became a voracious reader, to the displeasure of my grandmother: 'That boy's always got his head in a book. Why don't he find something to do?' She regarded reading as a form of escapism – which in my case it was. As I hadn't any live companions, I had to make do with literary ones. At first my reading was sprinkled with German enemies (*'Gott in Himmel! Donner und Blitzen!'*) and I rushed about the house hurling myself into bloody trenches where the Huns looked thickest. But, as time went by, I advanced via Andrew Lang's *Fairy Books*, with their pictures of long-necked king's daughters and ice maidens and goose girls, into the schoolboy world of the *Wizard* and the *Rover*, the *Boy's Own Paper* (faintly tinged with piety), Sexton Blake, Percy F. Westerman, Henty, Ballantyne, Rider Haggard and so on, until I came at last into possession of the shelves of books my father had accumulated for Mayna's education. Mayna was glad enough to leave them to me.

There was no television then, and the wireless was in its heyday. I listened to the wireless a lot: Henry Hall, the Palm Court orchestra, rugby matches ('England have the ball – Square 4, they're passing along the line – Square 7'), music hall, Elsie and Doris Waters, the Western Brothers, Flanagan and Allen, Percy Edwards ('Now we are in the farmyard – *moo-moo, baa-baa*'). Men in dinner jackets read the evening news in cultivated voices; baritones sang *The Road to Mandalay*. I enjoyed the programmes, but not enough. Afterwards I wished I hadn't listened.

Electricity arrived about this time and served both to help fend off the darkness on my way to bed and to provide a good light to read by when I got there. But each new thing exacts its price and I missed the friendly gas lamps in the road, tended first by a lamplighter and latterly turned on and off by clockwork. When I passed under them in the dusk I liked to hear the mechanism ticking. Sometimes I would hang about under the lamp on the corner waiting for it to light up with a whoosh (its tiny pilot flame and lacy mantle so inadequately protected, it seemed, against the pluck of wind from the sea). The electric street lamp which appeared instead, screwed to a pole, was an ugly thing, casting a hard light – precursor of an unromantic age.

I spent a lot of time swinging on the side gate of Stratton House. It was painted green and gave out a faint, disapproving squeak. I liked to watch the local world go by in the vain hope that something would happen to draw me into it. Passing children would be assessed as potential playmates or bullies, and adults categorised as sympathetic, like the local policeman, or hostile, like Mr Smith the schoolmaster. The police station was just beyond the council school, so I saw quite a lot of both. On weekdays about mid-morning, the milkman came. He made his rounds by pony trap and ladled out rich unpasteurised milk from a pail which he replenished from two churns. His face was tanned the same colour as the old leather pouch he wore over his shoulder to put the money in. The pony stopped at all the houses where milk was due to be delivered and refused to move on until it had been, so that if the householders were away a great flurry of shouts and crackings of the whip was needed to get him going again. One Christmas the milkman was treated rather too liberally by his customers, and elected to take his Christmas box with increasing frequency out of a glass. By the end of his round he was reeling drunk and singing. His pony would have taken him safely home had he not fallen out of the trap, along with a churn of milk, when they were coming down Redgate Hill. Whereupon he was dismissed. His successor was a dull fellow.

Every so often the scrap merchant would go by, a small, bowed man, pushing an empty cart draped with old sacks. I could hear his strange, mournful, unintelligible cry a long way off. Nobody came out to give him anything and I had a feeling he did not expect them to, that he was performing a ritual, a kind of lament for the transience of ordinary things, the collapse of bedsteads, the rusting of kettles. I would watch him trundle past and disappear round the corner by the council school, his lonely cry growing fainter and fainter on the wind.

A regular arrival through the side gate was the errand boy from Lambert's the grocer – a piercing whistler who seemed to regard me as a kind of sexual confidant, though half the time I'd no idea what he was talking about. Mayna used to go to Lambert's once a week to give her order. All orders were delivered, and accounts were settled monthly. The assistants in their white coats greeted her by name. If I went with her, I would be given a biscuit from one of the big tins arranged in rows under glass and mahogany lids which lifted up on brass hinges. A rich grocery smell conveyed the proper aroma of middle-class prosperity. It didn't do to be seen in the Co-op, which stood on the opposite side of the street. They didn't deliver, they gave you a 'divi' instead. Sometimes Lambert's would be out of a particular commodity and I would be sent to the Co-op to get it. It was a different world in there, making up in banter what it lacked in deference. Moreover, each counter was connected to the central cash desk by overhead wires on which a capsule containing your money and the bill was whizzed over to the cashier and then came whistling back again with your change and the divi. It was well worth the sacrifice of one of Lambert's biscuits to be sent to the Co-op and see it working.

Other favourite side-gaters were the dustmen and, above all, the coalmen with their grimed faces and startlingly white eyes. One day, to my extreme excitement, the coal came round in a chain-driven steam lorry with a fire blazing underneath. Unfortunately this form of delivery didn't last long; the pull-up from the station with a full load caused the machine deep mechanical distress and proved in the end too much for it. Occasionally a tramp came ('If your hedge don't need a clip, missus, I'll have to trouble you for a bob'), or a gipsy woman – mysterious and rather frightening figures who, I sensed, despised all the things we were supposed to believe in. The door to door salesmen, Kleen-eezee men and the like, of whom there were quite a lot, came to the front door; they probably despised those things, too, but had to pretend not to.

In the cottage next door lived Mr and Mrs Carter. Mrs Carter was a spritely, buck-toothed, cheerful woman who wore her hair tied up in a bow at the back. She would pop in from time to time for a chat, but there was a certain reserve between our households because her husband, Joe, suffered from a rare skin disease. She used to wheel him about, gloved and veiled, in a bath chair. The suspicion, unvoiced of course, was that his complaint might be contagious. Serious illnesses were never referred to by name; any mention of TB or cancer, for example, was taboo. Joe Carter was a gentle man who liked to stop and talk to me as I swung on my gate. But I was always uneasy lest he should raise his black veil. Had he not worn it, I wouldn't have been troubled by his ravaged face; but the veil endowed him with a sinister quality. Much later I came across a charming novel by L.P. Hartley called *The Shrimp and the Anemone*, set in a seaside town he calls 'Anchorstone'. Eustace, a sensitive, timid boy, is tormented by the duty to be kind to Miss Fothergill, a frightening figure whom he meets on the cliff path also being wheeled out, veiled and gloved, in a bath chair. Miss Fothergill reminded me of Joe Carter. Then the whole book fell into place! Anchorstone was Hunstanton; and all the familiar landmarks – the cliffs, the beach, the lighthouse, the rock pools, the winding steps, the wind-blown tamarisks, the Downs – came to life as they had been in my own childhood. I was back again where I began and glad, as Eustace was when he grew up, that I didn't still belong there.

In her younger days Mayna was a great walker, for lack, I suppose, of anything better to do. She had no goal except to tire herself. Each day we walked for miles along the cliffs and beside the sea, always towards Old Hunstanton and onwards to Holme, never the other way. As companions we had two dogs – Pat, an Airedale, and Sammy, a Sealyham.

Sammy was acquired at the insistence of my father on a visit to Bournemouth and his acquisition was not without its troubles. I still have two letters which my father drafted in pencil for Mayna to send to Miss Martin at the Dog Lover's Shop, 43 Westover Road. How strange that such ephemeral documents should have survived, and should bring back so clearly the memory of him, cigarette between his lips, gold pencil in hand, sitting in front of the fire at Stratton House on an autumn evening. The first letter was more sorrowful than angry:

Dear Madam,
The little dog Sammy arrived safely on Saturday. I am sorry to say that he does not appear to be in good condition. He is frequently scratching both his body and his ears. Has he been suffering from any skin trouble? I must take him to a veterinary surgeon.

You promised to send me Sammy's pedigree and also a chart shewing the best method of feeding him. Please let me have those two documents and let me know also whether he has been suffering from any trouble. I find that he has not been house trained *at all*.

My father's second draft was more imperious. The threat to bring in the police must have been unexpected from a country spinster!

Dear Madam,

I have not received any reply from you in answer to the letter I posted to you on Monday with respect to the little dog Sammy. I await an answer and I also await the promised pedigree and chart. I enclose a copy of the letter I sent you.

I presume that Miss Martin is the proprietor of the shop and responsible for the sale of the dog. If this be not so, please let me know the name of the actual proprietor. This will save me the trouble of having to ask the police at Bournemouth to make the necessary enquiries.

The little dog Sammy, however respectable his pedigree, grew into a low-slung, bad-tempered animal, with a habit of hopping every fourth step in an irritable way. He was, however, very intelligent; he didn't need Pavlov to tell him how to draw an inference. Pat, on the other hand, was not bright. He liked to rest his head in my lap while I fondled his silly ears and he would bring treasured, slobbery, useless objects to lay as gifts at my feet. The two dogs quarrelled often but not viciously, and without prejudice to total loyalty against a common foe. Their favourite enemy was a lurcher named Rex, whose owner was never to be seen. The method of dealing with Rex, and other local dogs, was for Sammy to go on ahead and pick a fight – which came naturally to him since he went about snarling at everything he met, even lamp-posts – whilst Pat hung back round the corner. As soon as Rex was committed to the attack, Pat, alerted by the sound of battle, would come bounding to the rescue and soon all three of them, and sometimes four if Rex's side-kick was about, would be rolled up in a snarling ball. It could be quite alarming. Since all the local dogs knew one another, however, it never became serious and, when Mayna's walking stick was liberally applied, they would prowl slowly off, stiff-legged and quivering, with lifted lips, careful not to stare but sneaking little glances, until they were out of sight of each other and could revert to their normal louche ways. On one occasion Sammy foolishly picked on a visiting Alsatian unfamiliar with the rules. He got badly mauled and Pat was put to flight. I was terrified, but Mayna stepped in with her stick and smote the Alsatian on the nose. When its owner ventured to demur, she was icy. (Very straight, in her well-cut tweeds and cloche hat, with her Rhianva accent, Mayna could be quite formidable. I think, looking back, I may have underestimated her.)

As he got old, Sammy found it burdensome to walk far and refused to go beyond the first shelter on the cliffs. His appetite, however, remained undiminished. Once, when Pat was out and my grandmother thought that Sammy had gone out as well, she left a joint of mutton unattended on the table. He jumped up on a chair, portly as he was, and grabbed it. As he was tucking into it behind the door, he heard her coming back. She found him apparently asleep on the hearthrug, snoring heavily. While she searched in the meat safe and the larder for the missing joint – 'I could have sworn I put that mutton out' – he remained deep in slumber. It has been suggested that one clear difference between men and animals is that men know how to lie. Sammy showed that to be false. It has also been suggested that animals can't see a joke. I exchanged many knowing glances, some of them suspiciously like a wink, with Sammy (though not with Pat) which led me to doubt that suggestion, too. He was a good, if grumpy, companion. He died in his basket, presumably of a heart attack. Pat pined for weeks, then became ill himself and had to be put down. Mayna never acquired another dog.

When I took the dogs for walks by myself, we forsook Mayna's immutable route and made off the other way towards the South Beach. This was the poorer end of town, reflected in much clearer class distinctions than now exist. Working men wore mufflers and caps and had a habit, when older, of addressing their wives as 'Mother' (thus blatantly exposing what Professor Freud, unfamiliar with the British psyche, thought everyone wanted to hide). Summer trippers on the beach still wore dark suits and, when the wind died down and the sun was hot, they basked in their braces to the pulse of the distant band. They paddled in the sea with the bottoms of their trousers rolled, like J. Alfred Prufrock.

We would make a diversion to go past the Cenotaph. During my first term the school had been taken there on Armistice Day and the ceremony made a profound impression on me. I didn't understand it, but it made me cry. Lines of men stood in silence with their hats off; men always wore hats in those days and their removal made them seem strangely vulnerable. Their hair blew in the wind. The notes of the Last Post, carried out over the sea, pierced my heart. Later on, the poetry of Owen was almost more than I could bear. The First War still seems to carry a charge of remembrance more poignant and more powerful than the Second War, which I and my companions in our shorts and red and grey school caps were being unsuspectingly groomed for. Armistice Day was the supreme festival of the year. No-one was to be seen without a poppy (which varied in size according to how much you paid). At eleven o'clock the siren sounded at the gas works. The traffic stopped. Drivers climbed from their vehicles and stood with bowed heads. For two minutes there was silence over England.

If I had any spare pennies, I would buy myself a choc bar from the 'Stop-Me-and-Buy-One' man who patrolled the area on his tricycle, and try my hand at some of the slot machines in front of the pier. I was fond of the pier, haunt of summer concert parties, sad co-optimists with bobbles in their pointed hats, and potent symbol of the Victorian seaside. The concert parties were replaced in autumn by less vulgar entertainments and Mayna and I would sometimes go to matinées. Once we went to see Jose Collins, who had been the toast of the town in the Great War when she sang in *The Maid of the Mountains*, or was it *Chu Chin Chow*? Mayna might have been to see her then; my father, who was partial to musicals, certainly had. She was getting old and fat now, and her voice was going. Two other women and ourselves were the only people there. We waited long after the advertised time, but no-one else came. The waves tumbled and hissed among the iron girders beneath our feet. I felt so ashamed.

Not far from the pier was the Sandringham Hotel, where my father used to stay – single room from three shillings a day, bath sixpence extra; though he, of course, had more palatial quarters, to which he never thought it fitting to invite Mayna or me. This prudent omission endowed the building, and the prodigious fire escape that zig-zagged up its backside, with a privileged, almost religious, significance in my eyes. It glowed with the kind of luxury and sophistication which only the mind of a child can invent...

Home again, suitably chastened: past the blacksmith who plied his trade amid galaxies of sparks at the back of Seagate, past Lynfield, now strangely quiet, past Carr's the greengrocer, where a warm wave of fruity vegetable scents engulfed me when I opened the door, through the side gate past the ant's nest into the garden. Finding it all just the same, I would feel the twinge of an inexplicable heart-ache, like the sudden memory of some lost happiness.

Mrs Carr, round and rosy, called me 'Pip', a nickname my father often used. Perhaps she did so because she knew my origins and wished to absolve me from them; or because there was some association in her mind with a comic strip popular at the time called 'Pip, Squeak and Wilfred'. She's unlikely to have been familiar with the character in *Great Expectations*. My father, knowing the book, may well have sensed subconsciously a certain aptness. Pip was a local boy who aspired to better himself and become a gentleman – an ideal recruit for a minor public school. It was appropriate, therefore, that in the autumn of 1932, when my father was struggling to stay financially afloat and politicians were trying to come to terms with the frightful business of going off the gold standard, my name should have been put down for one such school – Worksop College, formerly St Cuthbert's College, Nottinghamshire.

Ten

Worksop was the sort of school Miss Worthington might have proposed if asked for advice: Lynfield did not aspire to feed schools in the major league. However, the real reasons for its choice were more compelling. My father was in deep financial trouble. There was also the vexed question of paternity. He must have been wondering how much longer he could manage to keep his parental head below the parapet, especially when he was only too fond of going over the top when he had his ermine on. Worksop, tucked away in middle England, seemed a safe and relatively inexpensive compromise.

But these were adult problems, My father's visits held no hint of them for me, save near the very end when, worried and preoccupied, he would listen to the stock market prices on the wireless and make notes on a sheet of paper. This was the time of the great depression, when the value of money was actually rising if you were lucky enough to have some, but the worst possible scenario for someone heavily in debt. In the twenties things had been different, or seemed to be. Mr Hardie had patently not been strapped for cash and his visits were always a delight. He used to arrive about tea-time on Friday or Saturday evening. He returned each night to the Sandringham Hotel. On Sunday he went back to London again. I would watch for his stocky figure to come up the road, by which time, except in summer, fires would have been lit in both the dining room and the drawing room of Stratton House – rooms that were normally never used. He had a characteristic, determined walk, his feet slightly turned out, mackintosh and stick over his arm. At the door he would be met ceremoniously by my grandmother with a respectful, almost obsequious, air which always puzzled me as a child because it was so different from the way she normally behaved. She then disappeared and he took tea with Mayna and me. The silver teapot was brought out, and thin-cut sandwiches, cake on a silver stand – food much inferior in my view to the heavily buttered chunks of brown bread and freshly cooked winkles which I looked forward to when Uncle Fred came down. But, nice as Uncle Fred was, Mr Hardie brought deeper consolations – parental ones, though I didn't yet know that – and a reassuring air of privilege and authority. Our narrow household was suddenly more spacious.

He usually wore brown boots, knickerbockers, and tweed jacket, rather rumpled, all well used; and a wing collar with a silk tie. His mackintosh pockets would be stuffed with magazines – the *Strand*, the *Illustrated London News*, the *Tatler* – and gifts of sweets and cigarettes. Nestlé's chocolate in a cylindrical box, each piece wrapped in silver paper, was a special favourite. If there were colds about, he would unload one or two bottles of Lung Linctus which he purchased at Lenton the Chemist on his way up from the hotel. He regarded Lenton's Lung Linctus, not only as a matchless cough cure, but as a kind of restorative like Sanatogen ('to reconstruct the nervous system') or Phyllosan ('to fortify the over-forties'). With all medicines, patent or otherwise, he worked on the principle that three times the stated dose would do three times as much good. Often he would bring small painted tins of cachous, designed to sweeten the breath. Mayna had drawers full of them: an unnecessary precaution because both he, and to a lesser extent she, were heavy smokers. He smoked his Ardaths and she smoked State Express, the brand labelled 'My Darling' which had gold tips. His presence was charged with a tobacco-y, companionable, masculine quality quite different from anyone else's. He seemed a large man, though he was in fact quite small. He made jokes that I didn't fully understand.

His voice was musical and persuasive. His eyes were exceptionally bright and penetrating, yet full of amusement; they were hazel-brown, I think, but sometimes their colour seemed to change. Strangely, I have no recollection of his ever wearing glasses, even to read, but latterly he must have done. He was warm and loving and very patient with me and, as I've mentioned, he would make up those splendid stories about Richardson before I went to sleep.

Did I always call him 'Mr Hardie'? I didn't call him 'uncle', the favoured name for children's uncertain relationships. By the time I was nine or ten, I must surely have written thank-you letters. Perhaps the problem was got over by avoiding any term of endearment and writing something at the bottom of one of Mayna's letters. Of course I had begun to wonder whether...? But he fulfilled none of the paternal norms: he had a different name, he lived in a different place, his relationship to Mayna was not that of a husband. It couldn't be; and yet ... and yet...

On occasions like Christmas or Easter he never came down; I suppose he spent these with his family. I missed him most at Christmas. He tried to make up for this by a flood of parcels. I got bored with opening them and they did little to assuage the special loneliness, almost a dread, that comes with Christmas when all the world seems festive and you feel you've been left out; it was his presence I needed, not his presents. Mayna and my grandmother must have found it hard to put up with a small, silly boy who sulked at a spate of gifts.

One Christmas Eve my silliness was brought home to me. I was about to go to bed when someone knocked at the front door. The night was bitterly cold, with racing clouds and needle-bright stars. A dusting of snow blew about in the wind. An elderly woman stood outside. She sounded as if she was in some kind of despair, and asked to speak to my mother. When Mayna came to the door, she held out the little bundle of pictures: small, amateur paintings of conventional scenes, cheaply framed. Mayna didn't even look at them, she just handed them back. 'Thank you,' she said, 'but I'm afraid not.' Then she shut the door. I plucked at her arm. I longed to say, 'Please buy a picture, please invite her in, she has nowhere to go.' 'Come,' said Mayna, 'up to bed with you. It's Christmas tomorrow.' I remember nothing else about that Christmas, or the others of my childhood. They were unmarked by ritual – we had no Christmas tree, we never went to church; and we made no attempt, even the most mournful one, to celebrate New Year. But the woman shut out on that icy night I have never forgotten.

Mayna also received parcels, of course, which she appeared to value as little as I did mine. She had accumulated a large collection of beaded evening handbags, gold trinkets, enamel cigarette cases and the like which she never used. Like the remorseless accumulation of cachous, they were relegated to her bedroom drawers and lay unregarded among the Spirella corsets and the crèpe de Chine. Of far more interest to her were the hats and frocks she sent for 'on approval' from London. Marshall and Snelgrove was a favourite source of supply. They arrived in cardboard boxes, nestling in virginal sheets of tissue paper, and she would hasten upstairs to try them on. The hats usually made her laugh.

When he resumed his week-end visits, my father liked to play with some of the presents he'd given me, particularly a splendid roulette wheel with a green baize cloth on which we would pretend to gamble for high stakes. He would act as croupier, Ardath cigarette glowing. He insisted on using the proper formulae: '*Faîtes vos jeux*', '*Mesdames et messieurs, rien va plus!*' It had little appeal for me, or for Mayna, who reluctantly got roped in. Though I liked the slow circulation of the ball and its last tantalising hops before it dropped into a slot, I preferred the bagatelle machines on the pier where the stake was only a penny, but for real. My father loved the wheel. I think he bought it for himself.

A model steam engine which drove a small dynamo also attracted him – the more so, perhaps, as he had an ignorance of mechanical matters which, if he'd not been a Judge, would have seemed flabbergasting. One day when I was playing with the engine it began to show signs of incipient violence, like a miniature version of the geyser. I consulted my father, who, cigarette in hand, was reading the *Illustrated London News*. He joined me on the floor. I suggested that we withdraw the methylated spirit lamp from under the boiler. He brushed the suggestion aside. Instead he decided to lift up the spring-loaded safety valve, which seemed to have got stuck. Unfolding a small gold pocket knife, he tried to prise the spring open. By this time the apparatus was hissing from the joints and starting to jump about in an alarming way. My father, unperturbed but with rising irritation, bent himself to the task of easing the spring. At last he contrived to lift the valve a fraction, whereupon a thin jet of steam hissed out and a bright red spot appeared in the middle of his bald head. With a cry he leant back and clapped to the affected part one of the vast honey-coloured silk handkerchiefs he kept in his top pocket (handkerchiefs which served in winter to enable him to grapple with colds before Lenton's Lung Linctus took effect and in summer to wave away wasps if they came near him – though if they came near me he would say 'Keep still, Pip, keep still, they won't sting you if you let them alone'). The jet of steam stung him more effectively than any wasp – indeed, a hornet couldn't have done better. Dabbing his head and haranguing me on the folly of fooling with a machine that was plainly defective, he discovered that his cigarette had fallen from his lips when the jet struck and burnt a neat hole in his knickerbockers. Before he had time to blame me for this as well, the safety valve blew off with a kind of hollow shriek and embedded itself in the ceiling, followed by clouds of steam and boiling water which we only escaped by diving behind the easy chair.

Another Christmas present which took my father's fancy was a toy electric railway with a transformer that enabled it to run off the mains. In those days there were no built-in fuses, and the power plug (so called) was a piece of wood with two holes in it screwed to the skirting board. When a problem arose with the connection, my father advanced towards this plug with the wire from the transformer clutched in his hand. Very carefully he inserted the two bare ends of the wire into the holes of the plug, whereupon he was thrown on his back to the accompaniment of a loud bang and a sheet of blue flame, and all the lights went out. It was the only time I remember Mayna upbraiding him, which she did in no uncertain terms: a wigging of the kind he was more accustomed to give than receive. He was shaken and rather ashamed.

He was better at more orthodox games and, as soon as I was thought to be sufficiently adroit, he set out to teach me to play golf and tennis. We played tennis, or rather practised strokes, on the grass courts behind the pavilion at the recreation ground, where Dr Bull played his cricket. My father was a good tennis player, of county class as a young man, and it must have been excruciating for him to spend time on the court with me. But again he was endlessly patient. As a golfer he was less good and his patience less in evidence, for he had to cope with his own inadequacies on the links as well as mine. I still have a piece of note-paper on which he scribbled out a few basic instructions which begin with 'Keep your eye on the very bottom of the ball' (repeated twice, fiercely underlined) and end with 'ALWAYS keep in good temper'.

Naturally we didn't play golf on the championship course at Old Hunstanton, though he'd been a member there since 1908. We went to a nine-hole course (which doesn't exist any more) just beyond the lighthouse. The pleasant young professional there was very attentive – not surprisingly, for Mr Hardie was lavish in his tipping, handing out pound notes when a half-crown at most would have been expected. I recall one morning when the pro had given me a lesson and my game was, for once, spot on, the iron shots clicking into place. My father, on the other hand, had developed an appalling slice which made him more and more tetchy as we prowled about in the rough, searching for lost balls. In the end a man behind us became so impatient that he drove through. His ball bounded between us and came to rest some ten or fifteen yards ahead as we were making our way to the green. A shout of 'Fore' came down the wind. My father said nothing, but his lips tightened in a way I had learned to beware of. He strode ahead and, drawing out his brassie, smote the ball back again with all his force. It was a majestic stroke; there was no trace of a slice. The ball, boring low into the wind, sang like a bullet past the head of the offender, who was hastening forward to apologise, and disappeared towards the club house. A vigorous altercation followed. I think my father had the better of it: he was a difficult man to argue with. At any rate he was in high good humour for the rest of the day and his game took a marked turn for the better.

Once a year Mayna and I went away on a seaside holiday for a month to one or other of my father's chosen watering places. In England, of course; no question of our going abroad. Bournemouth was the favourite, but we also went to Torquay and Whitby. Apart from two holidays in Bournemouth at Silverdell Lodge (the bungalow where Mayna stayed after I was born), we would take rooms. They were of a reasonable standard as rooms go, but they did not go very far. My father, following precedent as befitted a lawyer, always stayed in the best hotel. In Bournemouth it was the Royal Bath. Needless to say, neither Mayna nor I was invited to join him there. It did not occur to me to question the fairness of these arrangements; and he did spend a lot of time with us. At Bournemouth he took me to a gymnasium three times a week to be taught some boxing and fencing: skills which, like riding, he considered to be appropriate for a young gentleman. The instructor was an ex-army man with a waxed moustache whose main aim seemed to be to instil aggression. He did not have much success with me. The other boys whom I was forced to contend with, whether with fist or foil, were bigger than I was and made short work of me. I was thoroughly humiliated – which may, of course, have been one purpose of the exercise.

When I wasn't being knocked about in the gym, I was hard put to know what to do with myself. I became acutely aware of what Dr Johnson called 'the tediousness of time'. Bournemouth seemed to bring this feeling on faster than anywhere else; my having been born in the place did nothing to assuage it. Mayna spent most of her time walking round the shops or going to the cinema, and I trailed about after her. I disliked shops and very soon I began to dislike cinemas. One cinema had a special section at the back where patrons were served tea and cakes whilst they watched the film – it was a wonder they didn't dance as well, for tea dances were then all the rage. I disliked this tea-serving place most of all. The talkies had come in by this time and I have a recollection, probably erroneous, of listening to George Arliss hamming away to the clink of cups. Mayna had a passion for George Arliss. I didn't share it.

The keenest memory I have of Bournemouth is of jumping off a moving tram. I had always admired men who did this and I finally screwed up courage to emulate them after a particularly shameful session at the gym. Unfortunately I hadn't appreciated that you had to jump off in the same direction as the tram was going. I jumped off in the opposite direction. The tram was still bowling along and the road rose up and hit me. I had to be assisted to the pavement by a passer-by, and a big blue bump the size of a pigeon's egg came up above one eye. After the headache went away, I was quite proud of it; but Mayna had a serious talk with my father about the violent boys at the gym. 'Pip must learn,' said my father sternly, 'to take the rough with the smooth.' I think he, too, was quite proud of my bump. He never asked me how I got it.

Torquay, birthplace of Agatha Christie, was a considerable improvement on Bournemouth, though I always felt de-energised. Partly this was the effect of the dopey Devon air after the east winds of Norfolk, partly the fact that we lived largely on mackerel. My father, descending in his knickerbockers from the Imperial Hotel and carrying his Burberry, used to hire a sailing boat, with a man to sail it, and we regularly went out fishing in the bay. Sometimes we caught pollock, but nearly always mackerel. They came in shoals and we hauled them in endlessly, iridescent, shot with green and blue. They flipped about in their death throes at the bottom of the boat. From time to time the old man who took us out would pick up a wriggling fish in his thick brown hand and cut slices from its flesh to act as bait. I was upset when he did this, but didn't like to protest for fear of being thought unmanly. Slow death from suffocation did not disturb me, slow death by the knife did – for the same reason, I suppose, one may tolerate hanging but draw a line at drawing and quartering. Most of the fish we caught we threw back into the sea, but they were dead by then. The weather always seemed to be fine at Torquay and much of the time I went about barefoot. By the end of the holiday it was strange to have to wear anything heavier than sandshoes.

I have only a vague recollection of the house we stayed at there or of the woman who ran it. She must have been tolerant and kind for she gave me the run of the place and cooked mackerel for us day after day. There was a patch of grass on which I used to sprawl out which gave off a salty, musty smell that was full of expectancy, yet sad. It prickled the bottoms of my feet when I stood up. We made trips to Dartmoor – an empty place then, little disturbed by coaches and cars. I liked going there, but I found it faintly sinister and threatening. Perhaps it was the prison. Or perhaps it was me. I got the same kind of feeling, but more powerfully, at home in Norfolk when the tide was right out and I was alone on the edge of the sea, far from the shore. The hugeness of the beach and the vastness of the sky would suddenly overwhelm me: I would be seized by a premonition that out of the receding sea a giant wave was about to surge in and engulf me. One evening, when thunder was muttering over the mussel beds and the purple-grey water, I seemed to see its white crest rearing up among the piled clouds on the horizon and to hear in the distance its terrible approaching roar. I ran back in panic to the safety of the land. It was a kind of waking nightmare. It shows how precarious my identity must have been, how easily overwhelmed by irrational anxieties.

Whitby was altogether different from Torquay. If Agatha Christie had been born there, she would have written very different books. There was still the sea, of course, but a colder, more insistent sea. I don't remember much about the geography of Whitby as it was then, but I remember the atmosphere: the harbour echoing with the ceaseless cry of gulls; the west cliff with its narrow streets, where you could buy jet, and its line of shallow steps – a hundred and ninety nine? – leading up to the abbey ruins and the Norman church on top, and Captain Cook staring out to sea with the moors stretching away behind him; and the east cliff, where we stayed, and its broad walks and bandstand and theatre. Mayna brought back a jet brooch for my grandmother, in keeping with her status as a widow. I thought it was a dreadful thing to wear.

We went boating at Whitby, but on a more modest scale than at Torquay, and without the benefit of professional help. On one occasion we made the mistake of taking out a rowing boat on a blustery day, when the wind was getting up and a strong ebb tide setting in. I elected to row and, with the tide in our favour, we made excellent speed towards the harbour mouth. Where the harbour funnels, however, we began to encounter short steep waves driven in by the rising wind against the ebb. Soon we were taking aboard a fair amount of water. Though the wind was against us, the tide was beginning to carry us out to sea. The time had come to turn about. My father stripped off his Norfolk jacket and prepared to take the oars. To change places while the boat drifted broadside on, rolling and tossing in the confused sea, proved both hazardous and undignified. A small crowd gathered on the quay to watch my father manfully trying to stem the tide. At one point, as he pulled hard at the top of a crest, he failed to make contact with the water and his left oar flew out of the rowlock and fell overboard. We both made a dive for it and came within an inch of capsizing before we managed, just, to get it back. Crouched at the helm in my shorts, I made a shivery pretence of steering while my father strained at the oars as we slowly reversed out to sea against a background of darkening cloud lit by viridian and gamboge. Luckily, before we reached open water, we contrived to get near enough to the harbour wall for someone to throw us a line as we bobbed up and down in the swell, and we were ignominiously hauled to safety.

I saw my first play at Whitby. I was kept up specially beyond my bed-time. We had seats in the front row. There was a small orchestra, with an uncertain fiddler who often took a while to settle on his note – an appropriate overture perhaps, because the play was *The Squeaker* by Edgar Wallace. My father knew Edgar Wallace and was once so impressed by one of his thrillers that he sent a copy to each of his judicial brethren! The fact that Wallace was the author of the play was no doubt why we went. Its eponymous hero (if he can be called that) is a young gangster who turns informer. In the last act he is 'executed' by his associates, pleading for mercy in the presence of his mother. It was all too much for me: by that time I was sobbing uncontrollably. When the lights went up, I could scarcely get my breath for tears. No-one else seemed to be in the least perturbed. There was polite clapping and the audience began to make their way to the exit, laughing and chatting. I couldn't believe they could be so cold-blooded;

Mayna and my father were as bad as the rest. I was bitterly ashamed, of myself, of humanity, of everything, as I stumbled out after them into the windy darkness and the thud of the sea.

Back at home we never went out in the evening, except now and again to the Capitol Cinema. Matinées were the general rule. Apart from Mr Hardie, virtually our only visitors (George having been forbidden the house) were my Uncles Ernest and Fred. They both worked in London, also on the railways but in a higher, clerical capacity, Ernest at Aldersgate (and later Billingsgate) and Fred at Woolwich. Once a year, usually in the summer, they came down by train to visit their mother. Ernest brought his wife and child – my Aunt Harrie and my cousin Gil, he of the crystal set. Fred came down alone, because he was separated from his wife and children. Though he now lived with another woman, she was unacceptable at Stratton House! Neither brother spoke about Mr Hardie. He remained unacknowledged, a kind of phantom brother-in-law, about whom the less said, the better.

Ernest was a frugal, conservative, utterly reliable citizen, dedicated to his garden, his pipe and the railways, grey hair kept at bay by Morgan's Pomade, a man who prided himself on never, literally never, having had a day off work in his life. He was anxious for the future of the country; at home, scroungers everywhere; abroad, waiting to take our jobs (which were disappearing fast enough already in all conscience), he saw the unimaginable millions of China and the Subcontinent happy to live off a handful of rice.

Fred was very different. He had the qualities of a second child in as full a measure as Ernest had those of a first. Fair-haired, amusing, with a light touch, unperturbed by the Yellow Peril, he had never felt the need which obsessed his brother to give each unforgiving minute its sixty seconds' worth of distance run. For some reason he clipped his g's like those women who used to frighten me at the hunt. He was full of tricks to amuse a child. Later in life he developed a dicky heart; but before that he used to take me crabbing and shrimping and winkling and cockling along the familiar shore he'd scampered over as a boy. Reaching for crabs under the rocks at low tide was a source of great excitement. Fumbles could provoke a painful nip. A more placid pleasure was shrimping on summer evenings in the warm shallow sea, pushing the wide net ahead of us and feeling all the little creatures pattering against our legs; and afterwards, skin still glowing from salt and sun, the savour of a fresh-cooked harvest of shrimps and the rustle of winkles and cockles ('Stewkey Blues', marvellously plump) cleaning themselves, unwitting victims, in a bucket of salt water under the sink.

I was always sorry to see Uncle Fred go. But sorrow was tempered by the ritual of departure. I would accompany him to the station and, as the train was drawing out, he would lean from the window and press a half-crown into my hand. It was a half-crown he could ill afford when he had alimony to pay and a new home to buy and a new companion to keep.

Eleven

I have mentioned my father's mounting debts. He had lost a great deal of money in the stock market crash of 1929. He went on losing a great deal more in efforts to recoup what he had lost, for the market went on falling through 1930, 1931 and 1932.

As time went on, his need for money became increasingly acute. He had grown accustomed to having more of it than he knew what to do with: in the heyday of his practice at the Bar he had drawers full of uncashed cheques. Though modest in his personal tastes – a small flat, abstemious in eating and drinking – he was an insouciant and prodigal spender. But prodigality would still have left him with plenty had it not been for one fatal flaw – gambling, and compulsive gambling at that. It wasn't until years later that I learned the full force of that compulsion, but as a boy I glimpsed its face when he took me once to a greyhound stadium and proceeded to bet heavily and unsuccessfully. I got extremely bored: all the races looked the same to me and nothing of interest seemed to happen in between. He knew no more about 'form' than I did, but this didn't deter him. He also knew little about stocks and shares. This didn't deter him either. He wasn't in stadium or market to make money, but to take risks. Money as such meant nothing; the 'buzz' was what he craved for.

It wasn't only money he was short of, it was goodwill, too. He was beginning to tax the patience of his colleagues. He delivered a number of rash judgements which incurred rebuke, and his well-publicised and unfashionable views on controversial matters like contraception and abortion were provoking wide criticism. I had no inkling of these things; they went on high over my head, distant reverberations of the adult world. Even if I'd known about them, they would have meant nothing to me at that age and in those unsophisticated days. Nor would I have associated them with Mr Hardie. There was no mention of any Mr Hardie in the *Daily Mail*, which I idly glanced at when it dropped through the letter box – the sports pages mainly, it must be admitted. Anyway, I had my own preoccupations – a Webley air pistol amongst others.

My father went on paying his usual visits to Stratton House. We played some tennis or golf as the season dictated. He seemed unchanged, if somewhat abstracted. I was old enough now to be able to give him some semblance of company. I also needed – and he must have sensed this – to bring out honestly into the open things which remained unspoken between us. The subject was not an easy one to raise at the best of times and he showed no anxiety to help. His mind was on other matters, reflecting an uneasiness which I was subconsciously troubled by, like the half thoughts that drift about under the commas in a book, and which made me reluctant to push forward my own minor concerns. Something significant was amiss. I could hear the murmur of talk in the drawing room after I'd gone to bed and knew that Mayna was trying to comfort and reassure him. I had no idea of the approaching catastrophe.

The Christmas of 1932, mild and rainy, brought its usual spate of presents from him, but they were significantly less lavish, mainly food parcels and game from the Army and Navy Stores just across Victoria Street from Queen Anne's Mansions. No wine, of course: with George's example before us, we didn't keep it in the house. I received a private present of my own: my voice was starting to break. After any long silence it would sink into a spooky bass of which I was very proud.

At the turn of the year my father had a bad bout of influenza, and then another and another. Over the following weeks he came only occasionally to see us. When he did, he was increasingly preoccupied. His last visit was just before Easter. He was as affectionate as ever, but depressed, restless and unwell, seriously out of sorts. I felt more than uneasiness, rather a sort of desolation – a feeling I was familiar with, but which usually vanished in his presence. It was as though I was somehow in the way. Mayna was plainly concerned. He kept on reverting to the differences with his colleagues and asking her for small sums of money which she could ill afford. But after Easter she began to speak more cheerfully about him. He was getting better, she told me; he was a resilient man, still strong. He wrote her a letter (now lost) which seemed to reassure her. Primroses and daffodils were coming out in the garden.

Then, very early on the morning of 27 April, there was a knock on the door. The dogs barked. Mayna put on her dressing gown and went down. A man was standing outside, a local reporter. He said: 'I'm afraid I have bad news for you', and handed her a copy of the day's paper. Across the front page was a banner headline: 'FAMOUS JUDGE TAKES HIS OWN LIFE'. Below was a large photograph labelled *Mr Justice McCardie*. It was a photograph of Mr Hardie. There was no mistaking it. All the unspoken things that had puzzled and worried me clicked at last into place. Mr Justice McCardie was my Mr Hardie; and Mr Hardie, bringer of gifts, was my father. I knew it: Mayna didn't have to tell me. She would never need to now – at about half past four on the previous afternoon, when we were sitting down to tea at Stratton House, my father had shot himself. He left no message, no letter, nothing.

It was a brutal good-bye to those who loved him, And a brutal way for Mayna to receive it, on the door-step in her dressing gown dandled by the cold morning wind, shocked, disbelieving, searching for words to say.

Within hours the Press descended en masse. They besieged

the house. A large group stood in a huddle outside the garage opposite, cameras at the ready. Mayna was bewildered and distraught. She didn't know whether to answer the door or what to say if she did. Luckily we had no telephone (my father always hated using it). She sheltered in the parlour, a shawl wrapped round her. She did not cry much: it would have been better if she had. My grandmother kept on making tea. I was told to lie low, and sat with Mayna, full of thoughts too difficult for my age, as bewildered as she was. Uncle Fred wired to say that he was coming down. After his arrival we felt protected; he skilfully parried all enquiries. The only reporter I remember was the man from *The Times*. He knocked and raised his hat and asked whether my mother had a statement to make. Uncle Fred said she hadn't. Whereupon he replaced his hat and went away again. The others did not go away, scenting scandal.

All the newspapers were full of my father's suicide, and the popular ones ran long articles about Mayna. Presumably the local man had tipped them off. Here are some extracts, typical of many:

> From the lips of those who knew and loved him, I have today heard the secret story of Mr Justice McCardie's life... It started over 30 years ago when Henry McCardie, a young and brilliant barrister overloaded with briefs, came to this quiet seaside town to forget work for a brief spell... While he did not mix with the town's society, he used to chat with fishermen, shopkeepers, railway men and farm workers in the neighbouring country. Through his friendship with humble people he came to know Mr Archer, a foreman porter at the railway station here, whose wife kept an apartment house. One day he met Mr Archer's daughter, Miss Mabel Archer, a strikingly beautiful and well-educated girl. A friendship sprang up between them. In her the young barrister found someone

to whom he could confide his hopes and ambitions. And so the friendship grew...

When I called at Stratton House, a double-fronted residence in Westgate where Miss Archer lives with her aged mother, Miss Archer came to the door. A tall and handsome woman, wearing a greenish jumper suit, her eyes told of tears. 'No,' she said, 'our friendship is too sacred a thing to talk about. The news came to me as a terrible shock. When he came down here last just before Easter he was recovering from influenza and very depressed. He was worried too about his work and the fact that some of his judgements had been criticised. But I never dreamed that this awful thing would happen.' Mrs Archer, who joined us, added, 'Yes, we have lost a very dear and a very old friend. He was one of the kindest men who ever lived.'

This was bad enough. It might have been far worse – and nearly was. For instance:

One of Sir Henry's constant companions was a youngster to whom he had taken a great fancy. The lad used to accompany him to golf and tennis, and the judge who could be so stern when the facts demanded it used to romp gleefully with his small friend.

This description of our relationship appealed to me then no more than it does now. In my new deep voice, I expressed my disgust. To my elders it was not just painful, it was perilously near the bone. The McCardie family, who were even more harassed by reporters than we were, must have been appalled by the sly suggestions of a 'secret' story hinting at disgrace. How much they knew about Mayna and me before my father's death I can't say; he was especially close to his younger sister Maggie, by then Mrs Bindley, and it seems unlikely that she was unaware of our existence, though it is possible. But she, so scrupulous to guard her brother's reputation and the family name, could only wait and see what we would do: she had no means of knowing how discreet or trustworthy we might prove to be. A liaison with the daughter of a railway porter did not bode well. Here was a girl who had, as it were, jumped out of her station. In such circumstances it is easy enough for a family to be persuaded that the girl is threatening to ruin their good name, not that one of them had ruined hers. Mayna was loyal and honourable, despite her deep hurt; if there was any dishonour, it was on my father's side. I suspect the McCardies didn't see it like that; no effort was made to get in touch with us, but the thought of what Mayna might say, or the Press winkle out, must have been a source of constant anxiety. As it was, the defences held. Neither the Archers nor the McCardies gave anything away. There was not a word in the newspapers of a natural child. Nor of my father's debts (save, later on, in some articles by his confidential clerk which the McCardies were also much upset about). Looking back, it seems extraordinary. Nowadays everything would have been avidly exposed.

Mayna read about the inquest in the papers. She learned of the date and place of my father's funeral the same way. No-one told her, let alone invited her. For the McCardies she might have been someone who did not exist; no doubt they fervently wished she didn't. Mayna did not want to be recognised; indeed she connived at her own obliteration. But it was cruel just the same. There was no ritual of departure, no chance to mourn. Her grief had to be hidden away and, because he had killed himself, guilt was mixed up in her grief: could she, she asked herself, have done more to help him? There was only the empty chair where he used to sit in the drawing room – no fire lit there any more, the person most dear to her suddenly out of reach, as though cased behind glass, like the books he had given her. She sent a bouquet of spring flowers bearing the unsigned inscription: 'A last tribute to a life-long and dear friend'. But there was no emotional release. She never got over his death. She became more and more solitary. Not long afterwards she developed asthma, and Stratton House was filled with the scent of Potter's Asthma Cure, a greenish-grey powder, the smoke of which she inhaled while it slowly smouldered, like a kind of incense to his memory, in a tiny tin tray.

As for me, I was full of conflicting emotions – a stunned apprehension of death and the strange ominousness of suicide, a sympathy for Mayna which I longed to express but didn't know how to, a sudden marvellous certainty that Mr Hardie really was my father. Subconsciously, of course, I'd known he was. Now I knew it consciously and could admit it openly. Joy bubbled up under the sadness. The loneliness of life with Mayna which had left me emotionally marooned didn't diminish but became different, part of a new pattern more bearable because more explicit. This realisation overtopped grief: I remember feeling ashamed that I wasn't showing enough sorrow. I needed time to comprehend that, at the moment I had found my father, I had also lost him, that he was on the other side of a door which would never open again; time for the hubbub to die down so that I could hear echoing in my mind, as it has so often since, the sound of that shot like the sound of a gun in the woods, empty and distant and irrevocable.

If I seem to have spoken ungratefully about the McCardie family, I should not have done. It is true they made no approach to Mayna, but they respected loyalty when they saw it; and they did not forget me. Despite having to find large sums from their own resources in order to settle my father's debts, they agreed to set up a small trust fund for my education. The arrangements were made by my father's solicitor,

Tom Cannon Brookes, 'T.C.B'. T.C.B was an old charmer with lidded eyes who came down to Norfolk to see me, presumably to find out what I was like. He brought me my father's silver hair brushes and toilet case, and his tie pin. I still have them.

T.C.B was a kind friend to me over many years. At the time I was only vaguely aware of what was happening. I had been told that I would not be able to go to Worksop College because there was no money to pay the fees. Mention was made of the grammar school at Lynn. I was all set to go there. But, thanks in large measure to my unknown 'uncle' and 'aunt', money for the fees turned up after all, and it was to Worksop that I duly went in the summer term of 1933.

III
ABOUT MY FATHER

'The more one sits here, the more one realises that it is only by gentleness that one can approach the truth.'

McCardie, in the King's Bench Division, 1932

Twelve

When I grew up, I naturally wanted to find out more about my father. On and off over the years I therefore put together a memoir about him. I had no thoughts of publication, it was written for the desk drawer. Even so, it didn't satisfy me. I felt instinctively that something was missing, something hidden. I knew that into my childhood world, which apart from occasional visits from my uncles was essentially a world of women – my mother and grandmother at home, mistresses at school – Mr Hardie descended like a god, a summer glow seemed to attend him. But he and Mr Justice McCardie didn't quite coalesce. There was a gap. Mr Justice McCardie remained a kind of historical figure, a paragon of legal learning, seemingly frank and certainly outspoken yet curiously baffling, always stepping into the limelight out of sight.

The name McCardie is an unusual one and no doubt the family would have been easy to trace had I been less reluctant to probe old scars, including my own. As it was, there seemed at first a plethora of information. A biography was published in 1934 by George Pollock. McCardie's important judgements are all dealt with there and they are, of course, enshrined more fully in the Law Reports. A separate collection of some of them, called *The Judicial Wisdom of Mr Justice McCardie*, was put together in 1932 by Albert Crew. Reprints of his lectures were to be found in various journals. There were references galore in the press of the time. These, however, are components of a *Life*, not of a life. My father as he really was is absent, even in Pollock's book, save sometimes faintly like the warm impress on a bed just left. Pollock was unwilling to let him in. As one legal historian has remarked: 'In general, Pollock was clearly prejudiced in favour of McCardie. His book may fairly be described as hagiography'.* A certain prejudice in favour of his subject is not unreasonable in a biographer, but there's no doubt that Pollock's book, being written just after McCardie's death, has a strong memorial ring about it. Of his unorthodox private life, of his gambling, of his errors of judgement nothing is said, and only the slenderest personal records still exist – a bare handful of papers. The rest have gone up in smoke. I've had, therefore, to rely all too often on hearsay and guesswork – the kind of evidence he would have laughed away. Nevertheless, I believe that the memoir which follows (and which incorporates some information gleaned from the McCardie family when in due course I met them) is essentially true in its particulars. But it doesn't tell the whole story. That I might never have known if it had not been for a surprising series of events which I shall come to later on.

---

*Shimon Stretreet: *Judges on Trial*, page 172.

Thirteen

Henry Alfred McCardie was born in Edgbaston, Birmingham, on 18 July, 1869. His father, Joseph William McCardie, was an Irishman whose family lived at Desertmartin, Co. Londonderry. A surviving photograph of Joseph shows a determined, easy sort of man, with a Celtic look and the promise of plenty of drive. He was a successful businessman and a local philanthropist, but little else about him has come down to us.

Joseph had a brother, James, and two sisters. The brothers emigrated to England as young men in 1840, when emigration was practically compulsory. They set up in business together in Birmingham, then in a phase of massive expansion. Their sisters, Mary Anne and Maria Theresa, remained in Ireland and married there. Mary Anne married a Presbyterian minister, John Martin, and Maria Theresa a draper, Samuel McCaw. Maria Theresa later suffered a severe break-down when her husband was thrown from his horse and killed only two days after the birth of her fourth child. The brothers brought her over to England and arranged for her to enter a retreat, where she died. Her children remained in Ireland and were brought up by their McCaw uncles. (At the time of the 1881 Census John Martin was staying with the McCardies at Edgbaston, and his son, James McCardie Martin, a naval surgeon, was later to become one of my father's few close friends.)

Joseph and James flourished in Birmingham at 24 Worcester Street, primarily as button makers (of which there were well over a hundred in the city at that time). Later they branched out as wholesalers and warehousemen. By the time Joseph reached his forties he was sufficiently prosperous to feel in need of a wife and, on 28 April, 1864, he married. In the preceding January his mother had died, aged eighty-one, and in September his brother James died at the age of forty-eight, so that in the year of his marriage Joseph was twice bereft. His bride was Jane Elizabeth Hunt. She was thirty – an age at which in those days women began to get a little worried if they were still single – she was the daughter of William Hunt of Wirksworth, Derbyshire, a well-to-do farmer who also owned a brickyard at Bolehill, formerly the site of a Roman lead mine, just outside the town. She had been educated at a private school in Derby, and was spoken of as being 'very shy – almost afraid to speak'. The shyness was deceptive. The new Mrs McCardie soon showed her quality and settled down with her husband and four servants in a substantial house, Wellington Grove, in Wellington Road, Edgbaston. There, over the next thirteen years, she produced seven children. Henry Alfred was (like my mother) the fourth. He was baptised at Carr's Lane Chapel by the Rev. Dr Dale with water Dr Dale had brought back from the river Jordan.

Edgbaston in the eighteen sixties was a semi-rural area, to which Birmingham's manufacturers and entrepreneurs moved out when they'd made their money.

> It was characterised [to quote a local historian] by large Georgian, Regency and Victorian houses set in acres of garden. Hagley Road, that most splendid of thoroughfares, rang to the clip-clop of horses hooves, their steady 5–10 miles an hour sometimes reduced on account of a flock of sheep being driven along the road to market. Even as late as the 1920s it was possible to see, from gardens in Wellington Road, green fields and grazing sheep...'

It's easy to forget that McCardie was born and grew up as a

Victorian, in the high noon of Empire, when gas jets popped along the corridors of the big houses and children learned over nursery tea that the British had a divine mission to bring betterment and justice to lesser peoples. Though unorthodox in many ways, he retained the impress of the age – in his passionate endorsement of eugenics, for example; in the strong patriotism of some of his public speeches; in his denunciations of extravagance in dress; in his belief that the English Common Law was the embodiment of human wisdom. Echoing through some of his judgements – sometimes not so faintly – can be heard the sounds of that gas-lit, horse-drawn world and the ringing tones of the Victorian Bar. Nor was he unaffected by the social distinctions so important to the Victorians, not least the line so carefully drawn between the careers of gentlemen and the vulgarity of trade. And lines were drawn within lines. Doctors were acceptable, but not dentists or vets. Shippers of wine might pass muster, but not people who made buttons; or farmers, unless like the Hunts they could aspire to call themselves landowners. An Irishman can slip through the English class system better than most; but there was no bilking these things. His own father, after all, was one of the nouveaux riches. And not unaware of it. The spacious solidity of Wellington Road helped to disguise the deficiency; and in the year Henry Alfred was born he took a further step towards that end by purchasing a substantial piece of ground in the local cemetery where his mother and brother were buried and laying in front of it a large stone slab engraved with the words *Entrance to the Vaults of J.W. McCardie, 1869.*

Certainly it was a source of deep satisfaction to Mrs McCardie when two of her sons became professional men. I get a distinct impression that the Hunts, despite the brickyard, regarded themselves as a cut above the McCardies – at least before Henry Alfred rose up to adorn the name – and that Miss Hunt was thought to have married beneath her. She had a reputation in later years of being a snob.

There is no doubt that she hankered after more distinguished forebears in the male line. The biographical section of 'Birmingham at the opening of the twentieth Century' in Pike's *New County Series No. 3* refers to H.A. McCardie as being 'descended from an ancient Irish family on his father's side' – a fishy piece of information that my father must have supplied himself. And among the few papers which have come down to me there is one, undated, which claims to be 'a McCardie Family History (with gaps and some dates indecipherable) made up from odd notes and letters of J.H. Rugg [a cousin] to H.A. McCardie ... taken from the Herald's Office, Dublin (about 1875) and also the English Peerage (about 145 years ago)'. Any document with this provenance, despite the mention of my father, needs to be taken with a pinch of salt. The history purports to go back to the seventeenth century and the Earl of Sutherland, one of whose daughters married Donough McCarty, Earl of Clancarty. Donough, having foolishly followed the fortunes of James II, was outlawed and his lands confiscated. He fled abroad, where he allegedly changed his name from McCarty to McCardie and, returning to Ireland, sought to re-establish himself. He managed to forge a connection with the thirteenth Lord de la Warr, but regrettably his grandson failed to learn from the grandfather's experience and got mixed up with the Irish rebellion of 1798, when he was informed against and thrown into prison. On his release he married Elizabeth Hessin, by whom he had numerous children, of whom Joseph William was supposed to be one. Among the others, so the story goes, was a certain Samuel II (Samuel I having died at birth) – a feckless, charming gambler who went out to New Orleans and died there, the sort of ancestor whom any family would be proud of at a sufficient distance. Reference to a strong vein of improvidence certainly rings true. But I have found no evidence that Elizabeth Hessin (born 1779 or 80), Joseph's mother, had more than the four children mentioned; and what is said about Donough is not borne out by other biographical information about him. More recent enquiries at the Herald's Office, Dublin, threw up a McCardie squireen from Duncannon, who seemed little nearer the mark. However, I've not pursued the matter further and Joseph's parents remain shadowy. I suppose they could have sprung from some ancient Irish line, but that's not much of a peg to hang one's hat on; I could equally claim descent from an ancient, if unsung, Norfolk family on my mother's side. Families branch out in algebraic progression to a tedious and bewildering number of contributory ancestors. Although my father liked to boast of his Irish blood when he heard himself described as 'the Judge with the ever-smiling eyes', it is by no means certain that his own father's family was genetically the more important. The evidence rather suggests that the Hunts of Wirksworth contributed to his natural abilities as much as or more than the McCardies of Desertmartin. His mother was a woman 'of outstanding intellect and personality', from whom, according to Pollock, he inherited 'his capacity for unceasing industry – and his inability to sleep for more than six hours a night'. He often spoke of the debt he owed her. There is no doubt that he was deeply – perhaps damagingly – influenced by her.

Mrs McCardie had need of all her strength of character when, in 1877, her husband died and was carried to his vaults. She was left to bring up her family alone. The eldest child was twelve; Henry was eight; the youngest child was a baby, only a few days old. Unlike her sister-in-law Maria Theresa, who broke down following a similar bereavement after childbirth, Mrs McCardie managed to cope bravely and well. No doubt her father, William Hunt, helped out. But funds were short. Family tradition has it that her husband was a gambler, or at least a spendthrift, reckless about money. Most entrepreneurs were if they wanted to make their mark in that dazzle of unrestricted capitalism which blazed as brightly as anywhere in Birmingham, 'home of the self-made man'. But he was more than that. His name appears among the lists of governors whose donations supported the voluntary hospitals. He was a member of the original committee, including the Chamberlains, which founded the Woman's Hospital in Birmingham where the work undertaken by Lawson Tait, its leading surgeon, led to the hospital being described as the birthplace of modern gynaecology. So Joseph McCardie showed himself to be both generous and far-sighted as well as successful in his business.

When he died, however, his finances were overextended and Mrs McCardie had to sell Wellington Grove and move to a much smaller house at 42 Wheeleys Road. The more ambitious plans she nursed for her children had to be dropped. There was enough money to see the eldest, William, through Cambridge and medical school. The rest had to make their own way.

The three other boys, including Henry, followed William to the local grammar school, King Edward's, then in New Street, Birmingham, having been rebuilt in 'Commissioner's Gothic' to the design of Charles Barry in 1833. Under the vigorous regime of Dr Vardy, it provided a first-class education. Two thirds of the pupils were admitted for a payment of £4 a year; the other third were given scholarships. Henry did not get a scholarship, nor did he otherwise distinguish himself there. Lively but not studious is perhaps the best way to describe him. He was in no way the prodigious worker he afterwards became. Except in his last year, when he competed for a form prize and suddenly shot to the top of the class, he was fairly low down the lists; scholastically he showed no evidence of unusual powers. At school it's not quite decent to be a swot and he hadn't that enviable kind of cleverness that absorbs knowledge without industry. His sporting prowess was more in evidence. He won the junior (under 15) championship at the school sports, in the course of which he threw a cricket ball 85 yards, 6 inches, and jumped 14 feet 11. Later he won two senior athletic medals – second in the long jump, third in the quarter mile. He boxed. He played cricket for the second XI. At age sixteen, he left. There was no expectation among staff or contemporaries that he would prove to be one of the school's most distinguished alumni.

The problem then was to find a job. When he was a small boy, his mother had taken him to a phrenologist who pronounced that he would become either a bishop or a judge. These seemed somewhat distant objectives in the light of his undistinguished career at King Edward's and he started by setting his sights somewhat lower. After some dithering he entered the office of a firm of Birmingham auctioneers, Messrs Bettridge and Thomas (who, curiously enough, celebrated the jubilee of their business association in the same year as he was elevated to the Bench). It soon became clear, however, that he wasn't cut out to be an auctioneer, though he did pick up some useful knowledge of commercial practice.

He also began to write poetry and to read widely. The year 1885, when he left school, saw a tremendous burst of poetic activity. Some of his verse has, alas, survived, demonstrating why he may have contemplated (according to Pollock) devoting his life to literature and why he was wise to decide not to. A commonplace book which he began a year later, in 1886, has also survived. This, too, opens with a few pages of young McCardie's verse, but soon it starts to fill up with literary quotations in Latin, French and Italian as well as English; there are even some carefully copied epigrams in Greek. Then the orientation alters again. Entries switch to such matters as the theory of cognition, land systems, taxation, Mill on political economy, the national debt (£736,278,685 on 5 April, 1857), the cost of seventy shillings to move an English piano from Liverpool to London as compared with only twenty-five shillings for a foreign one, and the like. The slow drift towards the worldly is interspersed with solemn excerpts about religion – the possibility of entering the Church, sprinkled no doubt by that water from the Jordan, was still in his mind. So were other things. He was becoming a good tennis player. He was sociable. A song he composed in August 1887 whilst on holiday in Aberystwyth opens with words (that ring a little hollow in the light of his meeting with my mother some twenty years later):

> Dust thou deem it such a pleasure
> To deceive with cunning art
> This poor maiden's richest treasure
> Her unstained and loving heart.

It seems pretty clear that, omnivorous reading apart, his basic interests were no different from those of other young men. But he was restless. The set of his mind was changing. His own contributions to the commonplace book fell away; he began instead to collect an extraordinary range of facts and quotations as assiduously as later he was to amass precedents. He remained a voracious reader. Like F.S. Boas, if he got a ticket in the tram, he would turn it over and read the back. I remember his telling me that he was once able to settle a recondite question of sport that came up in conversation because he had just read about it on a cigarette card. (That must have been before he switched to Ardath, which gave coupons instead.)

His first move towards the law was initiated by an old school friend, Philip Baker, by now a rising solicitor in Birmingham. Baker offered a partnership if McCardie became a solicitor, but told him that his abilities might be better suited to the Bar. Handsome, rebellious, confident, suddenly bursting with talent, McCardie had already begun honing his forensic gifts. According to the *Derbyshire Times*, he made his first speech at a political meeting in the Town Hall, Wirksworth, when he was seventeen. He continued to get as much experience as he could in public speaking. When he was twenty, his uncle Thomas Hunt donated a piece of land for the building of a Men's Institute at Bolehill and the memorial stone records that it was laid by Mr H.A. McCardie of Edgbaston on 19 October, 1889. After laying the stone, young McCardie delivered an address – somewhat prematurely, one might think – on 'Life and what can be made of it'. It was a wonder that his brothers and sisters allowed him to get away with it. But the theme may have fired his imagination. Soon he had made his mind up: the Bar it was to be.

He began reading in the chambers of J.J. Parfitt, later a County Court Judge. But he hadn't wholly given up the idea of entering the Church. In an expansive mood during one of the debates of the Birmingham Law Society, he told his listeners, perhaps recalling the message of his cranial bumps: 'You mark my words, I'll be either a judge or a bishop by the time I'm forty.' (He wasn't far out in his estimate. And his subsequent outspokenness on the Bench, where one of his homilies, on condonation, was actually referred to as 'a sermon in a judgement', may have reflected a lingering tendency to mix up the two roles!) He also joined the Birmingham and Edgbaston Debating Society, to which Joseph Chamberlain belonged. He first spoke there in 1892, and at once made his mark. In 1893, in a debate with the Central Library Association, he proposed the typically Victorian motion 'That the granting by the British Crown of Charters with sovereign power to Private Companies over territories in possession of native tribes is justifiable, and has been beneficial to the subject races'. The principal speaker had to withdraw through illness and McCardie was asked to take his place unexpectedly. The society's journal records that it was 'ably represented by Mr H.A. McCardie at an hour's notice' – a good augury for barristerial pressures to come. The motion was carried.

Already a glutton for work, endowed with readiness of repartee, that instant rapidity of perception called for in a first-class lawyer, a capacity to think on his feet and a musical and persuasive voice (though not a strong one – not the voice for a bishop!), young McCardie relished the cut and thrust of debate and sought it out wherever he could. He relished even more the intellectual tang of the law. He poured all his formidable energies, hitherto uncanalised, into gaining mastery of it. To unremitting industry he brought a remarkable memory. Whatever he read, he remembered. He was a 'natural'. He had found what he wanted. An intense love of and involvement in the law continued to the end of his life.

In 1894, having eaten his dinners and paid his dues, he was called to the Bar at the Middle Temple, with a Certificate of Honour from the Council of Legal Education and the Campbell Foster prize (for the best knowledge of criminal law) in his pocket. He began to practise on the Midland Circuit. He was twenty-five. In the same year his elder brother, after graduating at Caius College, Cambridge, qualified as a doctor and embarked on a medical career of considerable distinction.

McCardie's first brief came from a solicitor in Wirksworth, no doubt prompted by his uncle. But his first contested case was at the Birmingham Quarter Sessions, for which he was briefed by his friend Philip Baker. He appeared for the defence, largely unsuccessfully, in a case involving coinage offences. The case lasted two and a half days and he received a guinea for his pains. In the next Quarter Sessions he had a better chance to show his mettle. Three members of a family were charged with 'receiving' and Philip Baker had briefed a counsel for each defendant: Hugo Young, known as the 'Attorney General of Birmingham', Parfitt and McCardie. After Young and Parfitt had spoken, there seemed little for McCardie to say, but in a masterly analysis of the evidence he made several points his seniors had missed. All three defendants were acquitted.

Baker, who knew his quality, was always prepared to back him, but briefs at the start were few. He had no private means and he was as keen as anyone after 'soup' – prosecution briefs in minor criminal cases: pub brawls, stolen ducks and so on. But he lived at home, where his expenses were low and his mother was a tower of support. Meanwhile he didn't waste his time; Parfitt gave him plenty of devilling to do and he soaked himself in study of the law. Some indication of the intensity of his application has been given by a Mr Parsonage, a clerk at his chambers in Bennet Street:

> Mr McCardie was the most industrious man I ever worked with or ever hope to work with. He was at the office at 9 o'clock every morning and almost invariably worked until eleven at night. He would slip out for lunch at the Union Club, and then rush back to work and work... He lived and talked in a perpetual atmosphere of law cases and law books. The outside world seemed to mean nothing to him. His work was his god. No task was too big for him, no problem too involved.

The outside world did mean something to him, however; he had more energy than even Mr Parsonage gave him credit for. He didn't always stay at the office until eleven at night. No doubt there were girls: Aberystwyth had not been forgotten. But they were chaperoned and difficult to get at; and he was never an enthusiastic dancer. Nor had he much time to spare. Apart from debating and tennis, he was a founder member and secretary of a gymnastic club. He joined the King's Norton Golf Club. He was active in the Birmingham Law Students' Society and wrote the prize essay in 1893. He played a full part in the Old Edwardian Association and at their annual dinner in January 1897 he proposed the toast of 'the School' in 'a happy speech'. He was good company and often called upon to sing at smoking concerts held by the Old Edwardians and the local Bar association: he had a repertoire of popular songs, some of which, much later on, he would sing again with my mother in his pleasant tenor voice. But his main thrust, intensely focused and formidable, was the drive to succeed at the Bar.

Soon his reputation began to get about, not only as one of the more brilliant local juniors, but as having exceptional legal knowledge with which to press a case home. County Court Judges as well as lower tribunals were well aware that the soundness of their decisions depend a great deal on the quality of the legal arguments put forward by counsel who appear before them, and McCardie made it a rule that he would never advance a contention in law that he did not believe to be well-founded. He was lucky enough to have one of his early cases, in which he appeared for Plimmer, a young boxer who had been sued by another, quoted as an authority concerning the law of stakeholders under the Gaming Acts. He lost the case in the County Court, but appealed to the Divisional Court. Hugo Young was again his leader and spoke first. The Court was not convinced. McCardie was called and argued with such cogency that the judgement against Plimmer was reversed. This stood him in good stead and briefs with his name on them steadily increased in number.

It became clear that he was at his most effective in civil rather than criminal cases. He developed a relaxed style of his own. Nothing flustered him. His favourite stance when addressing the Court was to stand with one foot on the seat behind and use his knee as an arm rest. Constantly he toyed with his wig, alternately pushing it back from his forehead and readjusting it. His laughing eyes – everyone noticed their brightness – his youthful face and high-spirited manner made him a most engaging counsel; and his skill at getting straight to the heart of a case – a skill which was to make him the ablest drafter of pleadings in his day – was already manifest. His style was not rhetorical, but persuasive. He wove a logical net. His immense industry was worn lightly; it all seemed so easy. His personal charm made him, as he was later described, 'the nicest of cross-examiners'. Sometimes dangerously nice. There is a pleasant anecdote in Pollock's book about a breach of promise action in which he appeared for the defence. The plaintiff was an attractive actress. Corroborative evidence of such a promise had to be given, of course, either in the form of letters or the testimony of some other person. There was no written evidence, but there was a witness – the plaintiff's little sister, a pretty girl of thirteen with the same blonde hair and large blue eyes. Peeping shyly at the Judge, she described how, on a summer afternoon, she had seen the defendant kissing her sister and heard him promise to marry her. 'We'll not do much with this witness,' muttered the defending solicitor, as McCardie rose to cross-examine. 'You gave your evidence very nicely indeed, little lady,' he said in his friendly fashion, 'I'm sure you'll go on the stage like your sister and become a famous actress. Now, I wonder if you are clever enough to give your evidence all over again?' 'Oh, yes,' she replied, and proceeded to do so, with the same shy glances at the Judge, peep by peep and word for word. To shouts of laughter from the jury, the case was stopped in McCardie's favour.

As his practice grew, it became clear that the Midland Circuit provided too little scope for his talent. London beckoned. He was undecided at first whether to go or stay; but he knew he was going, much as a Judge, in giving judgement, goes through the motions of making up his mind when it is already made up. There was a risk, but he relished risk. Anyway, his name was by now well known; he was engaged in most of the important local cases at the County Court, the Quarter Sessions and the Assize. For example, he was 'led' by Lord Coleridge for the Birmingham Liberal Association when they sought to recover damages charged against them in respect of repairs required to Birmingham Town Hall after it was stormed by 40,000 of Joseph Chamberlain's supporters to stop

Lloyd George (who was lucky to escape with his life disguised as PC 87D) making a speech against the Boer War. Increasingly, though, McCardie's clients were content to brief him without a leader and take him to argue any appeal in London. There he was seen at his best. London solicitors, too, began to mark him.

The catalyst for his decision to move to London was provided by the death of his mother in the summer of 1903. He was deeply affected by her death; he had always been the child closest to her heart. By then all the family but himself had flown the nest. William, his elder brother, and Margaret, the sister with whom he was most intimate, had both married. Two other sisters had left Birmingham to take up nursing. Of his two younger brothers, one had already come to London to work in the City and the other, after an injury-strewn period of industrial apprenticeship, had emigrated to Canada as a marine engineer. There was nothing to detain him longer. Early in 1904 he made the move. He took chambers in the Temple at No. 2 The Cloisters – not unaware perhaps of its ecclesiastical ring – and never looked back.

Not long afterwards he received, at the instance of Joseph Chamberlain, a telegram offering him the constituency of South Birmingham, one of the safest seats in the country. This was an enormous compliment, for he had never belonged to any party. The telegram was handed to him in the middle of a heavy commercial case in the High Court. He was asked to make up his mind at once. After pacing up and down the corridor for a few minutes he decided to decline the offer. Chamberlain, when he was told, is reputed to have said: 'Tell that young man that, when the ball rolls at his feet, his duty is to kick it – it will never roll again.' Admirable advice, but misconceived. It was the wrong ball. McCardie wasn't a team player, and the trammels of party discipline would have irked him unendurably. He was aware that, by his refusal, he might have forfeited the chance of judicial preferment, but, as he remarked, 'If I went into politics, I should have to be a party unto myself. I cannot usefully do that and I will not pledge myself to a party creed in which I only half believe'. He remained unimpressed by politics, which he later referred to in one of his judgements as 'a somewhat clamorous branch of sociology'; and he was to have no cause to be grateful to politicians.

Fourteen

I have a faded photograph of my father taken in his Birmingham days. He is dressed in a light tussore suit and gazes romantically upwards towards the tops of trees. He is slim and elegant. I sense his charm and humour – the Irish side of him, amused at his own success. I sense also a vein of ostentation, even of femininity. He does not look at all like a man who, as he did, would carelessly fold up his clothes at night and shove them in a drawer; no doubt his mother ensured that he was well turned out. Nor does he look to be a man of indefatigable energy, but rather a flaneur, wearing his cleverness like a button-hole. On the basis of that photograph I would have put no bets on the move to London. How wrong a camera can be! – or does it show another McCardie, the one that fiddled with his wig, the one that nearly got away?

He certainly timed his move well. London provided rich pickings for the kind of legal work he was adept at. A wealthy society, with its satellite worlds of fashion and entertainment, is a happy hunting ground for libel and slander and breach of promise and matrimonial disputes, let alone commercial cases; and Edwardian society, led by a pleasure-loving king, was bursting with wealth – the new opulence of financiers, the old wealth of landowners, the lavish shooting parties, the enormous meals, the jingling hansoms, income tax at 9d in the pound. Once planted in the Temple, his practice soon took root. He found himself an able confidential clerk, Philip McCann, who became his friend, and a small service flat in Queen Anne's Mansions, which became his home. After 1904 this was his only home: a tiny hall, a sitting-room, a bedroom and a bathroom.

At 2 The Cloisters briefs began to tumble about his ears like the golden apples of the Hesperides. At Queen Anne's Mansions servants and meals could be whistled up like magic from below. In what spare time he had, he started to collect porcelain and watercolours (which he called his 'little bits of colour'). Soon the walls of his flat were covered with pictures – Cox, Hunt, Copley Fielding, Bonnington, Turner – their frames almost touching; seascapes were hung in the bathroom. Before long he was to collect a mistress, too – he felt no need for a wife. He became immensely busy. He saw his income treble and treble again. The money didn't matter much; he had drawers full of uncashed cheques. What mattered was the achievement, the sense of purpose, the camaraderie, the privilege of being a repository of innumerable confidences and, above all, the huge draughts of work. He was, in Lord Reith's words, 'fully stretched' at last, to the limit of his considerable powers. The next twelve years were the happiest of his life. When in February 1920, some three and a half years after he became a Judge, he was presented by the Derby Law Society with his portrait in oils – a portrait which seems to have disappeared – he referred nostalgically to his work as Counsel in London. The Bar, he said, had meant most of all to him – 'It was the life, the vitality and the struggle and the future that mattered; it was not the after-success in the administration of grave responsibilities.'

The weight of work he carried, the mastery of detail involved, in order to earn what he did year after year *as a junior* is hard to imagine. Perhaps only another barrister can get the full feel of it. His practice was one of the busiest the Bar has ever known, his earnings well in excess of £20,000 a year (equivalent to thirty times that sum today). Its extent may be estimated, said Pollock,

> when it is realised that his lay clients included practically every leading actor from Irving to Robey; nearly every

prominent actress; all the leading banks; all the principal railway companies with the exception of the old London and South-Eastern and the London Chatham and Dover Company; hundreds of big business concerns; and nearly every man or woman of title who went to law. There was hardly a prominent firm of solicitors who did not, at some time, send him a brief.

His chambers were nicknamed 'The Lighthouse': the lights were still burning there long after other inhabitants of the Temple had gone to bed. A minimum of six 'devils' made it possible for him to cope; the flow of work had to be organised like a production line. Once a week a table was booked at a West End restaurant and seats for a theatre or music hall. It was the duty of his clerk to make sure that McCardie went out that night, whether he wanted to or not. On every other night of the week 'devils' were in attendance, working until the early hours, the six taking it in rotation.

McCann has given an account of the daily routine. As was his custom at Birmingham, McCardie would arrive at his chambers promptly at nine o'clock for his first appointment. A client who failed to arrive at the time arranged did not see him at all. Clients would continue to come until twenty past ten, when he walked over to the Courts. Often he would have a 'conference' as he walked over, the client paying for the walk and the talk. His 'devils' would each be posted in a different Court, each with a carefully prepared note and thoroughly grounded in his case. McCardie, without any apparent haste, would move from Court to Court until half past one or thereabouts, when the Judges rose for lunch. But McCardie had no lunch. Instead, he would hurry, followed by acolytes bearing bulky briefs, to the 'bear-garden', the ante-room to the Judges' chambers, domain of the 'one thirty summons' where Masters of the High Court consider the pleadings that set out the issues upon which each party to a civil case relies. Such matters are vital, for a litigant is bound by his pleadings. In this esoteric area McCardie's subtlety and skill, combined with his extraordinary knowledge of case law and a hefty common sense, were unequalled. He needed only to read the papers once to remember them. He had a gift for putting his finger on the vital features of a case. He could summarise intricate arguments in a way which made them seem not only simple but incontrovertible. Those settling the preliminaries with him had to be on their closest guard or they would find their Statement of Claim struck out on the ground that it showed no cause of action. Three or four Masters would be ready to hear him on various cases and he would generally succeed in addressing them all. 'I appear for the defendant, Master, but my opponent does not seem to be here –' 'Perhaps your opponent is Mr McCardie. We have to allow him a certain amount of latitude.'

McCardie would still be arguing in the bear-garden when the Judges came back from luncheon. He would hasten back to one Court or another until the Judges rose again between four and half past. Then he would hurry back to his chambers for another stream of conferences: 'At four thirty,' he used to say, 'I start my day's work.' The conferences went on, day in day out, until half past seven or eight o'clock. At eight McCardie and the 'devils' on duty would go to the Cock to dine. Then they would return to toil away at the documents until one or two in the morning. When the work was done McCardie would walk home to Queen Anne's Mansions through the empty streets, in winter often shrouded in fog, the haloed lamps making the city more mysterious than one not lit at all. Six or seven hours later, at nine o'clock, he was back again in his chambers.

Four of those who worked there, first as pupils and then as 'devils', paid him a moving tribute in a letter to *The Times* shortly after his death. They felt that insufficient justice had been done –

...not only to his wealth of talent, his brilliance as an exponent of the law and his tireless industry, but above all to his great sagacity and his boundless generosity.

Industry and knowledge of the law were perhaps the most obvious of his great capacities; but the qualities which, we are convinced, secured him the greater part of his enormous practice were his almost uncanny judgement of the way in which a case was likely to develop and his brilliant judgement in foreseeing and averting difficulties.

The point, however, which we desire to emphasise above all others is his generosity. Apart from his actual beneficences to those in need, which were many and unpublished, there was never, we feel certain, a man more utterly devoid of any smallness, more ready to recognise and give its full reward to work adequately or well done, or more ready to encourage and inspire others to attempt to follow in his footsteps. He was equally bountiful with his money, his knowledge both of men and books, and his inspiration and advice. How many of us can look back with pride and gratitude to his actual personal teaching it is difficult to state. Several, one, at least, of the very best, did not return from the War. But we at least desire to state publicly what an enormous debt we owe him, and to say that there never was a better man for or with whom to work.

In lapidary inscriptions a man is not upon oath, as Dr Johnson said, but this is a splendid tribute.

In his more important cases McCardie was, of course, 'led' by a KC. Under the two-thirds rule which then prevailed, he would receive that proportion of the leader's fee – if it was five hundred guineas, he would receive three hundred and thirty-three, and so on. Many clients were reluctant to incur the extra expense and would have been content for him to take the case alone. But he insisted that a leader be briefed, if only because he was too busy to do it all himself. His frequent absence from the Court came to be taken for granted. Once Otto Danckwerts was leading McCardie in a vast and complicated case before Mr Justice Pickford and a special jury. 'My Lord and members of the jury,' he began, 'I appear for the plaintiff in this case with my learned friend Mr McCardie –' then turning round to McCardie, who was sitting behind him, he raised his hands and exclaimed in feigned astonishment '– *who is here!*' But he wasn't there for long.

This was a period when a fashionable divorce suit or libel action attracted enormous public attention and the leading advocates played a role akin to film and television stars today. Walk up Middle Temple Lane and across the Strand and it is easy to imagine them: Edward Carson, Serjeant Sullivan, John Simon, H.E Duke, F.E Smith, Rufus Isaacs, or the great Marshall Hall preceded into Court by a minion carrying his air-cushion and his nose-spray and his battery of prophylactics – 'Nobody,' said F.E. Smith, 'could have been as wonderful as Marshall Hall looked.' McCardie was not flamboyant; nimble-witted as he was, he didn't have the silver tongue of the top-flight advocate, and as a junior his name is not associated with the notable cases that are remembered from those days. It was the work he put in behind the scenes, his mastery of pleadings, as much as his ability on his feet, that drew solicitors to him like bees to honey. Even if he didn't open his mouth in Court, his clients knew they'd had their money's worth.

Only rarely did he catch wider attention, as when he was on the same side as Mashall Hall in a newspaper libel action before Mr Justice Bray. Marshall Hall had been interrupted several times by Bray in the course of cross-examination and his temper was rising. McCardie tried to avoid an explosion by tugging at his leader's gown, but in the end the storm burst. Marshall Hall flung down his papers: 'As I am not permitted to conduct the case according to my instructions, I will retire and leave my friend Mr McCardie to conduct it.' Whereupon he strode out. McCardie then got up and said: 'I associate myself with every question Mr Marshall Hall has put, and since my learned friend has retired I will retire also.' And he, too, walked out. He was one of the acknowledged leaders of the junior Bar and there was much argument as to whether he was right to do so; but Bray never held it against him.

Another case which brought him to public attention was that of *Lord Alfred Douglas v. Ransome and the Times Book Club* in April 1913. Arthur Ransome, who later became famous for his children's stories, had written a book about Oscar Wilde which Lord Alfred regarded as having traduced his honour by inferring that his degeneracy had been a main cause of Wilde's destruction. The defence, in which McCardie was led by J.H. Campbell, KC, called in evidence letters and other documents that Wilde had sent from prison, including many suppressed verses of *De Profundis*. The poignant handwritten sheets of blue prison paper were brought into a crowded court and it fell to McCardie to read out page after page of the unpublished verses. There were eighty pages and before long both Judge and jury had had enough. But the point was made. Lord Alfred, no longer a rose-lipped boy, sought to undo the damage by taking credit from the fact that he had won the school steeplechase at Winchester and by claiming also that he had inspired, without acknowledgement, much of the dialogue in Wilde's best plays. He lost the case. McCardie added to his reputation; and his reading of the verses made him more widely known.

He wasn't wholly taken up in his unwearying labours. There were week-ends – although in term time these, too, were burdened with briefs – and the legal vacations were generous. Without such breaks (and his regular night off) even he would have conked out. What did he do when he wasn't working? What friendships did he form, apart from the invigorating but limited comradeship of the Bar? No lasting ones, I think; but there is nothing to tell us. If only some letters had survived; they might have yielded some surprises. A simple engagement book would have been better than nothing – say, for 1908. That was the year he joined Hunstanton Golf Club. It might have been the year he met my mother.

This first link with Hunstanton brings him, and me, to more familiar ground. Yet is it not a strange place to find him? A professional man in his late thirties needing relaxation from the demands of an immensely stressful job might be expected to seek it in the whirr of partridges or the drumming of snipe, at least in more lively and sociable places than a small Norfolk seaside town. My father may have come down with fellow golfers at first, but all the evidence suggests that he was generally by himself. He wandered about among the local people. Later, no doubt, Mayna was the prime attraction; but the fact that it was she, living where she did, unsophisticated as she was, whom he elected to cultivate is significant. To be attracted, to make a girl giddy with tenderness, is one thing; to love is to choose.

More than once McCardie in his later years is referred to as a lonely man. For one so companionable and generous and easy, so sympathetic and full of curiosity, this may seem surprising. But there seems to have been a barrier beyond which others could not pass; he felt no need to share his inner self. None of his friends were really close. Again, although he took great pleasure in female company, he was unwilling to commit himself; whilst relishing the thrill of the chase, he deftly avoided entanglement. He dreaded an Edgbastonian domesticity that might gobble him up without trace. Nor was he a sensual man. In the matter of sex, food and wine he was abstemious. His addictions were work, gambling and cigarettes. If he had a passion, it was for justice. He was indifferent to the small comforts and intimacies of everyday life that are important to most of us. The idea of being a husband had no appeal. But he was capable of enduring loyalty to a woman, like Mayna, who, sensing his needs, kept her demands to a minimum.

When she was young and pretty, these demands were compelling enough and it is clear where my father spent many of his week-ends in the years after 1908. The time he spent with my mother is, as usual, undocumented, but it was considerable and, as my existence testifies, unexpectedly productive. What of the rest of his time? He remained a voracious reader. Blue books and books on history and sociology continued to be gutted and remembered. He told the Commerce Graduates' Association of Birmingham University in 1932 that he had read Adam Smith's *Wealth of Nations* when he was eighteen and since then had read 'with unfailing interest and pleasure almost every work of importance on economics, trade, industry and finance'. He had less time for fiction, other than whodunnits: the transaction of legal business is not always good for the literary taste buds. 'If I want fascinating reading,' he once said with some justification, 'I can find it in an old law report more easily than I can in the pages of a modern novel.' He continued to take vigorous exercise whenever he could. Like most Victorians he was a great walker and he retained his love for and skill at tennis. By the time he'd worked his way into *Who's Who*, shooting, fishing and golf are listed as his recreations. Golf dates from his Birmingham days, but shooting and fishing don't, unless his farming uncle in Wirksworth gave him a taste for rod and gun when he stayed at Bolehill. But they were, of course, proper recreations for a fast-rising, high-earning professional man who was expected to devote part of his leisure (which McCardie pronounced 'leesure') to the grouse moor and the salmon river. (In fairness it must be said that the same recreations were being pursued in humbler circumstances by some of the Archers – George shot duck in the winter on Snettisham marshes and Fred netted shrimps in the summer shallows of the Wash.)

I expect that my father, as a personable up-and-coming man

dealing with wealthy and fashionable people, would often be invited to country house parties. A good shot, an eligible bachelor and a witty talker, he was the ideal man to make up a party and, when he was elevated to the Bench, to adorn the guest list as well. In the long vacations he was a frequent visitor to Ireland – his home base, as it were – and no doubt went fishing there. He took many holidays abroad. There is mention, I don't know how well founded, of big-game hunting in India, though there were no tiger heads on the walls of Queen Anne's Mansions (he wouldn't have had room for them anyway). He certainly took many Continental holidays, mainly to France and Switzerland. It was the high age of Baedeker, but he preferred places with an international clientele like Monte Carlo or Vevey. He liked the freedom of Continental society, notably more relaxed as regards single women. He did a fair amount of gambling at the tables. He could afford to. He had acquired the habit of spending his money in the Irish manner, freely and generously, without thought, in the apparently secure knowledge that there was always more to be had. At the end of the vacation he went back to 2 The Cloisters and earned more. He enjoyed the earning as much as the spending. It was a good life, bathed in the unclouded confidence of imperial afternoon.

By 1910, by which time his practice as a junior had exceeded all previous limits, he decided that the time had come to apply for silk. He was ambitious and this was the way forward. There was the risk, of course, that his income might falter. He would have to compete four-square with those in the front rank of the profession and they were formidable opponents; his worth as an advocate had to be such that he could command the fee of his junior as well as his own. On the other hand, it would mean an escape from the relentless pressure of settling pleadings, which professional rules ordain must be done by juniors. One thinks of Rufus Isaacs forced to take silk in the vain hope of a few spare hours.

When McCardie applied, Lord Loreburn was Lord Chancellor. Lord Loreburn was a dilatory man who had a habit of taking a very long time to make up his mind about applications for silk. Sometimes he would make no new appointments for a couple of years. Unfortunately it was during one such period that McCardie put in his name. The fact that he had done so was generally known and he began to find his huge practice rapidly falling away as solicitors hesitated to deliver briefs to a junior who might soon be obliged to return them. It so happened also that he had invested large sums in South African shares, which had slumped. His response was decisive. He withdrew his application and publicly announced the reasons why – generating, not for the last time, a vigorous controversy in the Press. Lord Loreburn was thereupon provoked into producing a new list of silks, to which he added McCardie's name without any further action on his part. But McCardie, with a stubbornness as characteristic as his decision to withdraw, refused to be made a KC against his will. He therefore remained a junior until his promotion to the Bench. When war broke out he was much in demand by the banks. The legal consequences of a declaration of war were complicated and far-reaching. Typically McCardie mastered them in a very short time. He became busier than ever. More years of that inexorable regimen. It doesn't bear thinking about!

Fifteen

In October 1916, just after the battle of the Somme, as the leaves began to fall, Lord Buckmaster signalled his short Chancellorship by raising McCardie to the Bench. He was forty-seven. He succeeded Scrutton and took over Court IV of the King's Bench – 'King's Bench Four'. Scrutton, promoted to the Court of Appeal, was a tall, rude, spartan, orthodox, academically brilliant man, interested in opera and church architecture, who had never shaved in his life. Not surprisingly he and McCardie were incompatible and were later to clash in an unseemly manner. But no current asperities clouded McCardie's achievement. When a London paper rang up his brother William at Birmingham General Hospital to seek confirmation of his brother's appointment, Dr McCardie replied that he had heard nothing of the alleged appointment and didn't believe it.

His appointment was indeed a remarkable one. He had left school at sixteen. He had never been to university. He had remained a junior until he was promoted to the Bench; normally the only avenue for such direct promotion is appointment as Treasury Counsel. To change straight from his stuff gown into judicial ermine was a rare translation.

McCardie shared with two distinguished Victorian Judges, Colin Blackburn (Lord Blackburn) and James Shaw Willes, the honour of having ascended the Bench straight from the junior Bar. There are interesting parallels between them. All three were renowned for their deep knowledge of the common law; all had a reputation for wide reading, honesty of purpose and a determination to pursue every question to its roots. Like

McCardie, Blackburn remained a bachelor; Willes, like McCardie, was self-taught. Also, like McCardie alas, Willes committed suicide at the tag-end of a heavy Assize.

In 1916 the clouds which were to gather over his head had not yet appeared on the horizon. Full of beans, having skipped the silken gown, the freshly dubbed Sir Henry was content simply to relish his new status, in which he took a proper pride. There were only eighteen High Court Judges then, compared with over eighty now; and the Bench, as Lord Westbury said, 'is a damn fine thing to sit on'. He joined the Reform Club and the Athenaeum. ('All judges without exception are members of the Athenaeum,' Lord Cozens Hardy wrote to Lord Buckmaster on the latter's appointment as Lord Chancellor, 'and I presume you will wish to be a member.') His income was quartered, but he didn't care. He was on the crest of a wave. McCann, who stayed with him as his clerk despite a considerable financial sacrifice, recounts how they were standing together in the Judge's corridor at the Law Courts after he'd been sworn in. For the first time he was wearing his scarlet and ermine. The corridor was heavily carpeted, the silence almost tangible. McCardie glanced up and down and saw only a janitor in the distance. 'McCann,' he said with a twinkle, 'when I came here years ago to see a Judge in his room, I came on tip-toe in my best clothes, with trepidation in my heart. Look at us now – this is our promenade deck.'

McCardie never forgot what it was to be young. When inexperienced juniors appeared before him, he was always patient and ready to help; if one came to see him in his room, he would order tea and put him at his ease. His was the Court to which young men reading for the Bar or newly fledged came if they wanted to learn the tricks of the trade. 'The spontaneous tribute of young and fresh minds is the highest compliment a judge can receive' the *Law Journal* said of him, going on to speak of the 'air of youthful freshness which, notwithstanding the weight of his learning, [was] his most obvious characteristic'. He had a fund of sympathy and humour and there are many stories of his kindness. A young solicitor's clerk found himself unexpectedly ushered into the Judge's presence clutching a 'notice of motion' which he thought to be a mere formality and which proved on examination to be defective. McCardie sat him down and redrafted it for him: 'I expect,' he said, 'you were in rather a hurry when you did this.' When he himself was still a young barrister at the Birmingham Bar, prosecuting a man for murder, his opponent confessed when they adjourned for lunch that his nerve had gone and he didn't think he would be able to make his final submission to the jury. Over lunch McCardie went over the evidence with him and together they composed a speech for the defence. 'I found his points for him, one by one,' McCardie said later. 'I even wrote out a peroration of seven lines, and the speech proved so effective that the jury reduced the case from one of murder to one of manslaughter.'

With my father there was no question of 'pre-war' and 'post-war', no generation gap – even with me. Heaven knows, there should have been! But crouched side by side on the carpet in front of that hissing model engine, we were equals, though there was fifty years between us; indeed, in that situation I was more equal than he was. He showed no trace of condescension. In Court he never pleaded judicial ignorance or regarded himself as perched above the fads and fancies of the day. On the contrary, passing fashions of all kinds intrigued him. He was always ready to point a moral or express a personal view on matters great or small. When evidence was given about table manners in a case involving a couple charged with obtaining goods by false pretences at a restaurant, he remarked: 'I should not mind in the least eating fish with an ordinary knife and fork. A great many of our social affectations are absurd'. The remark was dismissed as quaint. It was simply honest and unpompous.

His humanity combined with a lively curiosity made him troublingly aware of the problems that beset people in their everyday lives – especially those at the bottom of the pile, 'the poor bloody infantry of the oppressed'. He offered help in secret out of his own pocket when it was needed. In the evenings on Assize he would often walk about to see things for himself. This awareness – combined, it must be admitted, with a certain contrariety of mind – set him chafing against the edges of the law. As a barrister the lives of others had come at him from an angle; his job was to take sides. As a Judge their lives came at him head on.

The law is a Roman occupation: it drives roads, and most lawyers, like most soldiers, are content to march down them. They like to hear their heels ring on the stone. My father loved this aspect of the law. But he also saw more clearly than most that roads need to be constantly repaired and extended to take account of new habitats and changing ways. Even then, the system can only work if subtler gradations of conduct – the little twisty private footpaths most of us follow – are disregarded: which is why it can sometimes make your flesh creep to hear two attorneys talking. McCardie had shown himself to be a master of the system, a sound, reliable man, apparently untroubled by originality: an ideal candidate for the Bench.

In fact, however, he was not a safe man. He loved the elucidation of a novel point of law as much as anyone; but there were springs in him that had been running deep underground through the busy years. Now they began to bubble up. For the first time he had leisure to reflect. He found he could not ignore or forget the misery and distress which the law as it stood and the conventional morality that buttressed it (that the poor deserved to be poor and the rich, rich) were too crude or insensitive to take account of – above all, in such areas as birth control, divorce and the status of women. He rightly wanted to see change and said so, though whether he was right to say it with such vehemence from the Bench is another thing. Many of his judgements were, in Pollock's words, 'at one and the same time, a mirror of the age and the reasoned pronouncements of a reformer'. Unlike most reformers, he started late and spoke out of experience. And he spoke as someone who owed nothing to privilege. In his Reading to the Middle Temple in 1927 he referred to the dictum of Lord Bramwell that 'one third of every judge is a common juror'. He went on to say, 'Remembering that, I venture to add that if there be any unconscious instinct to lean to one side rather than the other, it is an instinct not in favour of the strong or wealthy, but an instinct which tends to lean rather towards those who are weak and those who are poor.' He may have been talking of Judges in general, but he was thinking of himself.

His own appointment as a Judge was widely welcomed. The Temple, where he was liked and admired, approved it warmly. All his new brethren on the Bench wrote to congratulate him. One sent him a warning: 'To you the work will be easy. Your head was always straighter in court than your wig... Do not take your wig off or push it on one side as much as you used, it does not look dignified.' McCardie took the hint, but developed instead a trick of tugging at his ermine cuffs; and of chewing peppermints, presumably because he couldn't smoke. Had his new brothers known how far he would seek to enlarge his judicial function, some of them might have sent more sombre warnings.

Among the letters of congratulation he received was a charming note from Gordon Hewart (then a KC, later Lord Chief Justice) in reply to one of his own:

> I shall place your letter side by side with some verses you wrote at the Old Bailey in the Sitwell case, and, when you are captivating the House of Lords with your speeches, I shall read both letter and verses to my little

daughter and tell her that they were given to me by the great man and great lawyer whose position at the Bar was such that, in fairness to Juniors he could not remain a Junior, and in fairness to Silks he could not be made a Silk, and therefore he was appointed, for a little time, to be a Judge of the King's Bench Division.

This letter, with its sad, fairy-tale evocations of what might have been, is the only one my father kept from this time, except for the personal letter from Lord Buckmaster.

Like nearly all Judges newly appointed, McCardie missed the comradeship of the Bar. His initial sense of isolation was made worse by the sudden lifting from his shoulders of the huge burden of his practice. His enormous industry had by now become an addiction; he suffered withdrawal symptoms whenever he could not assuage its demands. This was so for the rest of his life. Mr Justice Avory told George Bancroft, 'Without my work, I should die'. The same was true of McCardie. And it wasn't merely a matter of habit. Work was necessary to keep at bay a destructive force, part melancholy, part ennui, part craving for risk and arousal, which drove him to gamble and, in his judicial life, to take up positions which were more foolhardy than courageous. In the end this force broke loose and destroyed him. The Bar had not only exacted unremitting labour, but its intellectual tourneys, its hazards, its successes, its hopeless defences, had also slaked his thirst for excitement. When he no longer had the Bar to make things happen for him, he had to make them happen himself.

In the winter of 1916 McCardie had no need to make things happen; he had stimulus enough in settling down to his new job, feeling his way. There were plenty of pitfalls. A Judge has to do constantly what most of us try to avoid – make decisions. He has no assistant to help him. He has to look up the law himself: the barristers who appear before him vary greatly in ability and their submissions may blur the issues rather than illuminate them. He has to make personal notes of every relevant piece of evidence or point of argument. He has to keep a close eye on the proceedings in Court and be ready to intervene if need be. After Counsel have finished their speeches, he has in most cases to sum up for the jury or give judgement straightaway, without any transcript to go by: only rarely can he enjoy the luxury of a reserved judgement. Then comes the question of sentence or of damages – always difficult. And afterwards both the judgement and the sentence is liable to be reassessed by others who have the benefit of hindsight. McCardie on the Bench must sometimes have thought, especially in cases (the great majority) where there was no conflict of law to spark his mind off, how much more interesting and rewarding it would be to be down there in his stuff gown doing it.

He did have one compensation – though with his temperament it was a doubtful one – and that was more time. Having no family, he had evenings to fill in. On circuit, where the Judge was a caged creature, this was particularly difficult. He couldn't go to a pub, or to the 'pictures', as the cinema was called, without a police escort. He had to rely on his marshal for entertainment. In London things were different. He liked the cinema: silent films in those days, with piano, even orchestral, accompaniment. He was fond of musicals and popular songs: some of the tunes of that war-time London still haunt us. He preferred operettas to opera – 'Most people do,' he said. He was no intellectual. But he was witty and sharp-minded and charming, and increasingly he was invited out to dine: a youngish bachelor Judge was an even more attractive dinner guest than a successful young barrister. Successful barristers, as Virginia Woolf said, 'are hardly worth sitting next to at dinner – they yawn so'. He began to be in demand as an after-dinner speaker, one of the best in London. He was good value both as guest and speaker. Before long his evening engagements had become an essential time-filling exercise – often five or six nights a week when he was in London. He took great care over his after-dinner speeches, especially the short ones) which are the most difficult, preparing them with as much assiduity as he prepared his judgements. Generally he made a rough draft, scribbling amendments and additions all over the page. Then it would be typed, and often amended and typed again. Every quotation would be scrupulously verified and he never made a speech at a banquet or any professional gathering without spending hours reading up the subject. As soon as he rose in Court, he would cross over to his private room and put the finishing touches to the speech he was to make that night. Often he didn't set out for his flat until the hour when most men had finished dressing. The speed at which he could undress, bathe and dress again was remarkable. Perhaps my ability to do the same is in part inherited.

But I'd not yet come upon the scene. It was still the third year of the War. The old, confident, boyish London had gone by then. Gone, too, were half the young men who had queued up to enlist in their cloth caps and jaunty boaters in that faraway summer of 1914. Now men younger still, boys only, were learning how short a time they had between reading Rider Haggard before a cosy fire in the upstairs nursery and dying as a second lieutenant in the Flanders mud. New poets were telling them what war was really like. The word 'goodby-ee' floated like a thin wail of despair above the gaiety and dancing to mask the reality of those final partings.

A case which came before McCardie at the Old Bailey in September 1917 illustrates vividly the temper of the times (and the sort of cant he was to come up against in his efforts to secure sexual reform). Today it seems unbelievable. War fever was at its height. The Court was crammed with fashionable women, who had queued for hours to get in. For the day and a half the trial lasted, large crowds also gathered outside. Lieutenant Douglas Malcolm was charged with murder. A man of substance in the City, he had married in June, 1914.

On the outbreak of war two months later he joined up. 'His wife was but a bride,' said his Counsel, Sir John Simon, whose mind opened and shut like the breech of a gun, but he knew when the time had come for vintage barristerial baroque, 'she needed his protection. But he did not hesitate and we may fairly put in his lips the famous words written two centuries and a half ago by another soldier going to the wars: "I could not love thee dear so much, loved I not honour more."' Unfortunately the same could not be said of Mrs Malcolm. While he was with his regiment in France, she became infatuated with a certain Anton Baumberg, a Russian emigré and a professional seducer 'with short soft legs' who called himself Count de Borch. Returning unexpectedly on leave Malcolm found his wife in a dressing-gown with Baumberg in his underclothes. To quote Sir John again: 'He was in time, but only just in time. He thrashed the man in the good old British way and left him there in his room, professing to faint, lying on the floor.' The man may well have fainted, for he was badly hurt. Before returning to the trenches Malcolm, not to be denied, challenged Baumberg to a duel. His splendid masculinity cut no ice with Mrs Malcolm, however, and within a week of his return she wrote to say that she could not give Baumberg up. Malcolm managed to get leave again. His wife was not at home and the servants had been given notice. He sat down and wrote a letter to his wife ('a letter', said Sir John, 'that will long remain in the annals of this court'):

> My dear, very own, darling Dorothy, ... Everything points to it that this creature is the most unutterable blackguard ever born ... I simply cannot stand it any longer. I am going to thrash him until he is unrecognisable. I may shoot him if he has got a gun. I expect he has, as he is too much of a coward to stand a thrashing. If the inevitable has got to happen, of course, I may get

it in the neck first ... If that happens, oh! believe me, my own little darling, my beloved soul whom I love so absolutely, believe me, it is for you only ... You are noble, honourable and upright, with what a beautiful soul! I believe in God, I thank Him from the bottom of my heart for having sent me over in time to save you from this devil incarnate.

Your honour is saved. Thank God, thank God! I know I shall meet you in the next world if the worst happens ... Yours for ever and ever, and also lovingly, your husband and your very own DUGGIE.

Taking a whip and a revolver, Malcolm then set out to track Baumberg down. He found him in a small, cheap flat on the top floor of a house in Porchester Place. This time he was wearing only a pyjama top. Malcolm whipped him, then he shot him. Beside Baumberg's bed a drawer was found half open. It contained an automatic pistol in a leather case, a tie pin and a tie. Letters from at least fifty women were found in the flat, including eight from Mrs Malcolm.

Sir John Simon announced that he would call no evidence. He scorned the suggestion that Mrs Malcolm 'had fallen' and that her husband had prayed in aid the so-called unwritten law and taken his revenge – 'never at any moment has he contemplated that in what he has done the purity of his wife has not been preserved unsmirched'. No, Malcolm had shot Baumberg in self-defence. Baumberg intended to shoot: Malcolm fired first. Why was the drawer open except to enable Baumberg to get at his automatic? 'A man who is dressed in nothing but the upper half of a suit of pyjamas does not want a tie pin or a tie.' Sir John drew an eloquent picture of a champion of whom his wife 'may well be proud, a man of honour, who has acted as all men of honour would wish to act – loyally, courageously, bravely, devoted to the most sacred service which a husband can take upon him at an hour of peril'.

Throughout his speech he referred to Baumberg as 'de Borch' (no doubt because it sounded like 'debauch').

McCardie stuck to 'Baumberg' and began his summing-up by trying to cool the temperature. He warned the jury that they must act on the facts. He drew a distinction between a husband who found his wife in flagrante, 'where the provocation is so grave and so sudden as to leave a jury to think that his self-control was overthrown and his capacity for judgement had gone', and one who is told by others of her adultery and then 'decides to seek out and kill the adulterer'. The first case might be manslaughter, the second was murder. He went on:

> The so-called unwritten law does not exist in England. It is the negation of law ... A husband has no property in the body of his wife. He cannot imprison her; he cannot chastise her. If she refuses to live with him he cannot, nor can the Courts, compel her to do so. She is mistress of her own physical destiny.
>
> If she sins and the husband can prove it, he may obtain a divorce, but if she decides to give her body to another, then the husband is not entitled to murder the lover either to punish the sin or to secure its correction. The law of England is settled, and you and I are here to administer it as it stands, and with loyalty to the oaths we have taken, and you will remember that the supremacy of the law is of more importance than the temporary indulgence of natural temper.
>
> I do not forget, nor will you forget, that beyond this Court, which must administer the law in accordance with the facts, there stands the right of the Crown to administer mercy. If you consider it your duty to find a verdict of murder against the defendant, the Crown by its advisers can still consider whether any mitigation can be extended to Lieutenant Malcolm. The duty of

administering the law rests on us: the exercise of mercy is the prerogative of the Crown.

It is said, and indeed has been proved, that the dead man was not an Englishman. True, but it matters not in what realm a man has been born. It matters not what colour foreign sun has burnt his cheek. The moment he sets foot on British soil he falls within the King's peace and the shackles of foreign nationality do not prevent him from asking that he shall be protected by the ordinary rules of British justice.

It has further been said that the dead man was a criminal. If he was a criminal let him be judged and punished according to law. The fact that he was a blackmailer, a white slave trafficker or a spy would not justify a murder by the hands of an irresponsible man.

If you think that Lieutenant Malcolm fired in necessary self-defence, as Baumberg had a loaded pistol in his hand and was about to fire at him, and if you think that the defendant honestly believed that the dead man meant to shoot him and he fired to save himself from grave personal injury, or to save his life, I think you are entitled to find a verdict of 'not guilty'.

It was not the dead man who visited Malcolm, but Malcolm who went to Baumberg's room. He went there with a whip. He went there with a pistol. And he announced: 'I will thrash him until I have maimed him for life'. The question might well have been raised by counsel for the Crown whether Baumberg was not himself entitled, if Malcolm was there with a whip to maim him for life, to fire so as to protect himself. The point has not been raised.

Therefore I say you are entitled to find a verdict of acquittal if you are satisfied that Malcolm honestly believed that Baumberg was about to seize a pistol and shoot at him, if you believe that he honestly shot him to protect his own person. It is quite clear that the dead man had a pistol and would have used it if he could have laid his hands upon it. The pistol was loaded and lay in an open drawer not far from the bed on which the Russian lay.

There is only one man living who could tell you what happened in that room, and that man has not gone into the witness box. Why not? He stands indicted with the gravest charge and offers not one word of testimony. He asks you to guess, to conjecture things which, if he desired, he could have proved on oath.

The result of the omission of Lieutenant Malcolm to appear as a witness is that there is no evidence that the dead man even tried to get the pistol. There is no evidence that he even threatened to use it. There is no evidence even that the pistol was in the room. The whole thing is left to conjecture. There is no suggestion of a single mark on the face or body of Lieutenant Malcolm. The evidence shows that the Russian was not a muscular man, whereas the defendant is a trained soldier in full possession of his physical power. He had overpowered the other man before. Is there any reason to doubt his ability to overpower him again?

The doubts sowed by McCardie in his summing-up created no difficulties for the jury. After only twenty-five minutes they returned to find Malcolm 'not guilty'. Simon's risk in not putting his client in the witness box had been fully vindicated. The Court erupted. Women leapt on their seats and cheered, waving umbrellas and handbags. The cheering was taken up outside, where crowds were waiting for the verdict. McCardie banged his gavel in vain. 'I am sorry,' he said, 'that the deliberation of the Court should be stained –' His words were drowned in further cheering.

When this judgement was delivered he had been on the

Bench for nearly a year. He spoke extempore; by now he was practised in the role. His language, as in other cases, is muscular and clear, only occasionally florid – 'to give her body to another', 'it matters not what colour foreign sun has burnt his cheek'. Lawyers' jargon is highly contagious, and he wasn't immune.

The issues in the Malcolm case were simple. But other cases in McCardie's early days as a Judge, when he was 'fresh to the Bench and at his best', brought into play his immense knowledge of case law and his capacity to apply the law to complicated facts and reduce both to seeming simplicity: 'What McCardie says seems so obvious – after he has said it' one advocate said of him. One of his earliest decisions, *Maclenan v. Segar*, became a classic authority on the extent of an innkeeper's liability to his guest for the safety of his premises. Two other cases may be mentioned. They still make good reading. Both are examples of the many judgements in which he re-affirmed the rights of the individual.

Heddon v. Evans came before him in July, 1919. He delivered a long, reserved judgement, heavily laced with legal history which must have given him great pleasure to dig out (and perhaps helped to take his mind off that little baby in Bournemouth, then four months old). An enormous parade of cases was drawn up, including *Johnstone v. Sutton* (1786), which he referred to with relish as 'a fount of unceasing ambiguity'. The story itself, that of a bolshie private who happened to be a solicitor, is – though ending in personal tragedy – one to delight anybody who has been in the services. McCardie set it out with humour and sympathy and, in his judgement, firmly asserted the right of civil judges to review, and if need be to overrule, the decisions of military tribunals; a man who becomes a soldier does not cease to be a citizen. How refreshing to hear that cool, judicial voice when the roar of sergeant majors and the bark of the pompous generals and pipsqueak officers has subsided into silence! 'There is but one law in

England and that is the civil law of the realm. It is for the ordinary courts of law to determine the extent of jurisdiction given to military tribunals and officers by Act of Parliament.' McCardie's luminous judgement dissolved the uncertainties that had previously surrounded a soldier's status under English law so compellingly that it prompted a book, *Military Law and the Supremacy of the Civil Courts*, edited by Richard O'Sullivan and published in 1921.

Not long before, in October 1918, McCardie had delivered another monumental judgement in *Pratt and others v. the BMA*, in which he upheld the right of the individual against the monopoly power of a professional association. The case especially concerned him because his brother was a doctor and it put in issue the entire system of discipline and regulation which the BMA sought to impose. The Association had mounted a boycott against three doctors who ran a dispensary in Coventry for poor people. There was no NHS in those days and membership of the dispensary grew rapidly. Local medical men began to murmur: their fees were in jeopardy. They were determined to put a stop to the dispensary by ruining the doctors who ran it. The services of other doctors and dentists were denied them. They and their predecessors and their wives and families were ostracised and vilified – the dying wife of one of them was actually refused treatment until her husband had sat down and written a letter formally resigning from the dispensary. The details of the case were complicated, but collective tyranny was the core of it, which McCardie relentlessly exposed. He spoke of a 'prolonged, deliberate and pitiless boycott'. He distinguished a long line of decisions with respect to actionable conspiracy and the unlawful molestation of another in his business or calling. Each of the plaintiffs, he pointed out, was free from professional stain. The alleged fault was financial not moral:

The pecuniary interests of the Coventry doctors lay at the

root of the matter. The question of ethics, as that word is normally understood, had nothing to do with the case... The assertion that the plaintiffs had been guilty of conduct against the honour of the profession cannot in my view be supported. The honour of the profession is amply protected, I think, by the wide powers entrusted by Parliament to the General Medical Council. I cannot view with favour the assumption by the BMA of a co-ordinate jurisdiction and the enforcement of varying views of medical honour with the deliberately framed weapons of ostracism, intimidation and threat... I feel compelled, with the deepest reluctance and abiding distress, to come to the conclusion on the material before me that the plaintiffs have established actual malice against the defendants.

He awarded substantial damages.

Although the atmosphere of war was pervasive and the voices of a million ghosts whispered in the air, the war did not touch McCardie in any direct and personal way. His age exempted him, and in London, apart from the occasional zeppelin raid, the battles were a long way off. The work of the Courts went on as usual: '...amid the clash of arms, the laws are not silent; they may be changed, but they speak the same language in war as in peace'. Social life went on as usual, too, with less formal occasions perhaps, but no rationing and few shortages. The week-end train ran down from Liverpool Street to Hunstanton as it had before, and more often than not McCardie was on it and Mayna was there to meet him at the other end.

But the other end was uncomfortably far. Deprived of the solace of being always overworked, her company became important to him. I can't be sure exactly when my father leased a second flat at Queen Anne's Mansions and she came to London. Probably early in 1918. Whether her parents objected to this final nail in the coffin of respectability or had given up hope of cherishing their daughter's good name, whether they still perhaps had expectations, I have no idea. For Mayna it was a great adventure. For my father it was an admirable way of filling in his evenings when he had no other engagement, or at least filling them in more completely after the dinner parties ended and the theatres closed. Is this unfair? I don't think so. Mayna was a kind of canary in a cage, like the bird which my grandmother used to cover up in the evening with a hood of green baize. She sang for him: she accepted his seed; she existed for his pleasure. She was simply available when he wanted her. He never took her anywhere, or introduced her to his friends. She does not seem to have expected that he would. It was wartime, he was affectionate, he needed emotional companionship: a restful presence and a compliant body. She was prepared to lead the life, almost of purdah, that he wished her to lead. He liked her to dress formally when he dined with her in the flat; he gave her jewels to wear. There must have been a risk in the relationship: the staff at the Mansions must have known about it. But he was generous, they were discreet. Gentlemen were entitled to their peccadillos. The risk was part of the pleasure. Perhaps it was for much the same reason that the accident happened and I was conceived. My arrival on the scene, or at least in the wings, put an end to the idyll. By the beginning of 1919, the War over, Mayna was gone, with me inside her, and my father began to catch a week-end train again, westward to Bournemouth instead of eastward to Hunstanton – at least until Stratton House was acquired and, with me outside her now, Mayna went back to Norfolk and the journeys east from Liverpool Street resumed.

From time to time he went on circuit. A new Judge is accorded the privilege of choosing his first circuit. McCardie chose his old stamping ground, the Midland Circuit. He went to Birmingham where, robed in the scarlet of the Red Judge, he was greeted with trumpeters and guarded by the javelin men: the Judge of the Assize had not then been shorn of his trappings. He took his butler and his cook, his clerk and his marshal. He was invited by the local Bar to join them at a circuit dinner. It was a far cry from the fifth form at St Edward's School and 46 Wheeleys Road and Messrs Bettridge and Thomas, then celebrating the jubilee of their business association and 'shining', as they wrote to say, 'with your reflected lustre'.

On this, his first Assize, a girl came before him charged with the murder of her illegitimate child. It was McCardie's duty to pass the mandatory sentence of death. His clerk prepared to put the black cap on his head, but McCardie motioned him away. 'It would be a hollow mockery,' he told the girl, 'for me to suggest that your life will be forfeit and to that pretence I will not be a party.' The girl served twelve months in prison and McCardie made a little legal history.

Sixteen

It is tempting to describe more of the cases which came before McCardie – truth being stranger than fiction and sometimes exceedingly odd. The trial in successive weeks of 1922, for instance, of two murderers, Henry Jacoby and Ronald True. Their convictions led to a major public row, in which happily McCardie was only peripherally involved. Jacoby, a young pantry boy who only meant to steal but killed a titled woman in panic, was hanged despite a recommendation to mercy, whereas True, a man of thirty whose mother was a titled woman and who killed in cold blood for money, was reprieved on psychiatric advice and sent to Broadmoor. In the eyes of the public, this was class distinction with a vengeance! And not only in the eyes of the public. A few days after True's reprieve Mr Justice Avory – a fellow workaholic nicknamed 'The Acid Drop' – told a Grand Jury at Exeter that the light calendar had led him to hope that crime was abating, but added: 'Whether it will continue to abate if the infliction of the penalties of the law is to be left to the discretion of experts in Harley Street I very much doubt.'

Accounts of these and other cases can be found in the books by Pollock and Crew and there is no point in repeating them. It is easy both to bury McCardie under piles of otherwise forgotten disputes which books about lawyers too often consist of and to lose sight of the steady flow of detailed work which comes before a Judge and which constitutes the stuff of ordinary living. One case, however, does call for special mention, *O'Dwyer v. Nair* – a libel action arising out of the so-called massacre at Amritsar in 1919. This is not only of great inherent interest, but had a traumatic effect on McCardie himself. It deserves the next chapter to itself.

Few of McCardie's cases broke fresh ground, but his judgements are full of legal history and they make excellent reading, for he was accustomed to season them with his own views, always robustly, often quirkily, expressed. He came to the Bench when new social forces were fizzing dangerously in old bottles. A Judge of first instance must administer the law as he finds it, but if, like McCardie, he has a restless and enquiring mind (as well as a mistress in the country), he is bound to find himself out of sympathy with many of the old rules. 'Social necessities and social opinion,' Maine said, 'are always more or less in advance of the law. We may come indefinitely near to closing the gap between them, but it has a perpetual tendency to re-open.' The trauma of the Great War had re-opened the gap and McCardie was determined to try to narrow it again. His sympathies ran deep and he'd not been subjected to the conformist pressures of public school and university. He was a Jack-judge, one who, seemingly the ideal cenobite, all at once refuses to conform to the discipline of the sect.

An early essay at gap-closing led to his first brush with Lord Justice Scrutton on the somewhat esoteric subject of agent of necessity, which allows action not otherwise expressly authorised to be taken in special circumstances, say, when a cargo is rotting. In *Prager v. Blatspiel* McCardie said:

> The object of the common law is to solve difficulties and adjust relations in social and commercial life. It must meet, so far as it can, sets of facts abnormal as well as normal. It must grow with the development of the nation. It must face and deal with novel and changing circumstances. Unless it can do that it fails in its function and declines in its dignity and value. An expanding society demands an expanding common law.

Scrutton, whose disquisition on *The Contract of Affreightment as Expressed in Charterparties and Bills of Lading* had already run through many editions, did not approve of too much zeal. He commented tartly that the Judge

> had proceeded to expand the doctrine of agent of necessity without clearly defining the limits, if any, of its expansion. The difficulty may be seen in considering the case of the finder of perishable goods or chattels which need expenditure to preserve them. If the finder incurs such expenditure, can he recover from the true owner when he finds him as his agent of necessity?

McCardie, however, was not unduly disturbed by this rebuff. He was after bigger game than agents of necessity. He wanted to bring about social reforms in areas – contraception, marriage, sexual relations and the like – that touch us more closely than charter parties and bills of lading, and he made no bones about saying so, with increasing vigour. Such questions generate high emotion. His embroilment in them – especially as one on whom the society he criticised had conferred distinction – didn't endear him to the ranks of the orthodox and those of his colleagues who liked a quiet life and who felt that confidence in the law was not enhanced when it was sniped at from the Bench. 'Reform? Reform?' cried Mr Justice Astbury. 'Are not things bad enough already?' McCardie realised the need for a proper measure of certainty in the law, but conceived it as his duty to draw attention to defects which, unremedied, would bring it into disrepute. He has been criticised for being better at expounding the law than applying it. There is more than a grain of truth in this. Though scrupulous in performing his judicial duty, he sometimes found himself caught up in a sort of double game in which he would take immense pains to cite one after another the earlier authorities, only to end up with a decision which he obviously regarded as contrary to the justice of the case!

His first sally into areas of controversy came in 1918. In May, the month when I was conceived, he was asked to help clear arrears in the Divorce Court, then clogged up with cases created by the War. Here some of his most polemical judgements were made. He saw the advantages of publicity – after all, if you don't go overboard sometimes, you never make a splash – and, indeed, he began to like it. He became known as the 'Bachelor Judge', a label which he rather relished. The popular Press could look to him for a steady supply of aphorisms about women, which had an added piquancy coming from a man who was unmarried and impenitent. He in turn enjoyed supplying them. He kept a scrap-book in which he pasted the reports of his bons mots, and he liked to anticipate others by giving an oblique hint to pressmen that something good was coming. This, again, found no favour at all with his more conservative brethren, who were inclined to share Lord Justice Mackinnon's view that the best Judge is 'one whose name is known to fewest readers of the *Daily Mail*'.

In the Divorce Court McCardie sat as a reformer reluctantly administering a system he wanted to alter. At the start he fell foul of the old doctrine of recrimination which, as he pointed out, had been rejected by Scotland two hundred years before. A soldier came back from Egypt to find that his wife had gone off with someone else. He met and fell in love with another girl and went to live with her. They were expecting a child and anxious to marry. When asked why he'd jumped the gun, the man replied very honestly that he had been away from a woman for four years and that he was human. If any circumstances called for a decree, these did; yet McCardie felt bound to refuse it. The result, he said,

> may seem strange indeed. For if the wife alone had committed adultery, then the husband could at once have

dissolved the marriage. Adultery is presumed to render further married life impossible. But inasmuch as the husband has here committed adultery also, and married life is therefore doubly impossible, the decree must in accordance with existing law be refused. The marriage must continue. I regret the result, but I must administer the law as it stands.

He had virtually unfettered discretion under Section 31 of the Matrimonial Causes Act, 1857, to grant relief, even though the petitioner had committed a matrimonial offence, where there were mitigating circumstances which did not offend against the established view of the interests of public morality, and he was strongly urged by counsel to use it. He decided he couldn't. His long rehearsal of previous authorities had snarled him up in the precedents. His call, in effect, for Parliament to intervene may have sounded a stirring trumpet note, but did not help the unfortunate petitioner.

In many other respects he found the existing principles of divorce distasteful, illogical and 'themselves utterly divorced from the opinion of educated clean-living people of the present day'. This did not prevent him from illuminating the law as it was by a masterly analysis of the doctrine of condonation – 'a sermon in a judgement'. But he had no time for the dingy, Brighton-hotel business of fabricating false evidence of adultery; he deplored the number of separation orders whereby husband and wife lived apart but remained married; he compared the task of placing a value on an erring wife as 'akin to that of an assessor in some of the markets of the eastern world'; he wanted to see 'the repulsive duties' of the King's Proctor swept away. Everything depended on proof of matrimonial offence and cases went on for days to determine who was to blame. The whole system seemed to him a relic of the past, touched 'by the dead hand of the old canon law'. Reference to canon law was perhaps misconceived, since once a bona fide marriage had been entered into under it, no question of divorce could arise. But the drift of his remarks was clear enough. In a humane common-sense way, he was moving towards the modern concept of divorce by consent, subject to the supervision of the Court for the protection of children. His own prime concern in marital disputes was for the children, whom he would invite to his room in order to find out over a fizzy lemonade what *they* thought – which was often quite different from what Counsel said they thought. The need for reform of the system was still in his mind when he delivered the Galton lecture that scandalised many people, a few months before his death. His widely publicised views on divorce particularly offended the Roman Catholic hierarchy and set off a long-running battle which lasted until his death. And not only his views on divorce. In *obiter dicta* from the Bench and in public speeches and lectures he was soon advancing radical ideas on abortion (which, had he been loyal to his principles, might well have done for me), birth control and the sterilisation of the unfit. Outspokenness of this sort on sexual matters not only provoked religious hostility, but cost him some old friends. Strong pressure was brought on him to desist. Equally there were many on his side, even if most were reluctant to go as far as advocating sterilisation. (In fairness it has to be remembered that this was before the Nazis had made racial purity a concept impossibly tainted and when men could still boast of the British Empire without embarrassment.) One enthusiastic ally was the Bishop of Birmingham, Dr Barnes, an Old Edwardian like himself – as, incidentally, was Francis Galton, who founded the study of eugenics. At the annual medical service in Liverpool Cathedral Dr Barnes declared, after quoting the Sermon on the Mount, that zeal for social justice had been allowed to outrun wisdom. He went on:

> Under the harsh social order which prevailed almost up to our own time the unfit, the defective and the degener-

ate were eliminated. But of late, at great cost to the community, we have not only preserved them but allowed them to propagate their like. I ask you to assent to my own conviction that such blind humanitarianism is neither Christian nor sensible. We ought not to allow those people in whom serious inheritable defects are apparent to have children.

Dr Barnes was exactly the sort of bishop McCardie might have become had he decided to enter the Church, a thorn in the ecclesiastical flesh.

In a society where sexual problems were still shrouded in hypocrisy and pretence McCardie, untrammelled by theology, sought to switch on the light of reason. He was appalled by some of the cases of rape, incest, endless pregnancies and back-street abortions that came before him. He developed a deep concern for the plight of the poor. 'As the law stands today,' he said, 'abortion is a crime for the poor but only a surgical operation for the rich.' He backed up his own experience, as always, with wide reading. He was ready with facts and figures which startled many of his contemporaries. And, like all those in advance of their time, he was relentlessly attacked and criticised. For a man of his temperament this was both a welcome challenge and difficult to bear: sometimes the one, sometimes the other. But he was never at home among that discreet class of people – higher civil servants, cautious dons, circumspect Judges – to whom the rightness of a position matters less than its tenability. He was determined to speak the truth as he saw it, free from sentiment and metaphysic.

McCardie also freely expressed views from the Bench on matters of lesser import. He relished human foibles; his curiosity was constant; his comments salty ('A husband is so unimportant these days that he is hardly worth mentioning'). He regarded it as a helpful part of his job to prescribe rules of guidance for men and women in their everyday affairs. This was an excellent source of copy for the reporters. A series of disputes concerning dress bills gave him a chance to expatiate on female fashions, which had always intrigued him. I was inspired by reading these cases to look through some contemporary copies of the *Tatler* and the *Bystander* and I could scarcely believe my eyes, though, like my father, I must have taken it all for granted then. Women wore hats like inverted chamber pots, their breasts were squashed flat, their dresses hung from their shoulders like sacks. The sight of these freakish modes, and the outrageous snobbery of the time – a report on the Royal Academy Summer Exhibition made no mention of the pictures (perhaps prudently) but listed in order of social importance those who attended the Private View – made me realise what layers of pretension McCardie's voice, often sounding so modern, had to penetrate, and to what extent also he was typical of his time. He was no puritan, he was all for attractive clothes which bring the magic of a minor art in the closest relation to ourselves ('How dreary life would be were it not for the elegance of well-dressed women'); and he spoke out strongly for the rights of women ('I must tell you that a woman's body does not belong to her husband. It is her own property, it is not his'). But he spoke of women themselves in terms of extraordinary complacency. It's not surprising that he never acquired, and perhaps couldn't have coped with, a high-spirited wife of the same calibre as himself.

Mrs Frankau, wife of the novelist, was a liberal pledger of her husband's credit to a degree which prompted McCardie to a lengthy homily. He goes on for many pages, but some excerpts will give the flavour:

> Plain speech is essential. There can, I think, be no doubt that, so far as concerns the actual physical necessity for warmth and the like, and so far as there is any needed or desired concealment of the female body, the ordinary

society woman could clothe herself quite well for one-fifth of the money she now expends on dress. She could buy a sufficiency of stout and long-wearing woollen or flannel garments for a very small sum per annum. Cotton fabrics for the summer time are extremely cheap...

Quite apart from the sacred trust of motherhood and the noble companionship she often gives, the function of a woman in modern society is largely utilitarian. Nature has decreed that leadership and physical strength and intellectual achievement shall belong to men, but women are the chief decorations of social life. Legitimate scope must be given to woman's instinct for dress as it may be exercised and permitted in present-day conditions. Women cannot be expected to renounce an essential feature of femininity or to abandon one of nature's solaces for a constant and insuperable physical handicap. A reasonable indulgence in dress is needed to counterbalance what I may call the inferiority complex of women...

Her natural vanity may seek a reasonable satisfaction. Her self-esteem must be reasonably gratified. The factor of sex allurement is not without its weight...

Dress, after all, is one of the chief methods of women's self-expression. I can well understand the fascination of a beautiful garment. It is, I conceive, important to remember the singular and tonic effect produced on a woman by a new and attractive dress or coat or hat. In matters of dress women often remain children to the end...

The extravagance of Mrs Frankau which incurred McCardie's long rebuke was as nothing compared with that of Mrs Nash. His denunciation of *her* dress bills was couched in the ringing tones of the Victorian Bar, with quotations from Ovid and Victor Hugo thrown in for good measure:

In Mrs Nash's numerous wardrobes there were always

fifty or sixty evening dresses... She would purchase shoes not in pairs, but in several dozen pairs of various sorts at a time... Everything was on the same scale, whether for hats, lingerie or the like. She threw herself beneath the fatal curse of luxury. She forgot that those who possess substantial means are trustees to use them with prudence, charity and propriety. She forgot that ostentation is the worst form of vulgarity. She ignored the sharp menace of future penury. Dress and dress alone seems to have been her end in life. She sought felicity in the ceaseless changes of trivial fashion. Self-decoration was her vision, her aim, her creed... She renounced her duties at the call of empty pleasure. She sacrificed her privileges of social service for the allurements of ignominious folly.

Such language must have been served up with an eye on the popular Press; and, if my father ever glanced through his old judgements, what he said here about the duty of those with substantial means and the menace of future penury may have come back to haunt him. To indulge in a rhetoric is often tempting, but to break a butterfly on the wheel like this is tawdry. And untypical. When dealing with factual matters, applying the law and reaching conclusions, he was refreshingly plain and unaffected. These had been his virtues at the Bar. He had never been one of the 'eloquent' counsels and the role didn't suit him.

On the question of punishment also he had strong views, which seemed to reflect apparent ambiguity: on the one hand, he condemned the effects of the prison system; on the other, he called for harsher penalties and longer sentences. He strongly supported flogging and hanging. Flogging was then much in vogue and George Bancroft, then Clerk of the Assize, tells the story of how McCardie had to deal with a man found guilty of a particularly brutal robbery with violence. When asked whether he had anything to say, the prisoner requested the Judge to sentence him to a flogging as the only punishment which would do him any good. McCardie asked Bancroft for his opinion. 'Surely, Judge,' replied Bancroft, 'you don't think he meant it?' McCardie said that this was exactly what his marshal thought, adding, somewhat portentously, 'I make it a rule never to accede to a prisoner's request.' He passed a long sentence without a flogging. The man was delighted: flogging was the one thing he feared.

McCardie remained troubled throughout his career as a Judge by the problems of sentencing, which caused more tugging of his cuffs than anything else. Most judges were, and still are. His wide reading didn't help much. 'Trying a man,' he once remarked, 'is as easy as falling off a log compared with deciding what to do with him when he has been found guilty.' If he sensed any hope of reform, he believed in avoiding imprisonment. He had been round prisons. He knew that they reinforced a criminal sub-culture and broke up family ties, one of the few things to make reconviction less likely, and that the chance of getting work on release was remote. He himself said: 'a prison sentence is a life sentence'. Nevertheless he was firmly convinced of its deterrent power. Deterrence was in his view the prime purpose of punishment. When imprisonment was merited, he believed in long sentences – a philosophy which was later to bring him into conflict with the Appeal Court. But his instinct was to temper justice with humanity and he would often send gifts of money to the families of those he had sent to jail. Mayna received a touching letter from one such family after his death:

> I wish to express my sympathy with you in the loss of Mr Justice McCardie. We have known now for some time his greatness of heart, in personal dealings with him. Some time ago my mother-in-law's hardship came to his hearing, she lives in Greenwich and he, dear Lady, is one

gone from the working class that will be felt more and more. What he did to help others he did without show and to mother to who he used to send 8/- a week for rent he was all kindness and goodness. What she will do now without his help I can not think.

It was among the few letters Mayna kept from that time – touching in more senses than one, no doubt, but a tribute nevertheless to the quiet and constant generosity that few people knew about.

These were fruitful years. Of course the work no longer came at him like a torrent as it had done when he was at the Bar, but he took the precaution of ensuring that he was always busy. How do you like being a Judge? he was once asked at dinner. 'Just as much or as little as I like life,' was his reply, 'for my work is to look upon life, except that at times I have a slight intellectual diversion when I am called upon to decide a point of law.' A bantering reply that went well with the soufflé, but hid the deep malaise that had been slumbering on and off under his long success. The truth was that, when the grandiosity was set aside, he didn't like life very much; depression, loneliness, boredom lay in wait under its admired and envied surface. His judicial duties made insufficient demands to keep them at bay; in most instances there was little law involved. So he increased the load. He drew on his huge knowledge of case law when an opportunity allowed and turned his judgements into little storehouses of legal information. He embellished them increasingly with moral homilies and calls for reform.

In other directions, too, he kept himself endlessly busy. He rarely declined an invitation to speak and he took immense trouble in the preparation – a series of readings at the Middle Temple (later published under the title *The Law, the Advocate and the Judge*), talks to university law societies, to the Royal Medico-Psychological Association, to divorce reform bodies, to the Discharged Prisoners Aid Society, the Horation Society, the Four Provinces Club, the Authors' Club ... the list is endless. As an after-dinner speaker he was in constant demand; few Judges, as someone remarked, can have dined out with such debilitating regularity or made such frequent after-dinner speeches. He continued to read widely. He had an enormous postbag, not only from people interested in social reform who wrote to praise or abuse him, but from ordinary members of the public seeking his advice and sometimes, it must be admitted, soliciting money; to bona fide enquirers, he made a point of replying personally. His week-ends were carefully taken care of – occasional visits to some house party, but mainly to Norfolk or to his family or to a particular friend, perhaps his only close male friend, his cousin Captain James McCardie Martin, at Alton. But despite all this, the 'craving void', as Byron called it, would again yawn in front of him and he would gamble. Then only the thrill of gambling could blot out the nothingness. There were no intimate ties of affection to hold him back.

Seventeen

The most controversial of McCardie's many well-known cases, and one which made him the target of deep political hostility, was *O'Dwyer v. Nair* in 1924 – about half way through his judicial career and pivotal in every sense.

Sir Michael O'Dwyer, Lieutenant-Governor of the Punjab from 1913 until 1919, had brought an action for libel against Sir Sankaran Nair. Nair was a former Judge of the Madras High Court and a member of the Executive Council of the Viceroy and later of the India Council in London. The alleged libel was contained in his book *Gandhi and Anarchy*, where he said: 'Before the reforms [of Indian administration] it was in the power of the Lieutenant-Governor, a single individual, to commit the atrocities in the Punjab that we know only too well.' He claimed in his defence that these words were true, and raised a further plea of fair comment. Most conspicuously he alleged that on 13 April, 1919, General Dyer committed an atrocity by ordering the shooting at Amritsar, when over 370 Indian civilians were killed, and that O'Dwyer caused it to be committed. The case came for trial before McCardie and a Special Jury on 30 April. One of the jurors was Harold Laski, the left wing academic from whom Clement Atlee once memorably requested a period of silence.

The shooting at Amritsar seems a small affair against the background of such horrors as the massacre of at least a million people at the time of partition in 1947, when the Punjab became a vast killing ground and Hindus, Muslims and Sikhs slaughtered one another on a scale comparable to the Somme. But it was carried out under the command of a British General and created a profound sense of shock. It formed a kind of watershed in our relations with India; things were never the same afterwards. No-one disputed that General Dyer had to act decisively. The rapidity with which disorder can spread in India is proverbial: 'India is quiet, as quiet as gunpowder', said John Lawrence after the Mutiny. Lawrence was an earlier Governor of the Punjab, then as now a potentially violent place. It nurtured the pick of India's fighting men and, perhaps as a consequence, produced a special breed of administrator who combined a strong sense of mission with a tradition of ruthlessness, the 'Punjab School'. It remained an article of faith for the Punjab School that swift use of force at the beginning means the least use of force in the end.

Michael O'Dwyer was a man cut out for the Punjab. He was one of fourteen children (nine boys) of an impoverished Irish landowner; his mother couldn't remember how many sons she had, only that there were 'fifty-three feet of them'. He was brought up in a hunting and snipe-shooting world in which a man soon learned to know his enemies from his friends. Physically fearless, he was a gifted linguist, a master of the vernacular, and highly intelligent. At Oxford he read a three-year course of law in one year and got a first. In India his rise was rapid. He distinguished himself as a settlement officer, and played a prominent part in organising the new North West Frontier Province, where he was mixed up in many a skirmish. In December 1912 he was appointed Lieutenant-Governor of the Punjab, with a warning that it was the province 'with which the Government was then most concerned; that there was much inflammable material lying about, which required very careful handling if an explosion was to be avoided.' He relished the task. The air was full of plots. The Ghadr conspiracy was fostered by Sikhs in America, and throughout the Great War German and Turkish agents were active in stirring up disaffection. The Frontier tribes were as usual itching for trouble.

After the War Indians expected to receive some recognition of their services during it: at least to be treated as equals and allowed to govern themselves. Instead they were offered a curious hybrid called 'dyarchy', a system of dual government operated partly by the Secretary of State and partly through Indian ministers in an elected assembly. It was described by Philip Mason as a technical term for handing over the steering wheel and retaining control of the accelerator, gear-lever and brake. Even this grudging concession was made to seem even more grudging by the Rowlatt Acts of 1919, which provided for an indefinite continuance of special war emergency powers. The result was a campaign of passive resistance organised by Mahatma Gandhi in the form of a hartal, or stoppage of work. Passive resistance was soon reinforced, however, by violence and intimidation. There were riots in Delhi. In the Punjab the violence was widespread. Telegraph lines were cut, railway tracks blown up and trains derailed. The police had to be withdrawn from Lahore. In Amritsar public buildings and banks were looted and set on fire, Europeans murdered, one smashed to pulp and his body burned, and an elderly woman missionary beaten up and left for dead. O'Dwyer regarded these events, not merely as riots, but as open rebellion. He asked the Government of India for the introduction of martial law. The Government (of whose Executive Council Sir Sankaran Nair was a member) agreed. But they refused to give O'Dwyer and his staff the military rank for which he had asked so that he might keep personal control. As it was, control was taken out of his hands; he could only advise.

General Dyer, the district commander, arrived at Amritsar to find all the British residents, including over a hundred woman and children, collected in the fort for safety. The city was in the hands of the mob with all communications cut off. The normal population of some 150,000 had been swollen by peasants who had come in for a fair. Most of them were Sikhs carrying the six-foot brass-shod quarterstaff; and, in the words of a contemporary dispatch, 'the peasants of the district are not of a type which will keep the law unless its guardians are able to enforce it'. It was a highly dangerous situation beyond police control, and Dyer took over. He had very few resources, and the mob knew it. When he marched with a drummer to strategic points in the city and issued orders forbidding all public meetings, he was followed by a cavalcade banging on kerosene tins and mocking him. The situation grew hourly more tense and in the forenoon of 13 April, after issuing a proclamation, he again marched round with his drum, warning now that any meetings would be fired on. Later that day, in defiance of these orders, a large crowd began to assemble in the Jallianwala Bagh, a piece of unused ground hemmed in by buildings. The entrance was narrow and the only other way to get out was to climb a gap about five feet high in a mud and brick wall at the back (a gap which was later filled up when the place was turned into a memorial). Dyer took personal command of a small force of Gurkhas – fifty riflemen and forty men with kukris – and confronted the crowd, estimated to be up to twenty thousand. They were being addressed by men, later convicted for incitement, who were working up their feelings and pooh-poohing Dyer's prohibition as mere bluff since he had only a handful of troops to enforce it. Dyer formed up his riflemen on each side of the entrance and, without further warning, ordered them to open fire. The crowd initially recoiled and then, finding there was no means of escape, surged forward again. Dyer told his men to continue firing. They fired until they had no more ammunition – 1,650 rounds. Over 370 people were killed and three times as many wounded. That evening the city was, in Dyer's words, 'absolutely quiet, not a soul to be seen'. Trouble elsewhere in the Punjab quickly subsided.

In his first report Dyer implied that his purpose had been only to disperse the crowd. There is evidence that he was 'dazed and shaken' and 'never knew there was no way out'. He told a friend that, when the crowd didn't scatter, he thought 'it was massing to attack him and kept on firing'. But later on he changed his ground. He learned that his superior, General Sir William Benyon, had asked the Governor whether he approved, and O'Dwyer, knowing that what had been done was irrevocable and believing that Dyer's action had saved the Punjab from open rebellion, had replied yes. There was praise from the English on all sides, partly as a revulsion against a passionate outcry in the Indian Press, and Dyer came to regard himself as the saviour of the country. He began to make up his own legend. When he appeared, ill-advised and unrepresented, before a committee of enquiry into the disturbances set up under Lord Hunter, he boasted in language tinged with racial arrogance that he had deliberately intended by the severity of his action to produce 'a moral effect' in all parts of India (though he was more circumspect in a subsequent statement to the Army Council which McCardie read out in Court). Moreover, he had done his reputation no good by a notorious order, for which O'Dwyer took him severely to task, that any Indian using the street where the English woman missionary had been attacked must crawl along it. The order was soon rescinded and the locals didn't take it very seriously. Though one man insisted on crawling down the street five times and had to be restrained by the piquet from doing so again, the people who lived there simply went home by the back way. But it had a disastrous effect on public opinion.

The Hunter Committee found against Dyer and, after receiving their report, the Secretary of State for India expressed the view that he had acted 'beyond the necessity of the case, beyond what any reasonable man could have thought to be necessary and that he did not act with as much humanity as the case permitted'. This view was communicated to the Commander-in-Chief, India, General Monro, with a request that he should take what action he thought appropriate.

General Monro was no sentimentalist – the Psalms of David came under his censure for being insufficiently martial: they showed, he said, a whining attitude. But he felt obliged to conclude that Dyer had not shown 'the wisdom and sense of proportion expected of a senior officer' and directed that he resign his command. The Army Council and the then Viceroy, Lord Chelmsford, concurred. Deprived of further employment in India, Dyer came home and bought a farm in Wiltshire with a purse of £26,000 raised for him by the *Morning Post* from those, including many in both Houses of Parliament, who believed he had been unjustly treated. This belief was exacerbated by the time – almost a year – which had by then elapsed, during which Dyer had distinguished himself on active service in the Third Afghan War despite being in continuous physical pain as the result of a riding accident in 1917, when his horse rolled on him. This accident, which produced severe and frequent headaches, may well also have impaired his judgement at Amritsar.

Such was the background to the libel case which came before McCardie in April, 1924. It was a matter on which feelings both here and in India were still running high. Dyer himself was by now seriously ill and unable to give evidence. He died without knowing that, in McCardie's eyes at any rate, he had been vindicated.

The trial lasted for nearly five weeks, during which Empire Day was celebrated with the customary waving of Union Jacks. Detailed evidence was taken from a procession of witnesses, including Lord Chelmsford. The ground covered by the Hunter Committee was gone over again, and the Committee, which did not take evidence on oath and had unfortunately divided upon racial lines, came out of it rather badly. McCardie's summing-up on 5 June took over five hours and filled 120 pages of shorthand notes, of which 30 related expressly to the Amritsar incident. The result was a verdict for O'Dwyer with agreed damages of £500. The jury found in his favour on all points by a majority of eleven to one. Needless to say, the dissentient juror was Harold Laski. He obtained leave at the end of the trial to address the court, when he paid McCardie an unusual compliment:

> My Lord, I think I ought to say on behalf of the jury that we are all of us very grateful to your Lordship for the care you have shown in helping us to a proper appreciation of this case during the long period we have had in sitting under you.

McCardie had been accused of intervening much too often in favour of the plaintiff and some thought that Laski was being ironic. But in his book *The Grammar of Politics* Laski referred generously to McCardie and spoke of a 'fault' which 'was, at the worst, an error of judgement made in all sincerity'.

Inevitably the trial aroused strong emotions and touched off powerful prejudices: but it was the words which McCardie used about the Amritsar episode in his summing-up that turned it into a *cause célèbre*. Addressing the jury, he said:

> Speaking with full deliberation and knowing the whole of the evidence given in this case, I express my view that General Dyer, under the grave and exceptional circumstances, acted rightly, and in my opinion, upon the evidence, he was wrongly punished by the Secretary of State for India.

McCardie was well aware that the Amritsar shooting was an acutely sensitive matter. Indeed he'd done his best early in the trial to avoid its becoming a main issue – with some justification, since to accuse O'Dwyer of having a hand in it was patently a nonsense as martial law prevailed, communications had been cut off and he had no knowledge of or control over what Dyer intended to do. 'Have *we* to decide,' McCardie

Mrs Jane Elizabeth McCardie (née Hunt) with her family, Henry Alfred on right, 1877

Henry A. McCardie, the barrister c.1895

Sir Henry McCardie, the newly appointed judge 1916

Henry Archer 1928

Henry Archer, Sir Henry McCardie and Mayna c. 1930

Sir Henry McCardie c.1932

Betty 1945

Henry Archer
1945

asked, 'whether General Dyer was right or wrong? If so I shall have to tell the jury that, when the safety of the Indian Empire was in question and through that the safety of the British Empire, perhaps it might be necessary to do things which would not be justified in other circumstances.' To which Sir Walter Schwabe, the defending Counsel, replied: 'We say that what General Dyer did was an atrocity from any point of view... And we say it was an atrocity which had the consent of Sir Michael O'Dwyer before it was committed and his practical approval afterwards. One of the questions which will have to be considered is whether the condemnation of General Dyer was right or wrong.' Here Sir Walter strayed beyond the pleadings. True, if O'Dwyer was accused of causing an atrocity at Amritsar, it was necessary to establish whether or not there'd been one; the conduct of General Dyer was, therefore, a direct issue and the Judge was bound to draw the attention of the jury to the evidence on the point. But it was unnecessary to decide whether Dyer had been wrongly or rightly condemned. That was not an issue strictly pertinent to the trial and, if passions were not to be further inflamed, there was every reason to tread delicately over it. McCardie elected to put on heavy boots. He'd made his own mind up and he never lacked courage: in that sense the judgement was a splendid example of his qualities. But did he really need to provoke a major political row? It was as if, not for the first time or the last, he was deliberately inviting trouble. If so, he didn't have long to wait for it.

The old controversies boiled up again. Those who spoke for Dyer rejoiced that, after five years of suppression, the truth had at last been established in an English court. On the other side, liberal opinion was outraged. The India Office were appalled at what they termed McCardie's 'indiscretion'. In India itself there was bitter resentment at what was less delicately described as 'this disgusting revelation of the jingo mind'. On 16 June Mr George Lansbury gave notice of his intention to ask the Prime Minister, then Ramsay MacDonald, 'Whether the Government will grant time for the discussion of a motion ... dealing with the remarks of Mr Justice McCardie.' The motion was for an Address by the House of Commons, as a first step towards a proposed Address by both Houses, for the removal of McCardie from the Bench as being in breach of that 'good behaviour' under which judges have held office since the Act of Settlement. Since the intention of that Act was to render them independent of the Executive, it was a little paradoxical that the power of removal should be prayed in aid because one of them had shown himself to be precisely that; judges are normally accused of an over-appreciation of executive difficulty.

Lansbury's aim was to call attention to the strength of public feeling rather than to press the motion home, and it was not proceeded with. But the Prime Minister's observations, when he replied, amounted in effect to a censure of McCardie. After remarking that 'a discussion on this subject would only add to the harm which has been done in India by the words complained of', he went on:

> However unfortunate the words may have been, they clearly do not constitute the kind of fault amounting to moral delinquency which constitutionally justifies an Address as proposed. It ought in fairness to be borne in mind that the objectionable passage occurred, not in a considered written judgement, but in an oral charge to a jury, delivered at the conclusion of a lengthened and somewhat heated trial, and the very form in which it was couched shows that the learned Judge was not informed as to what took place ... H.M. Government will always uphold the right of the Judiciary to pass judgement even on the Executive if it thinks fit, but, that being the right of the Judiciary, it is all the more necessary that it should guard itself against pronouncements upon issues

involving grave political consequences which are not themselves being tried... The *obiter dicta* which the learned Judge let fall were calculated to have a very serious effect upon Indian public opinion, and for these reasons I have couched the answer in the way I have.

Subsequently these observations were incorporated in a dispatch sent by Lord Olivier from the India Office to the Viceroy and published officially in the Press. McCardie's summing-up therefore remained – and remains – formally censured in the State archives, a matter on which he never entirely ceased to brood. Though many of his colleagues, and many others also, wrote privately to express approval of what he had done, he received a deluge of hostile letters, many of them vicious and hurtful.

Judicial etiquette precluded his replying to the Prime Minister's remarks, which he regarded as both unjust and inaccurate. He was profoundly upset. So much so that he immediately wrote a personal letter to the Attorney General, Sir Patrick Hastings, who had earlier been associated with the O'Dwyer case as Counsel for Nair and should, in McCardie's view, have advised the Prime Minister as a matter of law that the words complained of were not *obiter* but went to the heart of the case. McCardie indicated that he intended to resign his post and return to his practice at the Bar and to make 'a full, clear and public statement on the points at issue'. I have the letter beside me. In the end he decided not to send it and not to resign. (There is in any event an established tradition that judges do not go back to the Bar.) Instead he wrote a long letter, which he did send, to the Lord Chancellor, Lord Haldane, whom he felt he could properly look to as head of the Judiciary to put the record straight. Lord Haldane's reply was firmly discouraging. When McCardie pressed the matter, he received a plain snub, which must have been deeply wounding. Their exchange of letters is annexed at the end of the chapter.

Characteristically, McCardie refused to give up and prepared a detailed Statement, carefully annotated in his own hand, to justify his position. He never made this Statement public – I think wisely, for it savours of special pleading. Technically his handling of the trial cannot be faulted – he was as well versed in libel law as anyone in the country: latterly it had been his meat and drink at the Bar. The conduct of Dyer at Amritsar *was* a direct issue which, pursuant to the pleadings, fell to be tried irrespective of any 'political consequences'; neither the report of the Hunter Committee nor the condemnation by the Secretary of State was binding in this respect. Having regard to the volume of evidence taken, it was disingenuous of the Prime Minister to claim that 'the learned judge was not informed as to what took place' – though this was true to the extent that the Government refused to disclose details of the proceedings under which Dyer had been condemned. McCardie was also at liberty to make known his personal view of the matter, provided he made it plain, which he did, that it was up to the jury to sort out the facts. What was objectionable about that fateful sentence in his summing-up was the extreme form in which it was put and the fact that it went beyond what his duty strictly required. Whether Dyer committed an atrocity and whether he was rightly punished are, as Lord Haldane pointed out in his letter, very different questions. The reason why Dyer was relieved from his command (a punishment imposed by the Commander-in-Chief, India, not by the Secretary of State as McCardie asserted) was not because he opened fire, but because, by continuing to fire until his men had no more ammunition left, he was held to have been in gross breach of the doctrine of minimum force when military action is taken in support of the civil authority – a principle of civil administration consistently affirmed. No evidence as to the validity or otherwise of this doctrine, or the criteria adopted by the C-in-C in reaching his decision, was before the Court; nor were they matters for the jury to determine. To this extent, McCardie's remarks might reasonably be described as *obiter*.

Having decided to allow the Amritsar incident to be explored in detail, McCardie was in duty bound to draw attention to the many factors which might be advanced in Dyer's favour. He emphasised in his summing-up

> the prime duty of every government, be it in India, in England or elsewhere, is to maintain order and repress anarchy. Without the enforcement of law, there can be no good thing for the people... When I go from this country to the Punjab I begin to feel that all the treatises on civil government that I have read, all the political theories I have heard discussed, are really put to the test...

He makes the same point in his unpublished Statement with reference to Lord Olivier's dispatch: '...the words "the minimum force necessary" are difficult to interpret. Theoretic formulae may dissolve before the realities of a grave and exceptional emergency. The factor of deterrence may be a vital necessity in certain circumstances.' There is no doubt that Dyer, with his platoon of Gurkhas, was in extreme danger – confronting a huge hostile crowd in a city seething with revolt. How he acted was critical. That he acted decisively may well have avoided rebellion in a province where violence could spread like a forest fire. His immediate superiors approved his action and, strangely, the Sikh community insisted on his being baptised as a Sikh, a unique honour: Amritsar was their holy city, and one would have expected them to be outraged. This was a point to which McCardie attached great significance. He was also a Victorian by upbringing and had inhaled the mystique of Empire. The temper of the time and the consciousness of Imperial responsibilities inclined those in authority to take a more robust view of the repression of disorder than we do now. Use of aeroplanes to bomb recalcitrant civilians in the Punjab was numbered among the alleged atrocities cited by Sir Sankaran Nair, though little noticed. (Two years after the Amritsar affair Winston Churchill, then Secretary of State for War and Air, was urging the RAF in Iraq to use mustard gas, which had been employed 'with excellent moral effect' against the Shia rebels in 1920.)

McCardie remained convinced to the end of his life that he had acted in accordance with his judicial duty. It is true that he did not deviate from it as a matter of law; but to make as he did an unqualified assertion that General Dyer was 'wrongly punished' seems at the least perverse when the shooting at Jallianwala Bagh was continued long after its purpose had been effected and to a degree which, whether or not it could be called an 'atrocity', created widespread shock and horror. McCardie may be said in some sense to have made the same sort of error of judgement as Dyer did: he went beyond the necessity of the case. Like Dyer also, he had to pay the price.

Following the trial E.M. Forster, in indignation, sent McCardie a copy of *A Passage to India*, which had just come out. To his bafflement he received a courteous acknowledgement from McCardie saying that it had been 'an inspiration' and 'a help'. I wonder if my father ever read it. It was not exactly his kind of book.

He was still not prepared to let the matter go; he always found it difficult to give up. He took the opportunity in his Reader's Address to the Middle Temple some three years later to refer to *O'Dwyer v. Nair*. He did not mention the case as such, but his audience had no doubt that it was in his mind. He said:

> A further point is this – that a judge when sitting with a jury is more than a mere recorder of evidence or a mere pronouncer on points of technical law. He is far more than that. He is entitled – yes, fully entitled – to express

his personal opinion on the facts for the consideration of the jury, provided he leaves the issues of fact to them. Herein the State judges of the United States of America differ from the English judge. The right of my colleagues and myself on the matter was clearly formulated by the Court of Criminal Appeal in Rex v. O'Donnell, 1917, in these words: 'It is sufficient to say, as this Court has said on many occasions, that a judge when directing a jury is clearly entitled to express his opinion on the facts of the case, provided that he leaves the issues of fact to the jury to determine.' That right of the judge is, I venture to think, essential to the strength and independence of the English Bench.

A further matter I would mention is this: that the judges seek no popularity. They will not yield to the passing winds of popular excitement, whatever the direction in which those winds may blow. I recall to you tonight, once more, the spirit of Lord Mansfield, when he said: 'I will not do that which my conscience tells me is wrong, upon this occasion, to gain the huzzas of thousands or the daily praise of all the papers which come from the press. I will not avoid doing what I think right, though it should draw on me the whole artillery of libels.' (Case of John Wilkes, 1763.) Still a further point is this: that it is our duty to administer fearlessly the law as it stands. We follow, and we will continue to follow, the words of Mr Justice Littledale in Stockdale v. Hansard, 1837. He said there: 'If I am to pronounce a judgement at all in this or in any other case it must and shall be the judgement of my own mind, applying the law of the land as I understand it to the best of my abilities, and with full regard to the oath I have taken to administer justice truly and impartially.'

The steady rehearsal of cases is typical of my father's style, and the reference to *Rex v. O'Donnell* is especially apt because this precedent was laid down by the former Lord Chief Justice, Lord Reading, who happened to be the Viceroy of India to whom Lord Olivier's dispatch about Amritsar was sent. But the condemnation of General Dyer's action is not so easily dismissed as 'the passing winds of popular excitement'. The revulsion at the slaughter at Amritsar was something more than that, and it dealt a wound to our relations with India which is still not healed.

From Mr. Justice McCardie.   Royal Courts of Justice,
June 30/24.

Dear Lord Chancellor,

I send you this letter because of the statements made by the Prime Minister in the House of Commons on Monday last upon the O'Dwyer case and myself.

I feel sure that the Prime Minister made his observations under a *complete* misapprehension of the true facts. He stated (in substance) that my remarks on General Dyer were irrelevant to any issue in the case. The exact opposite is the truth. One of the libels complained of charged the Pltf. (Sir M. O'Dwyer) with having committed 'atrocities' in the Punjab. The deft's particulars of justification alleged (1) that Gen. Dyer committed an 'atrocity' on Ap.13/19 by ordering the shooting at Amritsar (2) that the pltf. caused that atrocity to be committed.

Those issues became the most conspicuous in the case. I was bound to deal with them in my summing up. I need not set out further the points I desire to make in this letter. They are dealt with clearly and fairly in the enclosed legal article in the Morning Post of June 23/24. I desire to adopt the observations in that article as representing substantially what I would wish to say here.

The Jury and myself had before us not only the whole of the material before the Hunter Committee and the Secretary of State but also a good deal of fresh evidence both oral and documentary. Those who heard the entire evidence in the action will realise the grounds of my summing up.

I myself feel (though opinions differ on the point) that the Prime Minister was *entitled* to say that he *differed* from my view. But I submit that he was not justified in saying that my observations as to General Dyer were irrelevant. They touched a vital issue. I expressed a view formed after carefully weighing every bit of the evidence. I may add that the Jury (by 11 to 1) took the view that I took for they *expressly* found for the pltf. on *all* points.

I realise the political difficulties of the Prime Minister – although I myself have never taken any part in politics.

I feel (as I have said) that he was entitled to say that he differed from the view of the Jury and myself.

But I am sure that he will wish (as a just and honourable man) to rectify so far as possible the wrong that he has unwittingly done one through the inaccuracy of the information supplied to him.

I have the pleadings beside me as I write. My summing up and the findings of the Jury are, I take it, on the shorthand notes of the trial. The report of the trial as set forth in 'The Times' is doubtless known to you. I feel it my duty to send you this letter as head of the Judiciary and *to place on record* the *true* facts.

I am, dear Lord Chancellor,
Yours very truly,
(Sgd) HENRY A. McCARDIE.

Copy of Article from "Morning Post," Tuesday, 13th October, 1925.

JUSTICE AND POLITICS.

The current number of the "Law Journal," in the course of an article on "Summing Up," brings into review that *cause célèbre* of last year, the famous case of *O'Dwyer* v. *Nair*, and we hope that the article will be read by at least four people whom it concerns— Mr. Justice McCardie, Mr. Ramsay MacDonald, Lord Olivier, and Sir Patrick Hastings. To the first it should give pleasure, since it completely justifies his direction to the jury, and we hope it may give a twinge to the sensitive consciences of the other three. The Judge, it will be remembered, in the course of his summing-up, said that "in the grave and exceptional circumstances, General Dyer acted rightly, and was wrongly punished by the Secretary of State for India." Thereupon, the Prime Minister of the day, in the House of Commons, publicly censured the Judge for *obiter dicta* outside any issue in the case, and therefore objectionable, and Lord Olivier embodied that opinion in a despatch to the Government of India, so that both in England and India an English Judge was censured and English justice slighted by the Executive Government. Now, the question which the "Law Journal" discusses is the legal question of whether the Judge was or was not within his right and duty.

It begins by pointing out that if there is one clear rule it is that a Judge can express his own view of the result of the evidence which has been led on any issue. That being so, was General Dyer's conduct an issue of the case? If it was, then the Judge had the right and duty to express his opinion upon it. The "Law Journal" turns to the pleadings and finds the Dyer "atrocities," both in the Statement of Claim and in the Particulars of Justification. Not only so, but the defendant's leading counsel, in his argument, put the issue thus:—

> "We say that what General Dyer did was an atrocity, and we say it was an atrocity which had the consent and the approval of Sir Michael O'Dwyer. One of the questions which will have to be considered in the case is whether the condemnation of General Dyer was right or wrong."

It was an issue of the case; it was covered by the evidence; it had to be considered by the jury. How, then, could it have been passed over by the Judge? We hope it will not be asserted that a Judge of our High Court in a civil trial was bound to accept the findings of the Amritsar Commission, where the proceedings were not even on oath and the General was not represented by Counsel! Nor will it be advanced in a free country that a Judge must not comment on an act of the Executive which is pertinent to the case on trial. Were that to be the rule, then no Civil Servant, nor anybody else, would have a remedy in our Courts from any action of the Government, which would make an end of one of the most cherished rights of the subject.

But who advised the late Prime Minister that the Amritsar affair was not an issue of the case? It must surely have been Sir Patrick Hastings, the then Attorney-General. Yet Sir Patrick must have been fully aware of the issues in the case, since before he became Attorney-General he acted as counsel for the defendant Nair, and when evidence was taken on commission Mr. Hastings (as he then was) cross-examined the witnesses on the various issues, including the issue of Amritsar. Was it, then, Sir Patrick Hastings who told Mr. Ramsay MacDonald that the Judge had gone outside the issues of the case? Or did Mr. Ramsay MacDonald censure an English Judge by the light of his native inspiration? We should like to know, and we hope that Sir Patrick Hastings, for the honour of the profession of which he is a member, will be so good as to inform us. In the meantime, as the "Law Journal" points out, the now famous summing-up is left in this peculiar position: it remains in the records as a reliable precedent of what a direction to a jury should be, but in Hansard and in State papers it remains condemned as something very much to be regretted, although not in itself warranting the removal of the learned Judge from the Bench! No man of sense would hesitate between the two yet as these political records do constitute an unjustified slight on the Judiciary—and we might even call it a threat or a menace—we think that the present Government should consider whether the wrong could not be set right.

Confidential.   3rd July, 1924.

Dear Mr. Justice McCardie,

When I originally read the observations in your summing up as to the rightfulness of General Dyer's action and the wrongfulness of his punishment, I formed the view that it was unnecessary for you to make such a pronouncement and that its consequences were likely to be unfortunate.

I realise that in the course which the trial took it may have been difficult and perhaps impossible, to shut out all consideration of General Dyer's action at Amritsar, but the question whether General Dyer was right or wrong was not directly in issue, nor was it an issue upon which the jury should, in my view, have been invited to express a judgment.

Statements were made, as I gather, in the course of the trial as to what happened upon the Hunter Commission and your observations convey a direct censure of the action of the Secretary of State. The members of the Hunter Commission were not present before you to state their view of the facts, nor was the Secretary of State represented, nor was it open to him to justify his action. Your words, therefore, seem to me to be what the Prime Minister described them, that is obiter dicta, and he seems to me to have been justified in his statement that "the main point and purpose of the trial did not concern itself with" them.

For these reasons, I considered carefully before Mr. Lansbury put down his motion whether I ought to write to you upon the subject. I came to the conclusion that I ought not. It did not seem to me that any useful purpose would be served by my doing so. The words once spoken could not be recalled, and I thought it best to leave the matter unnoticed. Nor should I now have expressed any opinion upon the matter if you had not yourself written to me upon the subject.

The form in which the Prime Minister cast his reply to Mr. Lansbury was settled by him without any consultation with me, but in substance I do not disagree with what he said.

I am, therefore, not prepared now to take any further step in the matter. It is an unfortunate circumstance that you should have pronounced a censure upon the action of the Secretary of State, whose conduct was not called in issue in the action before you. But, as you have done so, I fear that you cannot justly complain that the Prime Minister should have expressed a view which he is entitled to hold.

My own opinion is that further controversy upon the matter can do no good to anyone, and regrettable as the incident is from every point of view, I think that both your own dignity and the interests of the administration of justice will best be served by now allowing the whole matter to drop.

Yours sincerely,
(Sgd) HALDANE.

The Hon.
   Mr. Justice McCardie.

Judges' House,
WARWICK.

July 7/24.

Dear Lord Chancellor,
I have received your letter of the 3rd inst. I have read it with *regret*.

I dissent *emphatically* from your suggestion that Gen. Dyer's conduct was not directly in issue. It is obvious that you have not even read the pleadings or followed the course of the trial. The conduct of Gen. Dyer was a *direct and vital* issue in the case. This will be apparent to anyone who reads the pleadings and who is familiar with the law of libel and the law of pleading.

I gather that you suggest that the point as to Gen. Dyer's conduct was *concluded* either by the Hunter Report *or* the Despatch of the Secretary of State for India. *This view is utterly opposed to established law.*

The dft. pleaded various heads of so called "atrocities". Each side rejected both the Hunter Report and the Despatch of the Secretary of State except so far as they happened to *coincide* with the *contentions* respectively put forward. Do you seriously suggest that at the trial we were merely to *construe* the Report of the Hunter Committee and the Despatch of the Secretary of State with respect to the matters they covered. If they differed (as they did on some points) *which was to prevail*?

As to the condemnation of Gen. Dyer by the Secretary of State and the punishment announced by that minister, I beg to say that it was the *deft's. Csl.* who brought in this part of the Despatch and made it a part of the case. It was read and discussed and criticised repeatedly. It was the subject of vigorous comment by both Counsel either for or against.

True that the Secretary of State was not a party nor were the Hunter Committee parties. But does it therefor follow that their views were in any way conclusive – even *if* they *agreed*? Both the Report and Despatch were important – but only as points for consideration.

Many other persons (apart from pltf) for whose conduct the pltf was said to be responsible were attacked by deft's Counsel. Gen. Dyer was only *one* of them. They were not parties or represented. But to say that therefor we were not to consider *their conduct* would have reduced the trial to an *absurdity* and the deft would at once have moved for a new trial.

I repeat in plain fashion that my words (which the P.M. wrongly condemned) were *not* obiter dicta but dealt with a *vital* issue. I repeat what I said in my earlier letter. I reiterate what I said before, but I desire to add something more.

I think that it was *plainly* your *duty* when you knew of the Lansbury motion *to send for me and ask for my statement*. You should have examined the pleadings and noted the course of the trial. You should have ascertained the points which arose. You should have observed that the deft. (if he complained of misdirection) could have moved for a *new trial*.

Yet you did *nothing* altho' you knew that judicial etiquette prevented me from publicly replying to the P.Minister.

Had I been permitted to do so I would have vindicated myself *at once* and *completely*, and I would have shewn moreover that the Jury were right when they *expressly* found for the pltf. on *all* issues. I never dreamt that you would fail to ascertain the facts.

In answer to the last words of your letter I beg to say

that my own personal dignity is a small thing beside the truth and that the administration of Justice is never served by a regard to mere political motives.

I place *definitely on record* these points.

(1) That the course I took at the trial was *correct* in every way.
(2) That the views I expressed were *right*.
(3) That the verdict of the Jury was right.
(4) That the remarks of the Prime Minister were inaccurate and unjust.
(5) That you *failed* in your obligations towards me as one of His Majesty's Judges.

I shall never allow the matter to drop, either now or hereafter.

It is essential both for my brother Judges and myself that the *truth* should be known.

I am, Dear Lord Chancellor,
Yours truly
(Sgd) HENRY A. McCARDIE

9th July, 1924.

Dear Mr. Justice McCardie,
I am in receipt of your letter and have noted its contents. I remain of the opinion which I have already expressed and cannot continue this correspondence.

Yours sincerely,
(Sgd) HALDANE.

The Hon.
Mr. Justice McCardie.

Judges' House,
Edgbaston,
BIRMINGHAM.

July 16/24.

Dear Lord Chancellor,
In spite of your letter of the 9th I send you this final note.

It is *impossible* for you, as a *lawyer*, should you look at the pleadings and note the course of the trial to avoid the conclusion that the conduct of Gen. Dyer was a *vital issue* in the case of O'Dwyer v. Nair. I observe that you do not attempt to meet any of my points.

You intimate that you will not correspond further on the matter. I regret it. I merely state.

(1) That I have informed you of the true facts.
(2) That you have had an opportunity of taking the proper course.
(3) That, unless the wrong be rectified I shall regard myself as free to make appropriate public reference to the matter and to publicly state the truth.

I am, Dear Lord Chancellor,
Yours truly,
(Sgd) HENRY A. McCARDIE.

Eighteen

In his palmy days at the Bar my father worked on the principle that he could earn tomorrow what he spent today. He acquired habits of extravagance which he never shook off. Nor did he want to – they chimed with his own temperament. The wild oats he hadn't sown in his youth, he set about sowing now. Not primarily by way of personal pleasures, but by speculation. His own life style was relatively frugal, though he didn't stint himself – the best hotels and all that. Speculative investment, gambling if you will, straight gambling frequently (always, when the mood was on him), was the prime charge on his income. For many years, however, he had a comfortable overspill, more than enough to cover the costs of his picture collection, his clubs, his holidays, his financing of Mayna and me, and all the day-to-day demands of a very comfortable professional life. He gave substantial help to some of his own family – his brother Arthur, for instance. He was immensely generous, well known as someone who was always 'good for a touch'. He gave freely to charities and helped out of his own pocket the families of many prisoners whom he sentenced, often arranging to send a monthly remittance. He was an absurdly lavish tipper. Money was there to be spent, and he spent it, prodigally, carelessly.

Then suddenly he found he hadn't got any. All at once he was stripped down to the bone. His investments – or rather his bets – had become more and more notable for their rashness: indeed rashness was their *raison d'être*. In the Hatry crash in 1929, he lost the equivalent of five times and more his judicial salary. Shortly after that came the great American stock market crash, in which he lost more. Each time he tried to get it back by the same means on a declining market, and of course lost again. He knew it was folly, but he was hooked; and plagued at the same time by a sense of guilt profoundly corrosive in a man so open-hearted. When he was at the Bar and in such demand that he could pick up fees virtually for the asking, he could indulge his craving for play without much danger. The pressures and excitements of the Bar took the edge off it. But as a Judge he was on a fixed salary with the stimulus of constant competition gone, and when the coffers emptied, he could not replenish them.

I still have a touching letter he wrote to Mayna as early as November 1930:

My own darling

I have *tried* not to use the cheque you gave me in August last, for I wanted to save if possible any burden. But I *must* use some part of the £300 now. Please forgive me, my darling one.

I enclose the August cheque. Will you please tear it up, and please send me a cheque for *£150* instead. I do so hope and believe that that is all I shall now need.

You have been so good to me my sweet. Will you please post the cheque to me *tomorrow.*

I look forward so much to one of your dear little notes tomorrow. They *help* me.

With my *love.* Yours as always – Hy M.

Lots of kisses to you my sweet and to dear Pip.

This is the only letter to Mayna from my father which still exists. It shows how close they were; and it shows how pressed he was for money even then.

His position as a Judge put a brake on extra earnings – though it need not have done if the Lord Chief Justice, Lord Hewart, was anything to go by. Gordon Hewart, who had long since overtaken McCardie on his way to the top, wrote a series of controversial articles in the *News of the World*, for which he was exceedingly well paid; when told that this was no way for a Judge to behave, he replied that he wasn't writing as a Judge but as a Peer of the Realm. McCardie, having no such convenient alter ego, chose not to follow this example. He probably realised that, if he earned more, he would simply gamble more. Besides, he preferred to deliver his own even more controversial homilies from the Bench or the lecture platform. The annual salary of £5,000 he received as a Judge was nevertheless substantial at a time when the average wage was about £2 a week. Moreover, it could be relied on, or so he thought. He was wrong. In those pre-Keynesian days the stock response to an economic slump was to cut down expenditure – a theory that might have done wonders if McCardie had applied it to his own affairs – and in the early autumn of 1931 he was horrified to learn that an Order in Council was about to be laid under the new National Economy Act to reduce by twenty per cent the salaries of all State servants who received £5,000 a year or more.

He was abroad at the time – where I wonder? – and the news brought him back post-haste to London. He fired off a letter of protest to the Lord Chancellor, marking it '*Not private*' and sending copies to the entire Judiciary. They needed no prodding; they were also horrified. But, less sharply pinched than he, they baulked at any public protest and preferred to move away from the argument of 'sanctity of contract', on which he had based his case, to the more dignified ground of constitutional status. The Lord Chief Justice was in any event alert to possible encroachments by the Executive, having only eighteen months earlier published a somewhat unbalanced book entitled *The New Despotism*, designed, in a phrase which he quotes from North's translation of Plutarch, to 'pull down the pride and stomach of the clerks'. He foresaw the day when Judges would be 'reduced to the level of departmental solicitors'. And now came an Order in Council docking their salary, which implied that the House of Commons had authority over them. There was talk on the Bench of presenting a Petition of Right. My father, not to be outdone, dispatched another letter, this time to the Paymaster-General's office, pointing out that his pay packet was short and accusing the Paymaster-General of 'a grave constitutional impropriety'. It was possible, the letter went on, that the Paymaster was acting on the instructions of the Executive; in which case he should know that he had thereby repudiated an express statutory obligation and violated the principles of the Judicature Acts and the Act of Settlement, and that Mr Justice McCardie was considering the position. This attempted bouncer was met with a straight bat. A bland reply pointed out that the letter must have been sent 'in some misapprehension, since the determining of such issues as those raised form no part of the Paymaster-General's functions'.

The Executive, and the public, remained equally unmoved. Mr Justice McCardie's indignation and the groans of Mr Justice Avory that he and his colleagues were 'performing their duties under the shadow of a grievous wrong', and even a memorandum freighted with deep concern about the constitution which the Judges collectively prepared and presented to the Prime Minister in December 1931 went unregarded. Strictly, no doubt the Judges were right; it could well be argued that the Order in Council did not have the legal effect intended because they were not 'Persons in His Majesty's service'. But, as Mr Baldwin tersely remarked: 'I do not see why a judge should be excused his cuts any more than I am.' The cuts were duly imposed, and my father found himself that much closer to the edge of insolvency.

Worries about his mounting debts were compounded by his

intemperate excursions into areas of moral controversy like abortion and birth control and were taxing not only the tolerance of brother Judges who ran a tight ship and had no love of 'a loose cannon', but also the affection of some of his friends. Moods of depression became more frequent. He began to lose the sense of his own worth, as so often happens when spirits are low, and to think the others must feel the same way about him. The close camaraderie within the profession made the criticism of colleagues all the harder to bear. Nevertheless he continued to speak out with increasing vehemence from the Bench, where it would have been better to keep his views, however sincere, to himself. 'I should be false to my friends and to myself if I did not say what my reason demands I should say,' he declared. But he knew he was being both unjudicial and injudicious; it doesn't do for a Judge to be too far ahead of public opinion and set himself up as a censor of public morals. Might he possibly have felt that a rehearsal of these questions from the Bench would somehow compensate for the nagging consciousness of his own financial, and some would have said moral, improbity? In retirement he could have spoken out with complete freedom. But he let it be known that he was considering resignation – he'd done his fifteen years and was qualified for a pension; but in truth he loved the Bench and its trappings too much to leave it. Anyway, he couldn't afford to retire voluntarily and, were he forced to retire, there hung over his head the threat of disgrace – disgrace, what's more, that would vitiate irreparably his capacity to promote the causes he believed in.

He was no more prudent when it came to more trivial questions, like the niceties of matrimonial behaviour and women's dress. Here he showed more than an element of self-indulgence. He was only too ready to air his views and embellish his judgements. His bons mots delighted the popular Press, where, as the 'Bachelor Judge', he vied in the headlines with William Inge, the 'Gloomy Dean'. This didn't endear him to his colleagues either, whether or not they might have some sympathy with his opinions.

Neither did the Court of Appeal regard the length of his judgements as an unmixed blessing. They were often prolix to a fault. He showed a reluctance just to seize on the essential points and bang them home, as he had done at the Bar (when he had no time to do anything else). Sometimes, as was said of Lord Blackburn, 'a cloud of research seemed to obscure clear analysis'. On questions which interested him he would often reserve judgement and then draw upon his immense knowledge of case law to cite a stately procession of authorities that weren't always necessary for the determination of the issues ('How then does the old case of *Winsmore v. Greenbank*, decided two hundred years ago, stand at the present day?'). He was not averse to going back to Confucius. In an action about the ownership of an engagement ring he remarked: 'It is worthwhile to refer briefly to the law of Rome on the questions before me.' His colleagues, busy men, would not have thought so. Devlin, later on, put it succinctly – 'Lists of cases which have been decided one way, followed by lists of those decided the other way, are like irregular verbs: they make no grammar.'

The effect of criticism on my father, however much it hurt, was to make him even more determined to promote the causes he believed in, to a degree that latterly showed some lack of proportion. He was a stubborn man, on a short fuse. His social conscience would not allow him to be silent. He may also have got a gambler's pleasure from sticking his neck out. And stick it out he did. Whilst on circuit in 1931 he went out of his way to suggest that an abortion might sometimes be a moral duty. At Leeds Assizes in December of that year he said:

> I think that these abortion cases will continue as long as the knowledge of birth control is withheld. I am dealing with the grim realities of life: it is time the public knew

them. The question of birth control and amendment of the law of abortion must be looked at free from prejudice, whether theological or otherwise. The nation should be warned. I warn it today!

He was largely vindicated in 1939 by the famous case of *Rex v. Bourne*, where it was held that in all abortion trials the onus is on the Crown to prove that the operation was not performed with the object of preserving the life of the mother; but this was 1931, when *obiter* of such a kind could only divide him from his judicial brethren.

In the following year his feeling of estrangement was exacerbated by two cases which brought him in sharp conflict with the Court of Appeal and from which he did not emerge with credit. The first concerned a petty criminal named George Griffith who was charged with bigamy and breaking into an office. He pleaded guilty and asked for a number of other minor offences to be considered, some of which had never been formally recorded against him. Though he pleaded guilty to bigamy, he had in fact a good defence; his wife, who had left him after six months, had been absent for over seven years and he did not know then that she was still alive. McCardie unwisely, indeed unjustly, chose to make an example of him. Disregarding the fact that Griffith had already been punished for earlier offences – the principle was well established that previous convictions should not of themselves result in a more severe sentence for a new offence – and that there was no evidence on which he could be convicted of bigamy, he sentenced him to four years' penal servitude. He remarked:

> Your record illustrates the unfortunate effect of lenient sentences in the past, not only by magistrates but also by judges, and I think it illustrates, too, the unfortunate effect of unnecessary reductions of sentences by the Court of Criminal Appeal. I think that the wrong policy

has been adopted in the past with respect to men who are obviously intending to commit crimes from time to time in order to obtain a livelihood.

The Court of Criminal Appeal, needless to say, took strong exception to almost every aspect of his judgement. Mr Justice Avory described McCardie's remarks as 'a wholesale condemnation of the proceedings of this Court'. The conviction for bigamy was quashed and McCardie was admonished. As usual, he prepared notes for a counterblast, but sensibly kept them to himself. Nevertheless, he had put his finger on an important aspect of sentencing which is still a matter of controversy, namely whether, in considering the instant offence, it *is* reasonable to take account of a persistent refusal to respond to earlier punishments.

Later in 1932, another of his cases, *Place v. Searle*, found its way to the Court of Appeal. This was an action brought by a grocer's assistant, who alleged that his wife had been enticed away by a local doctor. During the hearing McCardie made a number of observations about conjugal life which had little to do with the case, and he called in his long summing-up for a review of the law relating to married women, referring unwisely in this context to 'the lawyer who possesses sociological vision', by which he clearly meant himself. The newspapers rejoiced, and the action became notorious as the 'Helen of Troy' case. McCardie found in favour of the defendant with costs, but, on appeal, his ruling was overturned on the ground that he had ignored evidence on which a jury might reasonably have returned a verdict for the plaintiff, and a new trial was ordered. In giving judgement on appeal, Lord Justice Scrutton described it as a squalid and not very interesting case which had been milked by the Press as a source of good copy. He found it difficult to conceive anything further removed from the god-like Hector and 'the face that launched a thousand ships' than Dr Searle and Mrs Place. Having seen photographs of the couple, I feel bound to agree with him. But Scrutton also took the occasion to say:

> Mr Justice McCardie referred to justices with sociological knowledge. I think that the less sociological knowledge that is brought into the discussion of these questions the better. If there is to be a discussion of the relationship of husbands and wives I think it would come better from judges who have more than a theoretical knowledge of husbands and wives. I am a little surprised that a gentleman who has never been married should, as he has done in another case, proceed to explain the proper underclothing that ladies should wear.

Scrutton was renowned for brusqueness and faults of temper and trial Judges had become accustomed to being 'scruttonised'. But this was an instance of exceptional rudeness which earned McCardie some sympathy. Unfortunately he behaved no better. He wasn't one to take such strictures lying down and he immediately dispatched a letter to the Master of the Rolls, Lord Hanworth, who was President of the Court of Appeal, to demand that no future appeal from any of his decisions should be heard by a tribunal of which Scrutton was a member. The next day, having taken care, as always, to find a precedent, in the form of a decision of the Privy Council in 1888 that Judges' notes of evidence are private memoranda, he announced in open Court at the start of a hearing: 'If there be an appeal I shall not supply any copy of my notes until I am satisfied that Lord Justice Scrutton will not be a member of any court which tries the appeal... I regret that it has become my duty to administer this public rebuke to Lord Justice Scrutton'. Lord Hanworth had to take rapid steps to resolve this unseemly dispute which, in a profession that is nothing if not discreet, was almost unheard of. McCardie was persuaded to withdraw his threat, but not before an Early Day

Motion had been put down in the House of Commons referring to 'regrettable conduct on the part of one of His Majesty's judges ... calculated to lower the prestige of the Judiciary'. The matter was then allowed to drop and Scrutton's remarks were omitted from the published report. But an unfortunate after-taste remained.

It is interesting incidentally that in 1971 a Committee on Legal Education chaired by Mr Justice Ormerod made the point, with caution appropriate to any lawyer coming to a view, that the profession needed to equip itself to make use of such disciplines as psychology, sociology and criminology 'in an informed and critical manner'. Once more legal opinion was belatedly catching up with McCardie. Scrutton may have been a better lawyer with a more subtle and penetrating mind than McCardie, whom he is said to have despised intellectually, but he was a less humane and far-seeing man.

A further case came before my father in April 1932 which, according to Sir Gervais Rentoul, may have raised in his mind a premonition of his death, now only a year away. It arose out of a bizarre libel action brought by a medium, Mrs Meurig Morris, against the *Daily Mail* for calling her a fraud. The case lasted several days and Norman Birkett, appearing for the newspaper, subjected Mrs Morris to a gruelling cross-examination during which she broke down twice and went into a trance. McCardie had grown more and more disturbed as the hearing went on – it may be indicative of his state of mind that he did not dismiss the rigmarole out of hand – and began his summing-up by saying: 'This action touches the very gravities of life and death and I say frankly that I dislike the action from beginning to end and every aspect of it.' Worse was to follow. When he went on to talk about the ease with which credulity can be exploited, Mrs Morris got to her feet, grasped the lapels of her coat and started to address him in booming tones: 'Thou, who art a brother Judge, hearken unto my voice.' After some unseemly altercations she was supported out of the Court for the third time and McCardie adjourned the proceedings for a quarter of an hour. On his return he said:

> I hope I have not upset the feelings of anyone unnecessarily, but as a judge I care not for all the incarnate or discarnate spirits in the world. As long as I remain on the Bench, I shall resolutely seek to reach the truth, and I advise the jury to do the same, although there may be ten thousand million discarnate spirits around us.

In the course of the case he received letters from the usual crackpots. One letter, however, was said to have made a deep impression on him. Purportedly dictated to a medium, it revealed a detailed knowledge of his private life and prophesied that he would die by his own hand, naming the date on which this would happen. Such a prophecy may well, as Rentoul said, have taken root in his mind. (A book also claiming that he was the victim of occult intervention was published a few months after his death. Its author, Dr Alexander Cannon, a psychiatrist at Colney Hatch, the big lunatic asylum run by the London County Council, asserted that my father had been warned, when travelling in India, that he would die in disgrace on a specified date. I suspect this was another version of the same story put about to explain a suicide which seemed otherwise inexplicable. It did Dr Cannon no good, for he told a string of even odder tales gleaned from his patients and was asked to resign on the ground that anyone who could write such a book was unfit to practise in a Western hospital.)

As the autumn days grew shorter and the year 1932 drew to its close, my father felt increasingly isolated. It is distressing for a naturally friendly man to be cold-shouldered by colleagues; it did not help to know that he had brought it on himself. He loved the law and in the closed world of the Courts and the Bar it was important to him that he should hold his head high within it. The whisper of gossip in the corridors is hard to bear. He had few, if any, intimates and no close family to come back to – a small service flat provided poor substitute for a home. And, of course, it wasn't only in his own profession that he met hostility. His outspoken advocacy in areas of moral controversy stirred up great animosity among those who opposed change. The Roman Church was especially vociferous. He was well used to abuse from their adherents and had learned to disregard it: 'I have been attacked,' he said, 'until I have forgotten what it feels like to be attacked.' But the constant hostile pressure made other worries more insistent. As always when tender points are touched on, mischievous stories were circulated about his private life: that he had a mistress in the country – which happened to be true; that a titled woman was pregnant by him; that he had a vast collection of erotica (a story still circulating, told to me by someone unaware of my connection with McCardie); that he had offered himself as a prize at the Malthusian Ball, and so on. His sponsoring of the Malthusian Ball in March 1933, and arranging for posters to be prominently displayed in the Inns of Court, provoked particular hostility. It was only a dance, after all. Father Woodlock, a well-known Catholic apologist of the time, declared that it 'would blazon the shame of England throughout the world'. 'The usual stuff,' was McCardie's response, 'I shall not answer it.'

In the summer of 1932 he had suffered another blow. He dined with his friend Captain McCardie Martin and stayed on talking until late, when he may well have confided something of the precariousness of his own situation. In the morning Captain Martin was found dead, of a heart attack. McCardie was deeply upset.

At the turn of the year, he went down with influenza. It was a bad attack, made worse by his depressed state. When he returned to the Courts on 12 January, after the Christmas vacation, he was still far from well. He was due to go on circuit on 20 February, when he had a second attack of influenza. He insisted on sitting, despite remonstrances. Whilst at Lewes he fell ill again, but again insisted on sitting, even with a high temperature. Moreover, he refused to give up his work for the causes he believed in. In February he delivered the Galton lecture to the Eugenics Society in which he not only reiterated his views about abortion and birth control, but called for the sterilisation of mental defectives. A month later – only a few weeks before he took his life – he carried out his promise to host the Malthusian Ball. He was finding it hard to sleep and complained of a lassitude so acute that he found it difficult to do his work. But he would not give up. One of the staff who looked after him at Queen Anne's Mansions spoke of how 'even during his illness he read voluminously and on several occasions asked me to reach down for him and take to his bedroom heavy legal volumes. On many occasions, too, the chambermaid who called him in the morning told me that legal volumes were in his bed, and the light on, as though he had fallen asleep from exhaustion.' His enormous industry made him an impossible patient. Work was not merely a solace, it was a necessity – anything was better than brooding on what might have been. He had never been ill, apart from an operation for gall stones in 1928, and he was as inept at dealing with lack of health as he was with lack of money, having had in his happier years a marvellous plethora of both. Post-influenzal exhaustion may last for weeks, in rare instances producing a severe depressive illness. My father was a man of deep reserves; had it been only influenza he would have thrown it off. But now it was cruelly compounded, and in the end he could no longer cope. He was forced to cancel most of his engagements. By April, having sent word to the Lord Chief Justice that he was too ill to sit, he was in a state verging on despair.

One of his neighbours in Queen Anne's Mansions was Norman Birkett, then a KC. He had often appeared before McCardie, as in the case of Mrs Morris, and, although there was a difference of fourteen years between them, they had common legal roots in the Midland Circuit and a common love of literature. They rarely met socially, however, and Birkett was surprised to receive an invitation from McCardie to visit him. He was appalled at his appearance. Haggard and grey, McCardie indicated that he was faced with financial ruin unless he got an immediate loan. He mentioned a sum of about £2,000 – an amount which in the ordinary way a man of his standing could have raised without the slightest difficulty. Birkett promised to make the money available at once, with the proviso, to avoid any appearance of impropriety since he was a practising barrister and McCardie was a Judge, that responsibility should be shared with a colleague. He suggested Stuart Bevan, also a KC, and a bencher of McCardie's Inn. McCardie agreed. Next day Birkett returned with Bevan, and the loan was made. My father's real debts were, of course, far greater. They ran well into five figures. He owed more than he could ever pay. The fact was that he had exhausted his credit. The bank would no longer honour his cheques. What he needed was, quite simply, ready money – money to pay the rent, to settle tradesmen's bills, to meet small, everyday expenses like meals and newspapers and cigarettes.

Most of the time he remained in his room, seeing no-one save for the household staff who attended him – and, once, his niece Ruth with her bunch of violets. Spring was greening the trees again in St James's Park, behind it the familiar reassuring shape of Horse Guards Parade and the Admiralty. But the eyes were dulled now.

On Wednesday, 26 April, he appeared to be better. He took lunch in the restaurant for the first time for some weeks. He seemed his old self; he chatted to the staff about the Budget introduced the day before by Mr Neville Chamberlain. Had they known, this apparent recovery was a danger signal. Those numbed by depression may be suicidal but incapable of suicide because the doing of the act demands more energy than they possess. When their strength begins to come back, initiative returns, but the depression stays. Indeed, it may get worse, endowed with a new persuasiveness while the natural love of life, which my father had in abundant measure, is still low. I think he seemed better because he had made up his mind. To be faced, after a lifetime of success, by resignation from the Bench and virtual ignominy was a prospect he could not accept. There was no road 'back to the warm and coloured past and away from the black avenue' that gaped in front of him – loneliness, broken ambitions, a private life in disarray. Everywhere he turned he was faced by impossible demands: the futile craving he could no longer hold at bay, the shameful begging for money, the long illness, the physical decline, the pathos of getting old, the barriers which had arisen between himself and his colleagues, the let-down for his family, for whom he had been a lode-star, the unassuageable need to work – so central to his life – still consuming but suddenly pointless, the terrible ennui yawning in wait for him. One shot would blow them all away.

The last letter he wrote was to Mrs Seaton-Tiedeman, secretary of the Divorce Law Reform Union, on the day before his death, regretting that he was unable, owing to ill health, to accept the Presidency of the Union in succession to Lord Birkenhead. The handwriting is firm: this was a man in full possession of his faculties. He must have wondered, as he wrote, what presidential weight would attach to a bankrupt 'Bachelor Judge' with a mistress and an illegitimate child. There was no lifetime companion with whom he could discuss the full extent of the mess he was in and from whom he might have received wise and informed advice that would put his position in perspective. Mayna could listen and give him consolation, but that was not enough. She was miles away and she was not a wife. His family – well, some things are impossible to say. There was no way out except to make an end of it, the quicker the better, just the raw, bare act, He left no note: a newspaper he had been reading lay beside him where he died. He made no attempt to pretend it was an accident; use of a shot-gun made it difficult to do so without risk of a terrible wound that might not have been fatal. The important thing was to make no mistake. He sat in an armchair, fully dressed, wearing a smoking jacket, the gun held between his legs. He put one end of a pull-through over his thumb with the other end passed round the trigger guard in such a way that by a movement of his foot the gun would be discharged. I wonder how long he waited before he pulled the trigger and what thoughts went through his mind. He was found drenched in blood, his head sunk on his chest. The shot had entered through his throat; part of his skull had been blown away. His elder brother, Dr William McCardie, identified the body.

The inquest was brief. The Westminster Coroner, Mr Ingleby Oddie, sat without a jury and the proceedings lasted barely fifteen minutes. Only four people gave evidence, including the pathologist who carried out the post-mortem: the organs, he said, were in average condition (how alike we all are under the skin!). The witnesses did not include a woman, referred to as a friend in one paper and as a typist in another, who had first alerted the staff of Queen Anne's Mansions that something might be amiss; my father, she said, had been expecting a telephone call from her and she was worried when she could get no answer. It seems strange that she was never questioned, but I suppose the circumstances were assumed to be so straightforward as not to require it. The coroner was brisk and in no doubt. He found that 'the judge's mind was unbalanced owing to his depression following upon influenza' and that 'he yielded to a sudden attack of compulsive insanity'. A verdict of suicide while of unsound mind was returned. So the due process was gone through neatly and quickly, much to everyone's relief. It was sufficient for the coroner to identify the prime cause, the *causa causans*; any contributory causes were best not gone into.

After the inquest my father's mutilated body was taken back to Birmingham. There it lay until the funeral in a mortuary chapel which, ironically enough, had been used forty years before as a gymnasium by a physical fitness club of which he had been secretary and principal organiser. Then, on 4 May, he who had since climbed so high in the world's eye and prized his place there was buried in secrecy, hugger-mugger almost. No intimation was given of the time and place. An empty hearse, followed by two black coaches, was used to keep hidden the actual route of the funeral. The real hearse, attended only by a closed brougham carrying the flowers, followed a different route to the cemetery where the mourners waited. It went through empty streets in pouring rain past the Law Courts where his first legal battles had been won and where only six months before he had come for the Assize, wigged and robed, heralded by trumpeters. Passers-by raised their hats, as they always did in those days when a coffin went by, but no-one knew whose funeral it was. A service was held in the small congregational chapel in Whitton Cemetery, not far from the McCardie vault where his father and mother lay and where he would lie, beside them. The service was conducted by a former minister of the church which McCardie had attended as a boy. Apart from the family, only his clerk, Philip McCann, was there. There were no more than a dozen wreaths; one came from the Birmingham and Edgbaston Debating Society – another link with his youth. And there was Mayna's bouquet of spring flowers.

Though Birmingham paid McCardie no final tribute, his

colleagues in London did not fail to pay theirs. On 28 April all twenty-eight Judges then sitting in London, a score or more of KCs and nearly a hundred members of the Junior Bar gathered in his memory in the Lord Chief Justice's Court before the ordinary business of the day. Speaking with great emotion, Lord Hewart, from whom he had received that charming note on his appointment, expressed 'profound sorrow at the loss of our dear brother McCardie. He was a man not only of the highest ability and integrity, and of quite phenomenal industry, but he was also a warm-hearted, trustworthy friend.' So my father was admitted again to the comradeship of Bench and Bar.

His debts were quietly paid. A lot of money had to be found, but both his elder brother and Mrs Bindley were well off, and it appears that other wealthy friends in Birmingham helped out and that some of his creditors agreed to waive what they were owed. T.C.B told me with a twinkle that the Jewish creditors were especially sympathetic when they learned there was a child. His personal possessions were disposed of. His china and some of his pictures had already gone. His remaining pictures, his library of some two thousand annotated law books, his furniture, realised a few hundred pounds. The chair in which he shot himself was knocked down for a paltry sum, giving rise to some indignation. He left no will because he had nothing to leave. He left no letter because he had nothing to say – and to whom, anyway, could he address such a letter without seeming to discriminate or disclosing what he did not wish to be known? The only document bearing on his suicide was a small piece of scrap paper found by his sister on the floor of the flat when she was sorting out his things. On it he had written: '*Suicide of Mr Eastman (Kodak) My work is done, why should I wait? March / 32*'. The quotation was underlined.

A year later Mr Jeffrey Williams of Edgbaston, a coal merchant and sports ground contractor, complained at Birmingham

Assizes that a judgement against him by Mr Justice McCardie had been delivered when the Judge was of unsound mind. He got short shrift from Mr Justice Parcq: 'You are not so foolish as you are hoping to make yourself out to be. I don't want to hear any more of that.' The ranks, with McCardie back in his place, had firmly closed again.

IV
GATHERING SPEED

'He looked more like a banana than an umbrella.'

Maurice Bowra, of Neville Chamberlain

Nineteen

At the time of my father's suicide, I was just thirteen. He was younger still when he lost his father, but his mother firmly took over in *loco patris*. Mayna showed no such dominance. Perhaps this was as well for me. But I was left rudderless and another thirteen years were to pass before I learned to steer a preferred course. By then the Second War was over and I was married and as grown-up as I'm ever likely to be.

The following pages give a brief account of what happened to me up to the age of twenty-six. After that, I will come back to the McCardies and the story of my father which, like the crumpled petals inside the poppy buds I used to pick from the hedgerow as a schoolboy on my way to church, was waiting to be liberated from its sheath.

First, back to Stratton House in April, 1933. Life slowly reverted to what passed for normal, except that money got tighter and the atmosphere more claustrophobic. Our main link with the outside world had gone. We were marooned. The car was sold; Eva no longer came three times a week; my grandmother was now approaching eighty. Mayna's asthma grew worse and the air was heavy with the smell of Potter's Asthma Cure and cigarette smoke. Grieving but not allowed to mourn, she became more and more solitary.

With the visit of Tom Cannon Brookes and the assurance that payment of the fees to Worksop were to be met by the setting up of a small trust, my own immediate future had assumed a clearer, if not a more enticing, shape. At least I had a complete set of parents, and I was bound for a school safely moored in the middle class, albeit at the shallower end. I didn't know much about snobbery and was still too young to despise it; but I sensed enough of the still meticulously layered society of the nineteen thirties to be thankful for a niche to creep into.

I set off for my new school with considerable misgivings, being naturally timid. Some eight years' boarding at Lynfield had, however, taught me to hide my timidity; and at least I knew Peter Vincent, one of my chums in the final class who had won a scholarship to Worksop: a charming freckled boy, much cleverer than I was, and much nicer.

Mayna having opted out, I had to take the train to Worksop by myself, a long and complicated journey. My clothes, too big as usual, felt horribly new. At Worksop I disembarked from a taxi (the first I had ever hailed) among a throng of shouting boys who fortunately ignored me. By some magical process I managed to find my way through a warren of corridors to the house to which I had been assigned. The housemaster was a harassed, kindly old bumble-bee in a worn sports jacket; in fact he must have been quite young. His name, he told me, was Mackie. He had a Forsterish moustache and his hair stuck up behind in a crest. Amid flashes of irritability he went out of his way to make sure that I wasn't left wholly stranded. But soon he vanished. I was alone in a long dormitory. My trunk, sent on in advance, lay beside me. I remembered the quiet evening when I'd helped Mayna to pack it; her neat, familiar writing was on the labels. I dreaded what would happen when all the other boys came in. I could hear a bell ringing. I did not know what it meant or where I ought to go next. I sat down on the bed. The silly euphoria of having got there without mishap faded away, and misery set in.

Because I had arrived in the summer term, I was the only new boy in my house. I was fortunate not to excite odium, but I was friendless – Peter Vincent was in a different house and I saw little of him. Only one boy, S., consorted with me. S. was ugly, and I disliked him. He knew that and only attached himself to me because no-one else wanted anything to do with him. He was constantly bullied. He wore thick glasses and, before the bullying started, he took them off so that they would not be broken. When this happened, I walked away and felt ashamed. Luckily I soon made a friend, 'Fishy' Pike, whose father worked for Heinz and provided a steady supply of baked beans, which added spice to our diet. Fishy had a long thin nose like Miss Worthington's that twitched and whitened when he laughed. We loved grappling together, a form of physical contact in which small boys delight.

The summer term proved an auspicious time. As the weeks went by and the first seethings of anxiety passed, I became familiar with the jargon and the totems. Speech Day was difficult, as it had been at Lynfield, because I had no visitors; I felt curiously conspicuous. But the work was easy and I enjoyed cricket, a game of white on green, and it was pleasant to lie in the sun with Fishy on a warm Saturday afternoon and watch the First XI playing. The tuck shop was nearby and a whipped cream walnut or a plate of egg and peas helped to plug any gaps left unfilled by Heinz beans.

We had no privacy and little leisure; and many silly rules, connived at by higher authority, were imposed on us until we reached a certain seniority. We were forbidden, for example, to put our hands in our trouser pockets – heaven knows what we might do with them there; it was even possible that the hands of other boys might find their way in. To make doubly sure, the pockets had to be sewn up. Periodically there was an inspection and those with open pockets were beaten by the Head of House. Quick work with needle and thread could sometimes save the day for those at the back of the queue, but otherwise it was four of the best. There had been no beating at Lynfield and my first experience of it resulted from this absurd offence. I expected it to hurt, but not to hurt so much. I was amazed. I thought that Philip Snow – for that ironically was his name – had by inadvertence laid a red-hot poker across my buttocks. When it was over, I scuttled away trying not to sob too loudly. In my time as a prefect we abolished the practice, which became the prerogative of masters only. One master, E.E. Peters – spelt by the cognoscenti e.e. peters – had a nervous habit of laughing if he had to administer punishment. Roars of amusement would ring out between the dull thwacks of the cane.

The most enthusiastic beater was the Headmaster, the Reverend F.J. Shirley. Later he became Canon Shirley and took charge of King's School, Canterbury, where he was held in high regard. He was the son of a carpenter, but shared few other characteristics of the Founder. Headmasters are supposed to inculcate awe. He inculcated fear instead. He was an alarming man. Short, clean-shaven, spring-heeled, moody, twitching his gown, smelling of cigars and often of drink, at one moment he could be immensely charming and at another dark with threat, a grenade fizzing. He was a remarkable administrator: the school flourished under his regime. New lavatories and science blocks sprang up all over the place. In 1934 he built a whole new wing and the then Prime Minister, Ramsay MacDonald, descended from an aeroplane to open it. Shirley was thought by parents to be a great Headmaster, and in many ways he was. His personality hovered over the school like a bird of prey. Sometimes after supper he would come round the studies, quietly, appearing suddenly at the door. Messages would be tapped out on the radiators to warn that he was on the prowl. On alternate Mondays, 'Black Mondays', he would put up a list of boys to be beaten, and he beat them savagely.

My friend F.N. Baird, a lanky hedonist with a narrow head but cleverer than he admitted, was once taxed by Shirley with smoking when on his way back from Clumber Park. Shirley was smoking a large cigar at the time. Baird had been smoking, of course, but denied it. 'Smell my breath, sir,' he said, and breathed heavily over the Headmaster. His breath reeked of tobacco, but Shirley couldn't smell it. Baird was an authority on masturbation and conspicuously lacking in deference: a natural suspect to all the staff. His only redeeming feature in their eyes was that he played an excellent game of rugby.

In the Christmas term of 1934 I had the misfortune to come up to Shirley for Latin in preparation for School Certificate – an examination familiar now only to the elderly. The class was held in a room just down from the Headmaster's house, which was linked to the main school by a special door. We would listen for the soft thump of this door and the echo of his approaching footsteps down the stone corridor. What sort of mood was he in? If benign, he would be jocular (though in a sinister way), tell stories, wave away mistakes. But if a bad mood was on him we could expect no mercy. He had compiled a little primer, *Memorabilia Latina*, which we had in effect to get by heart, and on such days he would draw out a cane from his gown and beat in front of the class anyone who happened to incur his disapproval. The punishment was arbitrary, the swish and wince of the cane sickening to the rest of us, forced to watch. It must be said, however, that the success rate in the exam was formidably high! Peter Vincent was in the class and absorbed the *Memorabilia* with enviable ease. He was held up as an exemplar, but no-one minded because he was so open-hearted. Shortly afterwards his parents lost their money and he left to work for an insurance company.

We were required twice a day to attend chapel. The Chaplain, Noble Fawcett, was small and neat, with a deep archidiaconal voice. His sermons were not lively, but he was a fan of Gilbert and Sullivan and possessed a complete set of the operettas on records, which he would invite boys to listen to. Between *Ruddigore* and the *Mikado*, I went to him for Confirmation classes. They must have gone well for I remember nothing of them; I did not, therefore, come stale to the post like so many candidates. Indeed, the reverse, for only a day or two before the ceremony it was discovered that I had never been baptised. For obvious reasons neither my father nor Mayna had thought a 'Publick Baptism' of the infant Archer expedient. A special service was therefore hurriedly arranged for the 'Baptism of such as are of riper years and able to answer for themselves', of whom I was now supposed to be one. Question: Dost thou renounce the devil and all his works, the vain pomp and glory of the world, with all covetous desires of the same, and the carnal desires of the flesh, so that thou wilt not follow nor be led by them? Answer: I renounce them all. Thus were my scrawny adolescent dreams knocked on the head at the end of a March day, chilly and desolate. The empty chapel, full of echoes, was lit by candles. Dear old Mackie, my housemaster, attended. It was all rather impressive. Much more so than the Confirmation which followed. I did my best to acknowledge the descent upon me of some spiritual power, but to no avail; I felt only the huge hands of the Bishop of Pretoria, an enormous man. After that, whilst I still relished the words of the Anglican offices and would have enjoyed the chapel music (which was very good) had I been taught how, I lapsed gently from partial to total disbelief. I did not disclose my feelings. In due course I played my part as a prefect in reading the lesson and the like. I took care not to repeat the Creed, for I did not wish to lie, but I still had a soft spot for sermons provided it wasn't the Chaplain's turn.

It would be tedious to give an account of my slow progress up the school, so much larger than the little stage of Lynfield. F.J. Shirley was succeeded as Headmaster by B.C. Maloney, a kindly but less dynamic man whose gentle regime did not always get the right response from boys accustomed to a harsher discipline. Meanwhile I slowly turned from a junior into a senior, passing on the way through the usual hoops – School Certificate, Higher School Certificate, Certificate 'A'. I made some friends, but I did not keep up with them, partly – perhaps mainly – because I could never bring them home to Stratton House, where loneliness and damp roved through the rooms and the atmosphere was symbolised for me by the marbled bowl which hung over the dining-room table (never used now) with its feeble bulb and a sprinkling of dead flies at the bottom.

Certain memories remain in my mind. The masters, of course, with all their oddities; the bare dormitories, the stone corridors, the echoing voices; the prickle of OTC uniform and the annual camp with its dew-tautened tents and its irresistible appeal to one's sense of the absurd; the communal rugger bath with its turbid steaming water; the excitement of defeating Trent College at rugby, when Prince Obolensky was playing for them on the wing and Shirley was stalking up and down the touch-line like a caged tiger; cross-country runs over the plough with every breath rasping and the cry of plover overhead; being taken out to lunch by Mackie and taught, unsuccessfully, how to drink; singing *Lord dismiss us with thy blessing* at the end of term, and being swept by a nostalgia at once phoney and overwhelming – 'Let thy Father-hand be shielding/All who here shall meet no more... Those returning/Make more faithful than before'. The memories come back arbitrarily, unnurtured, unwelcome almost, having a special sort of adolescent texture...

I must make special mention of John Anthony, a tall, shy man with a clear mind. He had given Shirley much help in preparing a thesis on Richard Hooker which earned him a doctorate. In my last year at school he taught a trio of us and we profited greatly. He became a Grenadier and was killed in the war. I owe a lot also to M.J. Wainwright, cynical and prematurely bald, who helped coach me for a scholarship in history at Cambridge. That I managed to get one – at Trinity Hall – was almost entirely due to him. He anticipated the questions brilliantly. Luckily there was no formal viva, otherwise my real ignorance would have been fatally exposed. I went to Cambridge for the exam in trepidation and found myself surrounded by frightening sophisticates from other schools. It is a measure of my inadequacy that I went out at the end of the first day's papers into the fenny gloom of a Cambridge winter evening and bought myself a book of Sherlock Holmes short stories. Oppressed by the acute minds at work about me, I was relieved to escape to the consoling company of Doctor Watson, who wasn't at all acute – exactly the sort of unpretentious citizen I wanted to be. I sat up half the night in my bare room reading about 'A Scandal in Bohemia' and 'The Golden Pince-Nez' while the mists curled up Senate House Passage and the bells sprinkled their quarters over the town. When I awoke next morning I felt even more of a fraud than usual – a skinny archetype of the hollow man, endowed with an illusion of solidity by Wainwright's clever straw stuffing.

That year also Ken Farnes, one of the masters, was playing cricket for England and the school basked in his reflected glory. Farnes, like Anthony, was killed in the War, whose first harbinger came to us in the form of an RAF biplane which landed on the playing fields as part of a recruiting campaign. I had a flight in it, spending most of it trying to adjust my goggles. I little thought that four years later I should be a pilot myself. I was glad to get back on the ground again. I still am.

Towards the end of my last term I developed pains in the joints. Scarlet fever was diagnosed, though no-one else in the school got it and (since I had no visitors) I'd had no contact with anybody outside. But I was confined to the sanatorium and at the end of term I was taken by ambulance to the local isolation hospital – a god-forsaken place surrounded by barbed wire. When I attempted on arrival to jump from the vehicle, my legs gave way, weakened by a fortnight in bed, and I tumbled to the ground, badly twisting my ankle. This marked me down as a trouble-maker. I was the only inmate, housed in a wooden hut with four beds and a desk in the middle. In the drawer of the desk I found the case notes of a former inhabitant who had died of yellow fever. The notes made gruesome reading. Geoffrey Newbould, a red-headed friend from school, came to see me. He wasn't allowed beyond the wire, of course, and when I hobbled out to meet him he would mow and gibber on the other side, much to the irritation of the nurse in charge, who thought that young public school boys should behave with more decorum. I had spent a week in North Wales with Newbould and we knew how to keep each other amused in difficult conditions. A ten-shilling weekly rail ticket had enabled us to travel on any train in the area for a week. We carried a volume of Nietzsche and we used to intone passages from *Thus Spake Zarathustra* in our lodgings. Bed and breakfast in cheap digs and supper in workmen's cafés were all we could afford. It rained most of the time. We spent our last afternoon playing billiards in Blaenau Ffestiniog, with huge cliffs of wet slate towering above us. By contrast, my recital through barbed wire of the terminal symptoms of yellow fever, while Newbould writhed about in appreciation, verged on the romantic.

In due course I was pronounced free from infection and sent home. Newbould had meanwhile gone on holiday and I never saw him again. It was a feeble ending to my schooldays.

Twenty

At home, between school terms, I led an isolated life. Mayna never went away on holiday after my father died. My grandmother had never taken a holiday and was too old to start. Besides, she had no money – 'When my ship comes home,' she used to say; but it never did. She continued to do the cooking and most of the housework. She and Mayna constantly quarrelled, which distressed me. It was frightening and demeaning to hear two adults abusing one another. When they were the two people closest to me, my sense of isolation was made more acute. Yet at the same time I experienced the obscure pleasure a child gets from witnessing misdemeanours of which it is innocent.

The tension grew as my grandmother moved towards her nineties, increasingly unable to hide the anger which bubbles up in each of us below the surface. She was like a beached ship with the bridge damaged and the timbers exposed. Mayna, like any other unmarried daughter, took the full brunt; and Mayna, too, contributed her own quota of hostility. Endlessly they fought the same futile battles. A rapid decline took place in my grandmother after she fell ill one winter with pneumonia. There were no antibiotics then: pneumonia was the old people's friend and generally took them off. I remember tip-toeing into her sickroom with its foetid, curtained smell. She was delirious, plucking at the sheets with bewildered hands. Her hoarse breathing would sometimes stop, then painfully resume. A kettle blew steam into the air to keep it moist, and the old oil heater fumed away at the foot of the bed, its reflections patterning the ceiling on which yellowy shadows from a night-light bobbed lazily about. It was Dantesque. Aunt Harrie came down when Mayna couldn't cope and everybody spoke in whispers.

Mayna must have been intensely lonely – cut off from her own generation and hard put to know how to pass the long, empty, unfulfilled days. My father had gone and she had only me: I was her present and her future, her only source of hope. And I wasn't up to it. I was dutiful, not loving. She could be enormous fun and I could see how she must have enchanted my father. But I could not forget the poignancy of her position, her unspoken cry for some sort of liberation. As I grew older, I felt it more and more; most of all when she came to the station at the start of each term to see me off. She was not a demonstrative woman – precisely the reverse – and I was a gauche adolescent. Neither of us could express our feelings easily: the love I owed her was a debt I couldn't pay. I gave sympathy instead – a poor substitute for love. Her position was so much worse than mine. She had no friends, literally none. Her only companion when the dogs had gone was an ageing mother, often hostile. I wanted to weep for her – and for myself, for I resented the lack of the emotional support I felt she should have given me. I had instead to provide support for her, which didn't seem fair. I wrote unfailingly every week. She rarely wrote back and showed scant appreciation of my achievements such as they were, either now or later. Her attention would begin to wander when I talked to her about my concerns; no doubt I was often a bit of a bore. This did not diminish the pain of our partings on the windy station, where I learned very early that the one who is left behind feels the pain more. As she waved good-bye I would pull up the train window by its heavy leather strap and sink back into the compartment with its smell of soot and dust and heated metal and moquette and its sepia photograph of Sheringham above the fishnet luggage rack. I would think of her making her lonely way back to Stratton House as the train clanked towards

Heacham past the gas works and the beach huts and the wheeling gulls. Her image would dwindle in my mind and then vanish into preoccupations with the coming term. She was the only person in the world then to whom it really mattered whether I lived or died. But I did not realise that.

Adolescence is an uneasy period at the best of times. Sometimes I would be seized by the peculiar horror of the normal, its weird shapes and sounds, its grotesque conventions, as though I was an alien. Everything was made worse by social inexperience. I was tormented by that promised sexual land which was always out of reach. I had my remote objects of desire, like Tallulah Bankhead, whose photograph I treasured as an icon. But I wanted the warmth of lips and flesh. On hot, hazy, aching summer days when the sea scrolled almost silent on the beach, I could think of little else but the girls who flowered about me in their patterned dresses – their careless breasts were pressed to the warm sand, their voices echoed in the shimmery air as though caught and reflected in some amorous medium, they coupled with their lovers in the long grass of the cliff top, the little bags of pleasure they had helped to fill sagged discarded among the dog-roses in the hedges. When the sun went down and there was no more hope, I would crank up the gramophone (bought with my father's Ardath cigarette coupons) and play the same old songs: *Priscilla, Priscilla, she smells like vanilla...*

I used to range the coast and countryside on my bicycle, taking sandwiches and a flask of coffee in a haversack. But all too often I would plunge into dunes or woods, so urgent were the claims of puberty. The rising excitement, the rending shudders, then the guilt. But desire was always stronger than the guilt and would not go away. 'Of sexual actions,' George Moore said, 'copulation is the least deleterious.' I had no chance to test the truth of this wise remark.

In the summer I went down to the sea every day, no matter what. I swam in high winds and in pouring rain. It became a duty. Its non-performance made me feel as guilty as did the performance of the other; I needed to have a substantial credit balance on the swim-side in order to feel reasonably at peace with myself. When it became too cold to swim, the moral settling-up was less straightforward. I read widely and set myself tasks, filling notebooks with quotations, as my father had. I flopped about among the Communist certainties and wrote down slogans which I didn't understand, like 'freedom is the consciousness of necessity', in capital letters. I bought a polo-necked jersey, badge of the intellectual, but the collar chafed my neck.

A boy from Worksop, David Wakefield, lived in Hunstanton and naturally I got to know him. He was the son of the local vicar, the St Edmunds one, a warm, friendly man who had spent many years in the West Indies. He had imbibed some of their easy ways and he wasn't averse to dropping into the local for a drink. This upset some of his parishioners who were racked by the dilemma of having to choose between taking their communion wine from the hands of an habitué of the public bar or going to worship at St Mary's in the old village, where the service was low and the journey tiresome. David Wakefield helped to draw me into a number of local activities. I hung about the fringes of Hunstanton café society, young men fooling around as bank clerks, trainee estate agents and the like while they waited for the War to start. I played some hockey. I was inveigled into the local amateur dramatic company run by the manager of Barclay's Bank – a weakness I tried to conceal when I met some of the boozy old professionals who played in repertory to sparse audiences at the town hall in the summer season. I did my best to join in, but I never quite succeeded. I was a pretender, a hanger-on, somebody tolerated but not really welcome. Was this an imagined exclusion? In part, yes: I got on well enough with most people. But not wholly imagined. I didn't belong, though I desperately wanted to.

Wakefield had an immaculately dressed wealthy friend who was as young as I was but seemed immeasurably older. Trousers, according to Arnold Bennett's tailor, 'should shiver on the shoe but not break'; his trousers did just that. I met him at a sherry party at the Vicarage, where he proffered Abdulla cigarettes from a gold case and invited Wakefield and me to dine next evening at the Sandringham Hotel. Black tie. On reporting in this unfamiliar regalia, I was horrified to find that I'd been invited not merely to dinner but to a dinner-dance, and that three girls were there, looking for a good time. It soon became apparent that, so far as I was concerned, they were looking in vain. Vaguely remembering dance lessons at Lynfield, I made some attempt at a foxtrot. My partner was quite unable to follow. Wakefield's friend pressed white wine upon me, which clashed with the aftertaste of too much sherry and made things worse. Between courses he took to the floor himself with his usual aplomb. Wakefield's own performance was undistinguished but no help to me: I spent the evening crushed under the weight of my seventeen years. My cuffs kept on disappearing relentlessly into my sleeves and I was in constant fear that the clasp of my made-up tie would ride up above the back of my collar. It was a profound relief when all was over. Providentially Mayna was asleep, or appeared to be, when I got home, so that I didn't have to pretend I'd enjoyed it. But I couldn't conceal from myself that it had been a disaster. At that time I was liable to fall into depressions and I duly fell into one.

As I grew less callow, my aspirations diminished. I went to Lausanne for eight weeks before going up to Cambridge in order to brush up my French. On the way I lost my money in Paris: stolen, not squandered, I hasten to add – there was little trace of my father in me. Then I got stranded in Vallorbe, because the last coach of the train was for no apparent reason dropped off there. I was the only person in the coach and the train went without me. It was raining heavily. I had no money to telephone or buy food, and such French as I had bore no resemblance to the language of a solitary porter to whom I tried to speak. Eventually, however, I managed to reach Lausanne, astonished by the scenery on the way – though I tried not to be, having read that the young Rilke thought the beauty of Switzerland too pretentious and would draw the blinds in his compartment when he travelled through.

I didn't learn much French in Lausanne, but I did learn to dance; and I fell in love for the first time. She was a girl from Beckenham. Her name was Muriel. We kissed and fondled, and I learned how warm and heavy a girl's light limbs can be, but I was too shy and she was too innocent to put George Moore's dictum to the test. We wrote to each other, and at the end of the year she obtained tickets for a ball at the Dorchester. White tie this time. By now I was at Cambridge and this seemed – just – to be within my compass. I obtained a special advance from my trustee to buy some tails, this being the sort of expense which appealed to him, and made my way to Beckenham, confident at least that I could tie an evening tie and, though no Astaire, make a fair stab at the foxtrot and the waltz. Muriel's brother and his girl friend came with us to the ball. She was a ballet dancer, tiny, wide-eyed, neat, with a strong straight neck and turned-out toes. When I danced with her she floated like thistledown.

Having a ball is a step up from having a good time and it was not to be expected that I would reach that eminence so soon after the earlier fiasco. But I did not disgrace myself. Beckenham, however, hadn't the same ambience as Lausanne and by degrees my affair with Muriel (if affair it can be called) gently fizzled out. I don't think her brother was sorry.

Twenty-one

In the Michaelmas Term 1937 I went up to Trinity Hall, Cambridge, to read history. The Hall was full of freshmen showing their parents around and carrying books and pictures and other paraphernalia into their rooms. Although my gyp, a painstakingly lugubrious man, had lit a fire in the grate, my own rooms seemed as bare as a cell – bleaker even than those I'd been given when I came up for the scholarship. Whereas they had been transitory, these seemed a simulacrum of my own inadequacy. I unpacked my clothes. I put out a photograph of Muriel taken on a tennis court in Lausanne. I arranged my few books on the shelves. Then I went out and bought a coloured portrait of Samuel Pepys and two prints of Cambridge colleges (coals to Newcastle), together with a second-hand copy of Stubbs' *Charters*, which I opened only once to shut again for ever. After hanging up the pictures, I sat down in front of the fire and ate some crumpets as the damp Cambridge evening began to close in. Outside I could hear the echo and bustle of ordinary life – voices, laughter, steps on the stairs. I half hoped, half feared that the steps would stop outside my door. But they didn't; the shadowy firelight wavered on the walls and that agonising wish of my childhood pierced me once more – to be wanted, to be like everyone else.

When the time came to dine, I was assailed by what therapists blandly describe as 'irrational fears', like one of Pavlov's dogs for whom the wrong bell has tolled. I put on my gown and prepared to plunge anew into the corporate life, whose password – despite having been thrown into the deep end at age four – I still hadn't (and haven't yet) discovered. Other new men were waiting about, joking and talking in loud, assured voices. No doubt most of them were as nervous as I was.

I was lucky with my college. Trinity Hall is small and intimate, flanked on one side by Clare and on the other side by Caius and backing on to the river by Garret Hostel Bridge, a good place for climbing in. William Bateman, Bishop of Norwich, founded it in 1350 to make good the loss of more than half his clergy as a result of the Black Death. By the time I got there some six hundred years later, although its conveniences were still largely mediaeval, baths and privies being tucked away in the basement of a newish court, it was better known for growing lawyers and oarsmen. The oarsmen sat at a special table in Hall. When they were drunk, they liked to make a lot of noise and, for some reason tolerated by authorities, unlike other hooligans, break things up. I preferred the lawyers, who were more amusing and less beefy. They touched, I suppose, some sympathetic chord in my genes.

My supervisor in history was Charles Crawley, 'Creepie' Crawley. He was a gentle, charming man, but dry. We sometimes played squash together. He soon found out that, like Merimée, my interest in history was really in the anecdotes and that my grasp of the subject was much less than Wainwright's clever coaching had led the college to believe. My own doubts had been amply fortified by that quick peep into Stubbs' *Charters* – Casaubon country, no place for me. I intimated as much to Crawley under the showers, where a naked confession seemed less out of place than in his study. I said I wanted to read English. I knew nothing about the English Tripos, but it seemed lusher territory, less exposed intellectually to the disagreeable east winds for which Cambridge is renowned. Few other subjects let you claim to be working whilst reading a novel with your feet on the fender. Crawley, if dismissive, was surprisingly kind – after all, I was repudiating his own subject. He allowed me to switch, but warned me that my scholarship might be in jeopardy. Indeed it was, for I made a complete hash of the May examinations. That disaster was generously held to be more the product of ignorance than incompetence and things came right in Part I of the Tripos when, to everyone's surprise including my own, I managed to scrape a First. So I kept my scholarship. I had a knack then, no doubt inherited from my father, of picking facts up quickly and – unlike him – as quickly forgetting them. (I still retain the latter facility, but I have lost the former.) This was a godsend in examinations. It helped less in the weekly essays because probing questions were apt to be asked, especially in my third year when I was 'farmed out' to Basil Willey. His gentle integrity cut me down to size and he taught me for the first time to say exactly what I meant. But there has to be some technique for papering over cracks. No student of English can hope to read more than a fraction of the literature he's supposed to pronounce on, so he has to read instead what other people have written about it.

But he has to be wary. There are fashions in critics as well as authors. In my day, I.A. Richards had shot his bolt and F.R. Leavis was the cult figure. Open-necked, acerbic, adenoidal, cantankerous, bullied by his wife, dourly bent to the common pursuit, Leavis secreted a natural camouflage which melted perfectly into the dingy background of the thirties, along with Marx's beard and Chamberlain's umbrella. He plucked at a particularly bleak string of the Cambridge intellectual tradition, a kind of dirge-like version of the Puritan Revolution. He was determined to smash the old revered images and, having no sense of humour, only a sense of the ridiculous, he took this task very seriously; he even, as Clive James said, had a serious way of being bald. I relished Leavis; I disliked him and needed him; he was the bran in the diet, the worm in the apple. His revaluations came to nothing in the end. He died in gloom, his worst fears realised – 'I'm not feeling chirpy,' was all he said.

Lionel Elvin, my supervisor in English, was not a Leavisite. He was an uncomplicated man, an athletics blue, positively un-donnish, very different from Charles Crawley. His manner was brisk: I got the impression that he had long ceased to be interested in English except as a piece of college business to be transacted as efficiently as possible. He was much more interested in politics; he had stood as the unsuccessful Socialist candidate for the university in 1935; later he became a Professor of Education. He liked to keep things simple in accordance with the old Cambridge adage that, if you can't put something into baby talk, you probably don't know what you're talking about. This matter-of-fact approach suited me down to the ground. I'd done no formal English since School Certificate. My ignorance was lamentable. I knew none of the tricks of the literary academic's trade, such as the capacity to sit in judgement on minds much greater than his own. I had read a lot during the lonely days at Stratton House, and I was familiar with classics like *Tom Jones* and *Tristram Shandy* and George Herbert and 'Lawn' Tennyson. I liked Aldous Huxley; Wilfred Owen moved me deeply. But I knew scarcely anything about Joyce and Eliot and Lawrence, or even Auden and Spender. Whilst my contemporaries regarded anything less textually or sexually abstruse than Donne or Empson as a bore, I was lapping up Herrick and splashing about in the Georgian shallows. Current modes of wit had completely passed me by. This may have irritated Elvin, but it stood me in good stead with the examiners who, expecting to be bombarded by the quotations of the day, found themselves caught in a time warp and sprayed with nostalgic references to the authors of their youth. Daudet said that the success of Maeterlinck's books was due to their being forty years behind the times. The same was true of my examination papers. I never did get on terms with the verse of the thirties, much of it written as if to be declaimed through a megaphone. It's ironic that the best English poem to come out of the Spanish civil war, John

Cornford's *Heart of the heartless world*, should be a simple love lyric – a bourgeois form which, till he became a soldier, he had affected to despise.

I shared Elvin's supervision with David Terry, a tall, lean, reticent South African who knew far more about English literature than I did. David remained my close friend until his death. He was partial to a glass of port before breakfast and smoked endless cigarettes in a short black holder, contemplating the British and their strange ways with amusement through the resultant haze. His deep chuckle was as good as a hot bath. He would have made a gifted reporter, having an acute, colonial eye for the bizarre: the flat-capped members of the Pitt Club, for instance, pink with innocence and insolence, cradled in the security of inherited money. At the same time he loved the traditional. Whatever happened, he made a point of entering into the spirit of the thing. After war broke out in September 1939, he always carried a gas mask, iron rations in the form of pemmican, and a revolver. On one occasion he left the revolver on a cinema seat and found himself in difficulties with the police. He had a friend called Turner, also South African, who was an expert in military history. Turner had a great respect for the German High Command, '*immer rasiert, immer bereit*', whose names – von Bock, von Runstedt, von Kleist – delighted him. In 1940, before France was invaded, he was convinced that we were about to lose the War. He had plotted the likely campaign on large-scale maps to prove it. He scorned the famous Maginot Line. He was right, of course. We *were* about to lose the war but, thanks to Churchill, we failed to notice; and, after Dunkirk and the Battle of Britain, found that we hadn't lost it after all. By that time both David and his friend had gone back home. The last time I saw David before his return he was being carried out of college on a stretcher to have his appendix out. He looked splendidly gaunt, relishing his role.

By then many men of my year had left to join up and part

of the college had been taken over for Army training, so that the rest of us had to share rooms. Cadets in uniform swarmed about in the quad. Their arrival meant that my last year at Cambridge was shorn of its trappings: no eights week, no May balls, no conferment of degrees. But at least we didn't have to decide what to do afterwards: that was a decision Herr Hitler made on our behalf. I took Part II of the English Tripos before going down and, upon my soul, I got another First! A feather in my hat, but of no use then – or for that matter afterwards, except for display on curricula vitae. Mayna was unmoved by my achievement. So far as she was concerned, it might as well have been a first-aid certificate; indeed she was much prouder when I was awarded that.

I did very well to land a double, because in both years I was distracted by pacifism – in 1939 trying to make up my mind about it, and in 1940 formally registering as a 'conchy'. This took some energy out of me, though not so much as it would have done had I been less of a loner or Mayna less unworldly. There were strong pacifist movements in Cambridge as elsewhere, but I didn't join them. I could not like the worthy men in the Peace Pledge Union. There was an even more distasteful group called Moral Rearmament, which originated in America but was marketed in England by 'Bunny' Austin, a well-known tennis player, also a Cambridge man. I seem to have acquired my pacifist belief all by myself, much as I had allegedly picked up scarlet fever during my last term at school. It also proved skin-deep, but was quite painful while it lasted.

War and the threat of war generally messed up these Cambridge years. Its lengthening shadow lay across them, creating sharp edges and false perspectives, partially eclipsing the sun at a time in our lives when, supposedly, it will never shine so splendidly again. Or so it was for me. For many, for most, a guffaw and a pint of beer provided as much pleasure as ever they had. Peter Studd, Captain of the university XI, told an interviewer in 1939 that he hoped to God the Führer wouldn't declare war before the cricket season was over. (Shortly afterwards his team made 531 against Leicestershire – which shows how long ago this was!) Nevertheless, everyone knew that war was coming and most men had no doubt what they had to do when it did. Others were caught up in implausible ideologies like Marxism and pacifism. Often these were illogically intertwined. Since war is the engine of capitalism, the argument ran, it was the duty of the working class and those who stood with them to oppose all armaments except those of the Soviet Union, which was by definition completely free of any aggressive intent. Pacifists had a complementary slogan: 'The bayonet is a weapon with a worker at each end'. Although the civil war in Spain and the takeover of Czechoslovakia made all this look pretty silly, it was given a fresh lease of life by the Russo–German pact. A young man tends to take ideas to heart and it's bad luck if he gets called to account whilst his blurred loyalties still seem more important than the truth.

Had there been no war, I still wouldn't have made the best of Cambridge. I didn't know how: I was too timid and naive. Perhaps Cambridge, like Oxford, is best in retrospect. You forget you were short of money, never quite keeping up, sexually frustrated and often worried about exams. You remember the wide lawns and the river's placid beauty.

What Cambridge had to give above all was unlimited time for friendship and talk. There were no mixed colleges then and scarcity of women is a great spur to friendship. I took some of what it had to give, of course – who could not? Occasionally, half drunk, I seemed to come within touching distance of the ideal life or, if rather more tipsy, of some enormous joke. Being happy, which calls for more secure roots, was a different matter; for all its beauty, there is a sadness in the Cambridge air. But there were enchanted moments: a marvellous sense of being alive under the chilly blue East Anglian sky, rain not long gone, the tall trees on the Backs mathematically precise;

or the sight of an Austin Seven deposited on the roof of the Senate House; or coming back to college in the winter dusk, mind swept clean by hard exercise, the big wooden gate with its narrow door in the middle, the shaft of light from the porter's lodge, old Grant in his bowler hat, haloes round the lamps, river smell mixed with the scent of damp leaves and bonfire smoke; or the moment before friends arrive, kettle on the fire, tea-cups set out, anchovy toast at the ready, curtains drawn, the sound of Schubert on the gramophone coming faintly from next door.

There was, too, the encounter with intellectual honesty, which I had tried to shy away from in my flight from history and from war, but which the remarkable privilege of tutorials – being alone with an able man prepared to turn his mind to the improvement of yours – taught me to recognise and respect. There's no point in pretending if you're going to be found out. What I wrote was always criticised, never praised. Praise would mean that you weren't being taken seriously.

Sometimes I didn't deserve to be. As when, in the rooms of one of the dons, I met the Headmaster of Rossall School. I do not remember him because I was so drunk that, as I was being introduced, I fell to the floor and had to be carried away. The occasion was Dr Eden's Feast, a college binge to which scholars were invited. I was wearing my tails and I was sick all over them. Next day I awoke in shame to the mother of all hangovers.

In one respect the War was providential for me. Had I been saddled with academic success in peace-time, I could easily have been persuaded to stay on and do 'research' in some trivial literary field – Byron's laundry bills and the like. It would have been a grave mistake. I was no proper scholar; I lacked the intellectual apparatus required, and detail fretted me like sand in my shoe. After the War was over, uncertain what to do with my life, I came back to Cambridge one windy afternoon to make sure. I had forgotten its penetrating beauty, its capacity to make things that had been important seem suddenly remote. I was invited to dine. The Master was there. He made a remark and paused for me to chime in with an apt response. I couldn't think of one and he had to provide his own. He went on to speak wittily for a little while and then grew bored. I had failed the test. I knew then that Cambridge was not for me: there is nothing worse than not being quite clever enough. That night I lay in my bed and listened to the bells being blown about the sky. I was reminded of the time I came up for my scholarship. I felt again the old loneliness: the thought of those bells ringing out year after year over the wide courts and the slow river was more than I could bear.

V
WAR

Once as we were sitting by
The falling sun, the thickening air,
The chaplain came against the sky
And quietly took a vacant chair.

And under the tobacco smoke
'Freedom', he said, and 'Good' and 'Duty'.
We stared as if a savage spoke.
The scene took on a singular beauty.

Roy Fuller

Twenty-two

The local Tribunal in Cambridge made no bones about allowing my name to be entered in the Register of Conscientious Objectors. They didn't even ask to see me. 'We accept the applicant's evidence and reasons for objecting to combatant service,' they said, 'and think he would be more usefully employed in the occupation specified below than in performing other duties.' The occupation specified below was training in wireless telegraphy for the merchant navy.

The statement I submitted in support of my application was not based on any religious belief, but rested in essence on the bald assertion that the effects of war would be more terrible than any alternative. Looking back into history, such an assertion is likely to be true more often than not. But in 1939 it wasn't true: it was naive and muddle-headed. Even more so was my volunteering for the merchant navy, whose cargoes were the sinews of a war I theoretically opposed. It was clear, moreover, that German U-boats were going to exact a fearsome toll – a prospect no doubt taken as evidence of sincerity. The truth is that I was terrified of being thought a coward.

I wasn't proud of being a pacifist; I wanted to stop each passer-by to apologise. Pacifism was not so much an ideal as a burden I found myself saddled with. I had grown up in a world of war memorials and pacifist declarations. A spate of influential books, such as Norman Angell's *The Grand Illusion* (which helped to win him the Nobel Peace Prize in 1933) and the writings of Huxley and Russell, encouraged a repudiation of war. But philosophical and ethical questions, the Hegelian 'slaughter bench of history' and all that, were not the things that moved me. What swayed me most was the literature of the 1914 War, the literature of disgust – Remarque, Barbusse, Graves, that marvellous book Frederik Manning's *The Middle Parts of Fortune*, and, above all, the poetry of Owen and Rosenberg and Sassoon. I couldn't get the poetry out of my head. Its emotional impact was boosted by films like *All Quiet on the Western Front* and Renoir's *La Grande Illusion*, a title curiously echoing Norman Angell's book. There is a kind of pity that makes you want to turn away; you cannot bear to look. It was really the 1914 War I was refusing to fight.

How innocent I was! If Germany had won that war, life in England or France would not have changed much; what lay in the balance in 1939 was profoundly different. The idea that, if we offered no physical opposition, Hitler could be persuaded by moral arguments is so silly that it seems impossible that I could have held such an opinion, even at the age of twenty. Gandhi was, of course, the exemplar. I overlooked the fact that the British, Amritsar notwithstanding, were a civilised power. Under the Nazis Gandhi wouldn't have lasted a minute. But I was unable to see beyond the horror of the killing fields of Passchendaele and the Somme: men up to their knees in mud, screaming with pain, blood gargling from their lungs, blown to pieces before the eyes of their mates. I knew it had become obscene to speak of the glory of war. I did not realise that what is obscene may also sometimes be necessary. If my father had been alive; or if I'd not been persuaded, *pace* 1914–18, that much of what was being said about the Nazis was propaganda, I might have seen sense earlier. None of my immediate family had fought in the War; I had no-one with a proper sense of the fitness of things to help me make up my mind. In the end, Hitler made it up for me, as he did so many other people's.

The choices we make are, of course, always more fishy than they seem – in my case the resentment of an illegitimate child against the society he feels excluded from. Torn between the wish to conform and the wish to rebel, which can suddenly rise up on a clear morning like the taste of last night's sardine, he has to reconcile a need to fulfil social norms with a sometimes stronger urge to break them. Pacifism offered an ideal paradigm. Secret anger – the same anger that surged inside me when I heard those high, confident middle-class voices that sank to a deeper note when they addressed their inferiors and would once have called for my grandmother to put coal on the fire – was magically transformed into a pledge of peace. Needless to say, it was too good to be true.

Things might have been easier if I'd met more hostility. I met scarcely any. Nearly everyone was tolerant and kind. Mayna was reconciled because she thought I was less likely to get killed. Tom Cannon Brookes, my trustee, took the view that I was old enough to make my own mistakes. Cambridge friends disappeared into khaki and wrote mournful letters from windy camps, leaving me with an uneasy sense of unrequited obligation. In blacked-out Trinity Hall I did my best to enjoy what was left of undergraduate life. The so-called phoney war had tipped us all into a curious cloud-cuckoo land – no drums, no flags, just sandbags and khaki and gas masks and identity cards and the careful voice of the BBC telling us what the Government thought we should be told. The war we all expected hadn't happened; the papier mâché coffins were quietly stored away.

Then suddenly the phoney war was over. By the time the future wireless operator, just down from Cambridge, reported for training at the School of Telegraphy, West Kensington, on a hot summer day in June 1940 when the blossoms were drifting down in the London parks, Denmark, Norway, Holland and Belgium had been overrun, the centre of Rotterdam had been obliterated, and the Panzers, as Turner foretold, had disembowelled Northern France. A defeated army had been taken off the Dunkirk beaches by Vice-Admiral Ramsay's motley force of little boats. The Battle of the Atlantic had begun; the Battle of Britain was a month away. A new voice, the voice of Churchill, came over the radio, telling us what we'd longed for but been unwilling to hear. In my pocket I had a letter from David Terry: 'You ought to be rather pleased that France is passing out. They'll have no more war. Or is that unkind?... I don't know how your conscience feels now, but I'm glad I haven't got it... Farewell, fortune attend thee.'

My trustee, who had a finger in many pies, had fixed up a room for me in one of the large stuccoed houses of Bayswater that spread out in wide terraces between Paddington and Hyde Park. The landlady was a spry, gossipy woman with bright teeth, well versed in the ways of men. Two couples, neither married, and a soldier lived there besides me. The soldier was a Baptist and gave me a book of Elizabethan homilies.

Each morning I would walk across Kensington Gardens to the Training School. Marvellous early mornings of sun through mist. It was a fine summer, pitilessly fine. People lay about in deck chairs; old women walked their dogs; model yachts glided among the ducks in the Round Pond. Only the throngs of servicemen – many of them the remnants of scattered Continental armies, Poles, Dutch, Norwegian, French – and the barrage balloons floating high in the sky, or lying wobbly and exhausted by their tethering posts like great silver elephants, brought reminders of war. But there was a growing tingle of apprehension in the air, pricking the nerves like the threat of thunder and mixed up in my mind with the exhilaration of being loose in London untrammelled by anybody else's expectations. Often at Hunstanton I had looked out over the sea and thought 'The world must offer more than this: I can't be caught in this trap for ever.' At school, even at Cambridge, I had still felt trapped: Skinner-box boy, Skinner-box man. Now I was unconfined. But it was draughty; I was very conscious of being on my own.

I remember little about the wireless course. It was run by a saturnine bureaucrat, wizard on the Morse key but obsessed with time-keeping and used to dealing with youths, not men. He would stand watch in hand by the door as we wandered in late. We had to spend long hours transmitting and taking down messages. The boredom was relieved by the fact that a number of my fellow students were musicians. They picked up Morse very quickly and rattled it off at high speed with a lovely, spaced rhythm. They took me to the Queen's Hall (then still unbombed) and on some evenings they invited me along while they played quartets together. At week-ends I liked to get away when I could afford it. I went down to Norfolk to cheer up Mayna. Tom Cannon Brookes invited me down to Frinton, where he had a house. Sometimes I would take a day trip to Surrey or Kent. The Battle of Britain had begun, the sky criss-crossed with vapour trails and falling plumes of smoke – a kind of lethal ballet. You could hear the drone of engines and sometimes the distant chatter of guns. I wondered what it was like to be up there. Later on I was to learn.

I met Eileen on the steps of St Paul's Cathedral. She was coming out; I was going in. She was slim and pretty, dusted with freckles; and she wore a fetching hat. We looked at each other and stopped and spoke. Then she turned round and went in with me. I told her I was a pacifist – something I always had to get off my chest. She didn't mind. She thought I was idealistic and compassionate, as I seemed to be; as indeed, in a jejune way, I was. I made her laugh. We spent the day together and, when we parted, she put her arms round my neck and kissed me. That same evening the soldier commended to me the homily against the superfluous Decking of Churches and the Peril of Idolatry. Had he known, he should have commended the one against ungodly affections of the heart, which vice, as his book said, 'in a manner among many is counted as no sin at all, but rather a pastime, a dalliance, and but a touch of youth; not rebuked, but winked at'.

After I met Eileen, I was reluctant to go away: London

contained all I wanted. But I was committed to regular visits to Mayna and it so happened that I was also away for part of the first week-end in September. I had just got back to Bayswater on the Saturday evening when the sirens went. It was the first night of the Blitz. The docks and the packed, mean streets of little houses round them were the target. We all climbed out on the roof and watched the docks burning. The flames, stabbed by searchlights and gunfire, lit up the eastern sky. The sound of the guns rolled out over the city. It seemed unreal, like a stage set. 'It will be us next,' said the soldier.

Shortly afterwards he was posted to the north and his room fell vacant. Eileen came to live there instead. She worked at the international telephone exchange in the City, often at night. When she was not on night duty there, she came on night duty with me. The edginess which marks the early stages of any love affair fused in a marvellous way with the edginess of the Blitz. Fear and inhibition (much stronger in those days) cancelled each other out and the Blitz became a kind of blanket beneath which we huddled for warmth: listening to the long, whistling strides of approaching bombs, the room gently rocking in the uproar of silence afterwards, bits of plaster flaking off the ceiling. As most young men do, I feared that I might not be worth loving. Eileen laid me and my fears to rest. Time no longer seemed to be slipping away from me. I looked at people, men and women, in a new, physical way and I kept on picturing Eileen with nothing on: 'Full nakedness, all joys are due to thee!' I remembered the smell of her like bergamot, sweet and sharp at once. We fitted together under the violent sky like the last two pieces of a jigsaw I thought I would never find.

As the nights drew in, the sirens wailed earlier. Searchlights probed and swung, and soon afterwards would come the uneven drone of the bombers and roar of the guns opening up. When I walked back through the Gardens in the lit dusk, shrapnel was already beginning to patter down and sometimes incendiaries would fizzle and blaze in the grass. But I didn't care, I felt invulnerable. And free: everything had become impermanent. The old order was rocking on its feet. Possessions, antecedents, respectability, top hats, no longer mattered any more. London had become an egalitarian city, the gas mask its badge. In the morning, when I passed the patient queues waiting for buses, the gutted terraces, the slabs of masonry like tilted tombs, the acrid smell of dust and fire, the sound of shovelled glass, severed water mains still pumping, I would feel a rush of love for the city and its people. To be there, to be one of them, to have my own girl, nothing could take this away!

I was not 'in love' with Eileen as I had been with Muriel. It was less than that, and more: more than affection, much more than sex. Though it sounds a supremely selfish thing to say, I loved the Blitz. It was wonderful to wake up each morning and to be able to say 'I'm happy'. There was eroticism in the air and we took what we wanted of it. She was an Irish Catholic and convent-educated, so guilt was there as well, to give a sharper edge. But not much guilt; she was a pagan really. '*Je suis catholique*,' she might have said, '*pas pratiquante, pas croyante, mais catholique.*' I was flirting with Catholicism then, as I had flirted earlier with Marxism, and we had discussions as we lay in bed together about the ethics of lying in bed together, which more pressing matters obliged us to interrupt.

We lived in the present, we didn't think about the future for there might not be one, the idea of marriage never crossed our minds. I could have gone overboard for Eileen, but I knew it would be a mistake. There were other men, for one thing. I was the preferred, but not the only, one. I don't think she slept with them, but they took her out when I was away. My landlady made a point of telling me. I met two of them. They were a rum pair. One was a detective inspector with an unpleasant bullying manner and his hair parted in the middle, who called me 'laddie'. The other was an army officer, thickly built, with a moustache, the sort of man who might have spent some years in Rangoon. He generously took us both out to a night club, where he danced a lot with Eileen and I felt out of it because I wasn't in uniform. I was jealous but not very; they both seemed so old and unattractive that I couldn't for the life of me imagine what Eileen saw in either. She never explained. Perhaps she didn't want to hurt me; it was a mined area and I wasn't fool enough to wander into it. One difference between the English and the Irish is supposed to be that the English tell less than the truth and the Irish tell more. Eileen would have told more and I wouldn't have believed her.

She was surprisingly domestic. She had to be, because I could rarely afford to take her out except to the flicks – her desire for an outing less austere may have been the simple explanation for the other men. We had picnic meals by the gas fire and she would sit with her feet curled under her bottom, mending my socks or sewing a button back on my jacket. It was then, with the barrage banging overhead, that I felt closest to her. Not the least thing I owe her, besides the happiness she gave me, is that she pricked my fantasies about women.

Just before Christmas I completed my wireless course and was duly awarded a certificate to say that I could transmit and receive twenty words a minute in plain language and sixteen words a minute in code groups, and that I knew something – I dread to think how little – about the practical working of the apparatus. I gave up my room in Bayswater and boarded the train for Norfolk on a raw cold evening. I didn't want to go – back to Mayna's sad world where the bed was cold and time was something to be killed. Probably the bombers were over again: I can't remember, only the great dark dingy echoing station. Eileen came to see me off in her best coat, trimmed with fur. Her breath formed a little cloud – 'You make me so sad, darling,' she said. She gave me a small silver pocket knife with my initials on it. I still have it: the last relic of our short idyll. But the darns in my socks, which bore the impress of her fingers, and the buttons she sewed on my jacket, meant more to me.

The train crawled interminably through Shoreditch and Hackney, now largely in ruins. The train, like all trains then, was packed and, as I sat wedged in the fug of my compartment lit only by a dim blue bulb in the ceiling and the occasional glow of a cigarette, I finally reached a decision that I'd really come to weeks ago, in Eileen's arms. I couldn't stay a pacifist any longer. I'd been plain wrong. My ideals, if that's what they were, were no use against the jackboot and the tank. The only reason why I was able to live in a decent ordered society was because others, like the Baptist soldier and the bobby on the street, were willing to use violence on my behalf. It wasn't fair to refuse to do what I expected others to do. I had no thoughts about making the world safe for democracy and the like; I just wanted to rid it of the Nazis and their tinpot myths. The thought of their goose-stepping into battered London as they had done into Paris was unbearable.

By the time we reached Lynn, I'd made up my mind to volunteer for aircrew. Tit for tat. Besides, I was still afraid of being thought afraid. It was a great relief. I didn't tell Mayna straightaway. I didn't want to spoil her Christmas.

Twenty-three

In January 1941 the sea froze near the shore. Ice tinkled on the beach. Everywhere burned bright with frost. On the Downs the rimed grass was as brittle as stubble and the twigs were all encased in crystal. Stratton House was like an ice-box, and damp too. Coal grew scarce, newspapers got smaller and food skimpier. My grandmother had suddenly grown old; she heard the voices of soldiers shouting outside when the street was empty. A stray German plane dropped a bomb near Mrs Carr's shop and the explosion blew our bedroom windows out. It was strange to hear that familiar crescent scream at Hunstanton of all places, like hearing a cockatoo on Snettisham marshes.

I lost no time after Christmas in informing the Air Ministry that I was at their disposal. They remained unmoved, so I had to find something else to do meanwhile. I experienced a paralysing sense of being back in the trap I thought I'd escaped from, where nothing was changed and, whatever I did, nothing would come of it. A feature of war which gets taken for granted is how much remains unaltered. Hunstanton remained deplorably the same. Its streets, tranced in the dingy glaze of a winter day, had the power to suck the meaning out of existence and, now I had ceased to be a pacifist, I felt even less able, oddly enough, to resist the apathy they could induce in me. But after a week or two I began to perk up. At least I no longer had to explain myself; a weight had been lifted from my shoulders and I could let myself be carried along by the easy, grumbling patriotism that infused ordinary life. Even Dr Bull made a point of stopping me early one morning outside the Town Hall to welcome me back into the fold. How he came to learn about my change of heart I don't know, but he did.

The Town Hall, heavily sand-bagged and with the air raid siren mounted on the roof, was manned all round the clock. Concern was not only about air raids; invasion was also regarded as a real possibility, the north Norfolk coast being marked down as a potential landing place. I put my name down for the night watch. My colleague was a fey, plump, kindly woman who judged people by the colour of their auras. From time to time her presence produced a flurry of loud rappings on the walls. She told me to pay no attention; it often happened. She grew fond of me and, protected by a disturbing sense of dissociation, consoled me in the early hours for the loss of Eileen. Later I met her husband, Geoff. He practised automatic writing and took down long messages allegedly from a Red Indian. I was reminded of Margot Asquith's remark after a lecture by Sir Oliver Lodge: 'I always knew the living talked rot, but it's nothing to the nonsense the dead talk.' Geoff, however, was a believer, Yet he was in no sense odd. On the contrary he was a rubicund, hearty man who sold fertilisers and was involved with an underground organisation called 'Auxiliary Units' – small guerilla groups set up at the initiative of a certain Major Gubbins when a German invasion was thought to be seriously on the cards, and recruited from men like gamekeepers and farmers who had an intimate knowledge of their locality. No unit knew where any other unit was. Their existence was never acknowledged. Training was given in terrorist arts at Coleshill House, near Swindon. Geoff Woodward, knowing that I was unlikely to be called up for some months, invited me to join one of these units and I did. Few pacifists can have gone so rapidly into reverse.

There were four in our group: a market gardener, a railway signalman, Futter and me. The market gardener, a fussy man with a sinuous moustache, having been a sergeant in the 1914

War, was our designated leader. Futter had a small farm, but for most of his life he'd been a poacher. We usually worked in pairs and Futter was the man for me; I did not put much faith in our leader. Futter was a sly man adept at keeping his mouth shut, small-eyed, suspicious, none too clean, bulky but light on his feet, utterly sceptical and deeply patriotic. His knowledge of birds and animals was extraordinary; and what he didn't know about threading a wood or crossing open country at night wasn't worth knowing. He liked to keep the wind in his face, from time to time sniffing the air like a dog. He would have disposed of a German with the same detachment as he would a partridge or a hare. He tolerated me because I was a 'scholar' and knew things he didn't. Education, I thought – that overblown trumpet!

A hideout was prepared for us in Ringstead Woods, near the Downs. Until recently its remains were still there. It was dug deep in the chalk, carefully camouflaged, timber lined and stocked with arms, ammunition, grenades, explosives, food and fuel. Some matériel, such as sticky bombs and plastic explosive, was issued to us ahead of the regular forces. Neither the local army or RAF units or the Home Guard knew anything about us. This lent a certain hazard to parts of our training. We used to go out in the dusk, as the barn owls were quartering the fields, to try to plant dummy explosives on searchlight sites or in a laager of army vehicles. The dummy was usually a potato primed with a timing device that exploded a detonator after a specified time. Since the 'enemy' had no idea that we were on a friendly exercise and there was often a risk of getting entangled in barbed wire, caution was called for. Sometimes you would have to stay motionless for long minutes, while a sentry prowled up and down a few yards away or yawned prodigiously. Like deer stalking, I imagine: 'Gang quiet,' as the ghillie said, 'gang as if ye were something growing.' If you took too long you wondered whether the bloody detonator would go off in your hand and take the end of your fingers with it. But if you did succeed in taping your potato to the target and, having got away unseen, lay safe nearby and heard it go off, the satisfaction was immense. Then you had to get back home; for obvious reasons the hideout was rarely used. Futter always seemed to know exactly where he was and, when he'd gone, it was like letting go of nurse's hand. Fitful moonlight playing over a countryside as dark and haunted as in mediaeval times. The cry of nightbirds, the wind soughing in the woods, the rustle of the high hedges, the sudden movement of a bullock by a gate, the long empty lanes – the old green lanes that smugglers had once used – could make me feel almost as panicky as I had as a child when I climbed the stairs alone to bed under the flickering gas: a feeling Coleridge has so exactly described:

> Like one that on a lonesome road/ Doth walk in fear and dread,/ And having once turned round walks on/ And turns no more his head;/ Because he knows a frightful fiend/ Doth close behind him tread.

I did not allow my mind to dwell on the deeper fear that the potato might become plastic explosive and the sentry German, and that I might be called on to use the knife I carried. It's as well I wasn't put to the test for I don't think I could have done.

In due course I was summoned to RAF Cardington, site of the old airship sheds, for interviews and a medical. We were given some elementary tests, in one of which, I remember, I made use of Pythagoras' theorem, the first time I discovered that such suppositions really could come in handy. Pressure was put on me to become a wireless operator – twenty words a minute seemed to them too good to miss – but, as all aircrew were volunteers, I was able to hold out for pilot training. One of the examining team fancied himself as a judge of men and after it was all over, having learned that I had been to Cambridge, expressed interest in my degree. 'Don't tell me,' he said, 'let me guess – a third in law.' He was nearer the mark than he knew!

In June 1941 Germany invaded the Soviet Union. Like Napoleon, who struck camp at Boulogne after the Battle of Trafalgar, Hitler abandoned plans to cross the Channel and recoiled eastwards to destruction. The purpose of our little group had gone. We used the hideout more as a miniature social club, letting off bangs from time to time for the sake of appearances and going home again to the caressing call of wood pigeons and the sight of rabbits hopping in the evening sunshine.

I helped Futter with the harvest, sharing the pleasure of seeing the golden stooks propped upright in threes to dry, the poignancy of that last little island of uncut barley with all the animals in it. I took home a rabbit and my grandmother rose from her armchair and skinned and gutted it and made a pie. When the time came for threshing and the traction engine had wheezed and clanked into position, Futter put me on the straw stack. He liked me well enough – he sent his wife round regularly with eggs – but he wasn't averse to getting some of his own back on a 'scholar'. For two days I waded thigh-deep in straw, drowned in a cloud of chaff and dust, deafened by the moan and thunder of the machinery and the clack of the moving belt. At the end of the day I had scarcely strength enough to bicycle back home. When it was all done I heard Futter say to his wife: 'I never thart he'd a-stood it.' It was a compliment worth having. Like Basil Willey, Futter didn't give praise easily. What's more, he insisted on paying me. The going rate produced a fraction of what my father in his heyday had been accustomed to earn in as many minutes. It made me think about social justice while I lay exhausted in my bath.

As the swallows gathered on the wires and the year began to draw towards its end, I became impatient for my call-up. Yet I was more than ever conscious of the lonely beauty of the coast, its dawns, its dusks, the cinnamon and scarlet skies when the sun went down over the marshes. I loved the moment when the tide turned and little sleepy waves floated off the weed on the mudflats, then slowly merged into a languid swell that lifted the beached dinghies and set their shrouds tapping. The air breathed with the murmur of the sea and the sad piping of redshanks, and the brent would come over in long black lines against the sky. Away from the coast the grass stayed damp all day and webbed mist hung about in the hedgerows until midday, forming again almost as soon as it had gone. Ghosts of frost glistered on the top of the stacks and the ploughing began. In the implacability of the everlasting cycle the War became irrelevant, almost impertinent, seeming to recede as it got nearer.

But it arrived eventually. At the beginning of December, my call-up papers came. When it was time to go, Mayna had a streaming cold and my grandmother gave me breakfast. She was agitated and burnt the toast: she didn't seem to be quite sure where I was going and why. She had the curious hostility of old people, once so confident, whose identity is leaking away. I went upstairs to say good-bye to Mayna. 'I won't kiss you,' she said, 'in case you get my cold.' She got up and waved to me from the window as I went off to war at last.

Twenty-four

At the Aircrew Reception Centre near Regent's Park, I began my service life as a 'trickle posting', having arrived before my papers did ('We don't want you 'ere yet, lad. If I was you, I'd piss off for a bit'). Piss off I did; but Eileen unfortunately had departed, and loafing about the metropolis with very little money soon became boring. I was glad when my papers turned up and I became a number I've never forgotten: 1612791. We were billeted in a block of flats and fed in batches at the Zoo. Three times a day long lines of airmen, at first in civvies and then in uniform with little white flashes in their caps, formed up in squads along Prince Albert Road and moved in a slow procession to the Zoo restaurant. The first squads assembled before dawn, with a man in front carrying a yellow oil lamp and a man at the back carrying a red one, waiting for breakfast. Squads were still there after dark, similarly lit up, waiting for supper. The process of feeding and kitting out, and the other rigmaroles of induction like pudding-basin hair cuts and inoculations and lectures on VD, occupied most of the day. In between we were taken for drill by a corporal, which meant in effect being marched round the corner to a 'caff' (from which he got a rake-off) for char and a wad. I shared a room with an actor with curly hair who had the gift of making everything and everyone seem extremely funny, as of course they were.

I had assumed that the RAF, as a fairly new service, would be less encrusted with 'bull' than the older ones. How wrong I was! Budding pilots were sent first to an Initial Training Wing (ITW) to receive a deluge of it. My ITW was at

Scarborough. We were quartered in the Crown Hotel on top of the cliffs, where the east wind blew ferociously during our morning inspections. The winter was nearly as severe as the previous one – cold enough, the driver informed us on arrival, to freeze your fucking balls off, mate. It was almost as cold inside as out; I slept with a hot-water bottle, a sad come-down from Eileen. We had classes on navigation, theory of flight, aircraft recognition and so on, not forgetting sanitation in the field. But the important part was the polishing and the drill. Drill I enjoyed: the ring of heels on a frosty road. The rest was ridiculous, and my new room-mate, James Crawford, elegant and short-tempered, kept on saying so in an imperious voice, which didn't help. Chased by screaming corporals, we were required to polish everything – taps, light switches, handles, water pipes, floors, basins, as well as badges, buttons, webbing and, of course, boots, boned up for hours. What couldn't be boned up had to be lined up. It was a world of obsessionals, in which we were punished for sins we hadn't committed. NCOs were always right: if they set you to scrub a floor and you scrubbed it clean, they would say it was dirty. This was understood by all, even by James in the end.

On completion of the course, we were given yet more inoculations and I went down with a high fever. During the resultant spell in sick quarters my friends were posted away. I was tacked on to a new mob, all strangers, and sent to Brough, a sad little airfield beside the Humber, to which we were bussed each morning from scattered parish rooms and village halls. There we had to show we could fly solo in a Tiger Moth before being sent overseas – in our case to the United States.

It was a stroke of luck being sent to the States. Ours was the last draft under a training scheme devised by General Arnold of the Army Air Corps before they came into the War. We were taught by Americans and trained with them. After the primary course British and American cadets were sensibly mixed up, sharing rooms together, so that no petty nationalism developed; indeed there was more friction between the descendants of Yankees and Confederates than between us and them. The flying training was first class, but we had to come to terms with a strong dose of West Point – hazing, gigs, square meals, pettifogging inspections and so forth, a second dose of ITW, as it were – and with the natural tendency of Americans to over-egg their pudding. But no-one can go to the States without being astonished by its size and power and the generosity of the people.

All our training was done in Florida and Georgia and I remember the long slow mid-summer train journey from Canada to the south, everything new, everything strange – the transcontinental wailing of the engine, the neat countryside of Ohio, the black waiters, the growing heat, the red soil of Tennessee, the final grimy arrival in the firefly-twinkling, cricket-shrilling dusk at Turner Field, Georgia. The big white eye of its beacon swept round and round a bruised, peach-coloured sky. Mail was waiting for us; one of our party received his calling-up papers.

Turner Field was enormous, acres of brown tents (where we lived) interspersed with huge barrack blocks with common showers and long lines of loos back to back, no doors, no partitions, where we all sat side by side in bondage to the morning stool, against which, even as infants, we had bawled in protest. Part of our acclimatisation to the American way of service life! Like the different food – more meat at a meal than a week's ration at home – and the gassy beer and the mosquitoes and the lowering of the flag each evening when we paraded for Retreat and the bugles blew. The heat was formidable; we became slaves to the Coke machines. I'd brought *War and Peace* and *Candide* with me to read. *Candide* proved the better prophylactic.

Lakeland, Florida, was our first Flying School. By some absurd colonial quirk, we were issued with pith helmets which, needless to say, we never wore. There was no let-up in 'bull', but its application was less efficient. Many of the flying instructors were leathery crop dusters or fairground flyers, who didn't know what discipline meant and, when they weren't in the air, lolled around in cane chairs smoking. My instructor, old Smithy, was one such. A reveille bell blasted off at 5.15 a.m. and we had to be at attention on parade outside within five minutes. There was a lake on the east side of the airfield and the dawnrise over it was beautiful, a ghostlike green with palm trees pasted against the sky like pieces of black paper: a magical moment between the shrill bell and the first coarse command – ' "But an instant",' remarked Alan, our philosopher, ' "and the fairy tale is over, and once again the actual fills the soul." ' Alan borrowed £12 from me, a significant sum in those days, and never paid it back.

The aircraft we flew were Stearman biplanes, painted yellow, built to last and very stable (Tiger Moths were skittish by comparison). They had open cockpits and the air, the medium you flew in, was always streaming past; there was nothing between you and the sky or, at the top of a loop, between you and the earth. There was no airspeed indicator either, so you had to fly from the start by the seat of your pants. Communication with the instructor was one-way only, down a tube; he could speak to you, but you couldn't answer back and on bad days you were on the end of a stream of abuse: 'Goddam it, fella, will ya stop fooling about. Hold that goddam left wing up – O dear Jesus Christ, will ya hold it up!' Rusty Bowditch, another pupil of Smithy, had a cold one day and took up a roll of lavatory paper to blow his nose on. When brought into play, it began to uncoil and got deflected into the front cockpit, where it wrapped itself round the controls. Smithy was tearing off paper right and left and trying to throw it over the side. 'He must have thought he was over Hamburg,' said Rusty afterwards, 'I've never had such a bollocking.'

I wasn't a 'natural' like Rusty, who said he preferred flying upside down. I was nervous and tense. I had to think about flying the aeroplane all the time, to learn to coax it through a manoeuvre, not bang it about. I should have remembered Howling and the little mare, Cigarette; or what Walford Davies used to say about singing hymns: 'Don't try and sing it, just think of the tune and let it sing itself.' I knew I could become a good pilot, but I was haunted by the fear that I might be 'washed out' first. This was a constant threat if you didn't come good quickly enough. You can't cram for a check ride or pretend to a competence you haven't got – either you can do it or you can't.

As I slowly got the feel of the air and its wide horizons, I began also to get the feel of ordinary life outside the base, the drug stores, the main street, the girls, the jacaranda trees, the southern voices. We went swimming and riding and played golf, when my little black caddie was not averse to improving the lie unobtrusively, if need be. (Whether this was a gesture of hospitality to a foreigner or normal practice, I never discovered.) During longer spells of leave we used to hitch quite a long way; all sorts of people would give us a lift. In some areas cotton was being picked and bits of white would blow like snow along the roadside. Segregation was still rampant: special seats for blacks in buses, special toilets, special eating places. We soon learned that the prime social disease was race, not class, which is ours. Curiously, though, the negroes – their rich laughter, their music, their broken-down shanties – seemed more at home than the whites, whose standardised, ghostless towns were somehow superimposed on the land, not part of it.

I've spoken a lot about the primary training school because this remains most clearly in my memory. But experience was much the same on other airfields. We went north to Macon and Valdosta. The flying became more advanced, the aeroplanes more demanding. We learned to fly on instruments, we learned to fly at night. There were occasional funerals, and a steady proportion of men who got thumbs down after a final check ride and passed out of our lives.

I developed a love-hate relationship with flying. Often I was afraid. If we had days without flying, I would dread going back to it again. But once in the air I would feel exhilarated, especially on a fine day solo in the Stearman, snap rolls, lazy eights, chandelles, with the wind blowing past and the shadow of the aeroplane flitting over the fields below. On the other hand, flying alone at night across country, when the weather was closing in and I had to navigate as well, didn't appeal to me at all. If someone else was with me – albeit no less a novice than I was – most of the fear went away. Later, as a bomber pilot, I felt strangely secure in the responsibility I had for my crew and in the support I got from them. Though skinny, I was essentially a 'heavies' man; I found satisfaction in the long haul and comfort in the glimmering instruments. I would have been no good as a fighter pilot, my hunting instincts undeveloped, my reflexes too slow.

At the end of February, just before my twenty-fourth birthday, we proudly paraded to have our wings pinned on and become honorary Second Lieutenants of the US Army Air Corps. The next day we caught the train back to Canada, where a considerably colder air embraced us. I handed in my comfortable pale khaki uniform and resumed the familiar blue serge and sewed on three stripes and a brevet: Sergeant Archer, 791, sir.

Twenty-five

After North America, England seemed absurdly small: drab, lustreless, over-ordered, overactive, overtired. Stratton House was still the same, but more so. The garden which my grandfather used to tend was now in decay. My grandmother was surly; she hadn't long to live. She would sit for hours behind the net curtains in her bedroom, watching and brooding. Mayna held me tight – I realised how much I meant to her; I was the baby she had cradled in her arms, his unsteady little head against her cheek. In ten days' time I would walk out of her sight once more and her heart would squeeze up. She would be always anxious, waiting for the knock on the door, like the knock she'd heard that chilly April morning ten years before. But she said little; and when she hinted at her love and concern I grew irritated, struggled against the too-much feeling she had for me, because I was ashamed. We had little to talk about. I had so much to tell her, yet it seemed impossible to communicate except in the most superficial way. When my leave was over, I was glad to escape.

Training began again. We had to adapt to the different English conditions. We flew about in Oxfords – plump twin-engined workhorses. I was sent on a navigation course at Bridgnorth and I slowly moved nearer to the sharp end of the War. Early in November I was posted to No. 14 Operational Training Unit, Husband's Bosworth. The Unit was equipped with old clapped-out Mark I Wellingtons. The airfield was in the middle of nowhere. Nissen huts, crouching in the desolate slanting light of a winter afternoon, bulged out of a lake of mud like fungi. To taxi off the runway was to sink into a morass. Accidents were frequent. It was not the sort of place to spend your last days in. Here bomber crews were farmed by an uncomfortable process of natural selection – changed around to see who would gel with whom – and I met the men I was to fly with on ops, except for the engineer and mid-upper gunner, who would join us at a Conversion Unit, where we would graduate from two to four engines. Shortly after we came together we went out for a meal to The Three Swans, an inn at nearby Market Harborough run by a man called Fothergill who wore shoes with silver buckles and had written a book and liked his pub to be frequented by the best people. Four young sergeants, not out of the top drawer, were received with marked coolness. We walked out and got drunk in a friendlier hostelry. This helped our bonding.

In due course we became a competent crew; more important, we had one priceless advantage – luck. For ten months we flew together: nobody missed a trip. When our tour of operations ended, we had a drink and separated and have never met since, which is strange because I have never felt closer to a group of men than I did to them. We hadn't much in common, but what we did have was intensely strong. Bomber crews have to rely on each other totally, whatever class they come from, whatever rank they happen to be. I was the Skipper because I was the pilot – an accident of trade; a gong was given to me but belonged to all of us. J.W. Halley (Hal) was the navigator, a Scot, gingery and precise; Bob Howie the wireless operator, wry, lazy, self-sufficient; Bob Adam the bomb-aimer, aloof and jumpy, in need of reassurance; Chris Foscolo (Taffy) the rear-gunner, tubby, garrulous, black-haired. Taffy came from Barry Docks and raced dogs and played the accordion. The two others we collected later were Alf Scott, the mid-upper gunner, a long-jawed, cynical Lancastrian, and Bob Read, the engineer, youngest of us, a Birmingham boy like my father. The ones I knew best were the navigator and the rear-gunner. Hal was a splendid, unflappable man: we plied our trades harmoniously together. Taffy was very flappable but resilient as a rubber ball. He played his squeeze box on the edgy afternoons of waiting, and he smoked like a chimney. I would often wake at night in the billet to see his cigarette-end glowing as he took a drag. If he had bad dreams, he never let on. There is a natural affinity between the pilot under his perspex canopy up front and the rear-gunner wedged in his turret at the back, the coldest, loneliest place of all.

It seems long ago now – a time as remote to my children as the Punic Wars – since we turned up in a truck at 106 Squadron, seven apprehensive sprogs, and were shown to the beds of seven other men who hadn't come back to claim them. The Squadron, part of Five Group, was based at Metheringham, another temporary station like Husband's Bosworth – the same Nissen huts, the same hangars, the same fuel bowsers, the same erks cycling about, the same scattered aircraft silhouetted against the bare horizon. Thank God, it was no longer winter, with the wind moaning off the flatlands, but June – the week of D-Day. The mud was dry. If we'd taken off and climbed a little we would have seen Lincoln Cathedral, triple-towered on its hill, built in a world that had never heard an engine. We felt lonely as we sat on our beds. We could hear the bomb trolleys rattling round the perimeter track. Even Taffy was subdued. This was our turn on the wheel: once it started moving there was no honourable escape until either you fell off or its circle was completed.

On a night bomber station you develop a lasting distaste for pomposity. You learn how precarious existence is – a persistent niggle in the gut erodes the flavour of the traditional bacon and egg. But death is rarely a physical presence as it is on the battlefield; it is an explosion to starboard, a crater in the ground, the sickly smell of burning, empty places at the table – no more mysterious really than a game of cards, perhaps for that reason the more arbitrary and senseless. You never know if you're going to be next and you wonder vaguely what form it will take and how much it will hurt. The best palliative is mockery and a due sense of proportion – and moments of intensity which hang like flares in the sky over tracts of time long since forgotten. Sometimes moments of exultation – the nightmare splendour of a burning city, the blossoming of the bombs, the flares sailing down slowly, beautifully, the flicker of the guns, the winking haze of the flak cloud, the searchlights swinging and swaying... More often, at any rate for me, moments of quietness and thankfulness. Coming back in the dawn, for instance, eyes still prickly from searching the darkness, the sea below vague as an expanse of silk, the cool commodious morning sky sprinkled with insect aircraft. It was marvellous to be alive, and, when the sun came up, to be still there.

We went through our thirty-five trips without a scratch, though not without alarm. In coping with this I was better off than some. The process of learning how to fly had been a struggle with the jitters. On ops, with my skill consolidated and a crew I was responsible for, I became in a funny way much 'happier'; I went almost with a sense of homecoming to my funk-hole in the cockpit. The fear I felt didn't penetrate to the quick like the fear that hummed in the telephone wires of my childhood. That was metaphysical fear, *Urmutterfurcht*, beyond the reach of reason. This was a containable one (or at least, so long as our luck held, it seemed to be). I thought about my father and the despair he must have suffered at the end, and how fortunate I was by comparison. I no longer felt 'different' and almost for the first time found myself in the same boat, as it were, as everyone else.

But not entirely so. On one of my leaves, after a night op followed by a wearisome journey in overcrowded trains, I arrived home late to find my grandmother asleep in a chair, her false teeth half out of her mouth, and Mayna ill in bed. Perhaps this was the moment at which each of us most abjectly let down the other. I had forty-eight hours' leave; for all I knew it might be my last. The rest of my crew had gone on a spree in London. I wanted – well, I don't know what I wanted. Not 'a good time', for sure – I was hopeless at that. Some illusion of security, perhaps, some harbour to come back to. There was scarcely any food in the house. The shops were closed. Beside Mayna's bed were some books of romantic fiction. She didn't want to know about life on a squadron. If she had, I couldn't have told her anything. She had no idea I'd been over Germany a few hours before. I felt like a small boy again, lost and lonely behind my so-called achievements, no golliwog to comfort me. Yet, paradoxically, the fact that this was the way things were provided a kind of rickety scaffolding which would sag but not break; gave to everything a spikier, more mordant outline, like Elizabethan handwriting. It was obscurely satisfying to have no expectations of a future which had such a lugubrious backside. I remember one evening, after a daylight raid on Brest where the flak had been especially bad, lying back on the grass embraced by the warm summer air, the roar of the Merlins distant in my head, looking up at the 'old star-eaten blanket of the sky' and wondering what life would be like when it was all over and the sky was just the sky again and not the arena where we played our deadly games. The sound of Taffy's accordion came floating through the dusk: one of those silly poignant wartime tunes. The others were talking about girls. We wanted girls constantly, of course, but this was the time we needed them – 'I love you in your negligee/ I love you in your nightie/ But when moonlight flits across your tits/ Christ all-bloody mighty!' In the fields round the station the ripe poppy-freckled corn was gently waving, as no doubt it was in Norfolk where Futter, nervous for the harvest, would be sniffing the air for rain. A day of summer slow to die. In my memory it still hasn't died.

Our last trip was to Darmstadt on 11 September – 1,100 track miles there and back, five-and-a-half hours. It was exclusively a Five Group show: 218 Lancs and 14 Mosquitoes.

Bombing was at varying heights from seven different directions, a new technique designed to spread the attack evenly over the city – what the Darmstadters were to call *Der Todesfächer*, The Death Fan. The night was clear, with a strong westerly wind. Flak was light over the target, but there were fighters about on the way back.

Twelve aircraft were lost. As we celebrated the end of our tour, we were as happy as sandboys. We had no real idea what we had helped to do. We knew it had been a successful raid. It had been more than that: we had left behind a fire storm, a little Dresden. The centre of Darmstadt had ceased to exist; it was now a smoking wilderness of shattered buildings and melted bodies. Eight thousand people had died, many of them children. We did not know this. If our masters knew, they did not think it expedient to tell us.

It's easy to say that we should have used our imaginations. But anyone with an imagination was wise to forget it. It was superfluous to requirements in a world where scores of our chums, themselves not long out of childhood, fell out of the sky in blazing aeroplanes. The flak, the searchlights, the fighters, and that eternal enemy the weather, were enough to go on with – spare us the philosophy! Operational flying is a young man's game: most of us were in our teens or early twenties. We gave little thought to what was happening underneath. It has been given to other people to feel the more noble emotions they think – and I once thought – we should have felt. Which may be the reason why Bomber Command was never given a campaign medal although, out of a total of some 125,000 aircrew, 55,500 were killed (almost a seventh of British servicemen's deaths in the war), over 9,800 taken prisoner and a further 8,400 wounded. Only the German U-boat crews suffered greater proportionate losses. I'm no believer in medals, but that was an ungenerous decision.

* * *

In the autumn of 1944 my grandmother died and was taken to join her husband in the peaceful graveyard of St Mary's, Old Hunstanton. Her death was a relief, but it left Mayna even lonelier than before.

During our tour an edict had gone out from Group Headquarters that all bomber captains were to be commissioned. I was summoned before an Air Commodore to be told so: he advised me with some asperity to get my hair cut. It made no difference to us as a crew except that I had to put on another uniform, sleep in another hut and use another mess. But it made a difference to me afterwards because, about the time we finished, it was decided to pep up the training of new crews coming on to squadrons and the records were duly trawled to find an officer with a good degree who might be able to inject some new ideas (though it's not apparent why a good degree should be much of a recommendation in this context). My name was fished up, I was summoned before yet another Air Commodore, jacked up a rank and told to do something about it.

As it happened, I did have some ideas. There were many things I would like to have been told, and hadn't been, before coming on to ops. I was lucky enough to discover that I had a capacity – no doubt inherited – to get on my feet and put them across compellingly. Of course, I had a captive audience. But they were intelligent men and I talked not only about what they needed to know in order to give a good account of themselves, but also about unformulated anxieties which nagged at their minds – in essence, I suppose, the numbing sense under the laughter and the comradeship of being caught up in an impersonal machine without control over one's destiny, and what could be done about *that*. It was the sort of thing the RAF fought shy of; they thought it was unnecessary and would undermine morale – a good binge would do the trick.

Unnecessary it might have been for the first rich flush of crews, but most of those had gone. By 1944 war came less easily. Courage needs to be open-eyed or it slides into its counterfeit, foolhardiness – fool's gold. Bomber crews had no myth to sustain them. Though part of a squadron, they functioned alone, seven ordinary men in an extreme position.

I think I must have done some good because I got an oak leaf to ornament my ribbon. When my stint was over, I was sent on a Flying Instructor's course. Back to stooging about in Oxfords, in the West Country somewhere. Could it have been Lulsgate Bottom? – it sounds appropriate. I thoroughly enjoyed it.

With the coming of peace, I felt, like many others, unaccountably sad, stranded in a strange interlude when the RAF was emptying itself of temporary combatants before returning thankfully to its old bullish existence. The process took an inordinate time but proved a marvellous blessing for me because I met Betty, the girl who became my wife. We spent our honeymoon at Blakeney wandering naked one hot afternoon among the terns' nests on Scolt Head while they dived down on us, screaming defiance. We're old now, but I still get a lift of the spirit when I see her coming into the room. Whatever modern pundits may say, and they say a very great deal on the subject, love in marriage surpasses anything else – 'For nothing is better and more precious than when two of one heart and mind keep house together, husband and wife...'

Betty and I had both been switched into an 'Educational and Vocational Training Scheme' designed to help bridge the gap between the safe war years, when decisions were made for us, and the hazardous post-war England where, back in mufti, many of us would feel diminished and most of us would be poor. I did no more flying, but spent my time trying to organise courses and giving lectures on themes like citizenship and the Beveridge Report – sad pennants these of a brave new world that nobody believed in, least of all bored airmen waiting to be demobbed. They had a vague interest in Beveridge because he offered them a modicum of social justice which they'd never had before, but otherwise they just wanted to go home. However, they needed jobs when they got there and we laid on many useful trade courses with the aid of that astounding pool of talent always to be found in the RAF. Betty set up a Domestic Science School in a commandeered house. The food there was so good that the Group Captain and the Senior Administrative Officer couldn't keep away and this enabled us to get backing for projects that would otherwise have been refused. I liked going there too, and not only for the food.

Eventually the time came for me to collect my trilby hat and my grey suit and my small gratuity and join the ranks of the unemployed. I toyed with things to do – reporter? (I'd taken a book called *Teach Yourself Shorthand* on our honeymoon, but other things had occupied my mind.) Doctor, following my unknown uncle William? Lawyer, in the footsteps of my father? Ghost tracks, plum stones on the side of the plate, dreams on a windy coast. I went hopefully to Cambridge, as I have described, and was disabused. I tried to pass myself off unsuccessfully at John Lewis's as a trainee manager. I rejected advertising on grounds of principle; I rejected schoolmastering on grounds of incompatibility. I went to the Ministry of Labour and asked what I should do. They suggested the Civil Service. This seemed by then as good as anything else and we came to London. We had no money; Betty was expecting a baby and we depended, heaven help us, on what I could earn. It wasn't the London we remembered. It was a drab, diminished city. Wild flowers had invaded the bomb sites and the gutted basements. Rationing – meat, eggs, cheese, milk, sugar, tea, fuel, clothing, even furniture – was more severe than in the War. Spivs haunted the street corners. People were grey and disgruntled, the elation of victory forgotten. The Civil Service was not life-enhancing: I had the wrong sort of mind and, as with all my jobs, it took me a long time to learn how to do it properly. There were no flats to be had. We lived in two rooms in the small semi-detached house of a cousin, who himself had a wife and two children. It was a grim initiation to married life, for Betty especially. I learned from her that pain and discomfort and even pleasure have nothing to do with the essence of love; they ruffle its surface but don't touch its depths. We had each other and, soon, the baby; and, when the coal ration permitted, we sat in front of our own fire and drank cheap Italian wine. We had finished with war and could look forward to an ordinary, blessed, humdrum tomorrow.

VI
SHIFTING SANDS

'We lie more often than we need for lack of imagination: the truth is likewise invented.

Antonio Machado

Twenty-six

Of course our marriage wasn't all plain sailing. Two adults can't settle down together as easily as puppies in a box. Quarrels, tensions, long silences, sexual frustrations, crying children, the cosy sitting room suddenly claustrophobic and afterwards lying side by side in bed having no comfort to give and unwilling to touch, wondering whether it wasn't a terrible mistake. Then marvellously it would all come right. Or nearly right. For Betty, as may be imagined, had some difficulty in getting on terms with my mother. Mayna at first was a woman wounded and jealous, for whose son all other women were unworthy or sly rivals for her own place. But honesty and affection prevailed and, when our first baby grinned toothlessly at her, he healed the wound. For a little while her reclusiveness was set aside, her old gaiety returned and she proudly wheeled him about in his pram along the lanes where she had once wheeled me.

The Civil Service wasn't all plain sailing for me either. After passing the exam, I was left largely to my own devices. We had moved into a little wooden house by the river near Staines and it took a long time to get to the office and back. Sometimes an old ferrymen would row me across the river for a penny. Everyone worked on Saturdays then. When I got to the office, people seemed to get on very well without me and I spent most of my time idly. I read James's *Varieties of Religious Experience* there, and Popper's *Open Society and its Enemies* and Gibbon's *Decline and Fall*. The latter was perhaps a portent, for, at the end of my period of probation, I was summoned again to the big room in Burlington Gardens with a view to being thrown out. By luck I had recently prepared a long memorandum on the doctrinal differences between Orthodox and Liberal Jews arising out of a refusal by the Board of Deputies to allow Liberal Jews to register marriages in their synagogues according to their own rites and ceremonies. This so intrigued the interviewing board that they decided to give me another chance. Duly chastened, I learned to accept that, if life as a civil servant is not real life, at least it is an honourable substitute, and very demanding at times too. I began to speak of 'Our Masters' and acquired the habit of treating them like members of the opposite sex – 'Take this corner seat, Minister, it's less draughty'. In this fashion, as a paid-up member of the bowler hat brigade, I embarked on the long delaying action of the middle years when you are always busy and from which you emerge to find that the options have nearly all closed and the hands which stick out of your sleeves look like your father's.

In February 1951 Mayna died suddenly from a perforated ulcer. We had paid regular visits to Stratton House and brought our babies to console her. She was not well. Her asthma was bad. She suffered from a painful neuralgia. High blood pressure had caused arteries to rupture in the retina so that she was nearly blind. She could no longer live alone and her brother Ernest and his wife came down to look after her. She slept on the ground floor and, when the pain came, her calls weren't heard by the two old people upstairs drowsy with opiates. It was not until morning, after she'd foolishly had a cup of tea, that she was taken to Lynn hospital.

When I reached the hospital she was dead. It was already evening, a scarlet sunset in an ashen sky. I asked to see her. She lay in the morgue, lonely as ever, but peaceful. When I bent to kiss her forehead, it was ice-cold; cotton wool was stuffed in her nostrils. I stayed a little while, an intruder in the silent world of death. Mayna had gone; she wasn't there any more. My status had changed, too: with both father and mother dead, I had ceased to be anybody's son. I went back to Hunstanton and walked for a while by the sea. The waves gleamed in the darkness and the swish of the surf on the shore was like the sound of grieving.

Betty could not come to the funeral because of the children. There was only Ernest and Harrie and me, and one of those stray women in old-fashioned hats who always come to funerals. The service was taken by Charles Wakefield, Vicar of St Edmunds, in whose house I'd drunk South African sherry all those years ago. We took Mayna to be buried in the town cemetery, overlooking the sea. It was a blowy day. Wakefield's cassock swirled about at the graveside and his voice came and went in the gusts. He was old, too, and hadn't long to live. He picked up a handful of the wet, raw earth and it fell with a soft pocking noise on the coffin lid. I thought of the moaning wind in the telephone wires on Redgate Hill above us, and of my childhood.

Mayna was sixty-six. My father had been the centre of her life. After his death, the heart went out of her. Because she had no chance to mourn, she remained locked in a kind of unobtrusive grief. Had you not known her history and heard her spontaneous laughter, you might have seen her as the eternal spinster left at home with mother. She had to bear that burden also, a burden which steadily increased as her mother got older and turned into an unloved and unloving old woman, hostile and suspicious. But nothing could take away the memory of those marvellous stolen years. 'Mac' held the prime place, always, immutably. He may not have deserved such devotion, but he had loved her, as the Russians say, *po-svoyemu*, in his own way, and this sufficed. She loved me too, but I was second best. I knew that and didn't feel let down. In my own heart, curiously perhaps, 'Mr Hardie' also took precedence. I was not conscious of any jealousy, only of my failure to support her when she needed it. She did not find it easy to express her love. Nor did I. This may have led me to think her unfeeling when she was simply shy. She did me the brave courtesy of concealing the worry she must have felt when I was flying. I think in this she was partly protected by ignorance, which also prevented her recognition of my other achievements. There were times when I longed for warmth and never got it. She may have felt the same.

She really did nothing all her life except for my father's sake. She played the piano for him, not for herself. She did not knit or sew. She hated housework and cooking and did only what her mother couldn't do right at the end. When we had the dogs, they, and I, provided company. She had no other friends. She was an inveterate cinema-goer in middle life.

Afterwards it became a matter of organising her day in patterns of idleness. A long time was spent in the lavatory each morning, sitting on the comfortable mahogany seat and smoking. She read romantic novels until her sight became too bad, and listened endlessly to the radio. Latterly she became unwilling to leave the house, agoraphobic almost, wearing dark glasses, as if fearing again the ostracism of the unmarried mother; yet reluctant to come back to a house where nothing awaited her.

The arrival of Harrie and Ernest, whose opinions remained unwaveringly reactionary, helped to liven things up; and our visits with the children meant a great deal to her and turned her mind to the future instead of the past. She did not seem to be bored or especially lonely or unhappy, but I expect she was. At the end she accepted illness and pain without complaint. I wish I'd had a chance to tell her what I never managed to tell, to hug her and to say good-bye.

Twenty-seven

For many years the draft memoir of my father remained in its drawer. And there it might have stayed had I not, in 1973, happened by chance to see an announcement in the deaths column of *The Times*: 'McCARDIE, Esther May, widow of Dr W.J. McCardie of Edgbaston, and beloved mother of Jane, Harry and Derek, in her 90th year' – my father's sister-in-law, and technically my aunt! Allowing no time for second thoughts, I wrote off to the family explaining who I was. I need not have worried. I received by return a welcoming and friendly letter and a few days later, at the age of fifty-four, I met my long-lost cousins for the first time. They were marvellously hospitable. Champagne was broached; the gap closed as if it had never been; I was made to feel like the prodigal son.

Derek, head of the family, was the son of my father's eldest brother, William, the 'uncle' who had been a prime mover in setting up a trust for my education: distinguished in the field of anaesthetics and a pioneer in the use of ethyl chloride, which he is said to have sprayed on his moustache before administering it! I wish I'd known him, for he was a delightful man who 'loved company, easy, gentle, dignified, reliable, skilful, patient and long suffering', with a special sympathy with children (keeping a pocketful of barley sugar sticks for visits to the children's wards). This sympathy was one of a number of characteristics – including a refusal to drive a car, and always sitting in the front seat – that he shared with my father. They were proud of each other's achievements. William was quite content to see his brother garner the greater acclaim; they remained close throughout their lives. Of the other members of the family, only Margaret, my father's favourite sister, seems to have shared in this nearness of participation. The three formed a kind of triumvirate in which decisions of family import were resolved. They shared a lavish life style. Henry's income, before he become a Judge and finally gambled it away, was remarkable, even at the Bar. William had at one time almost a monopoly of anaesthesia for wealthy patients in the Midlands and stories of his professional income were legendary. And Margaret had married a wealthy man, William Allen Bindley, chairman of a successful Birmingham firm which made umbrella frames. It was as well for my father's reputation that his brother and sister were close and protective and determined to preserve the family name, for when the extent of his massive debts became known it was they who were substantially called upon to meet them. He squandered enough for all three and dangerously drained their coffers.

Derek McCardie, who welcomed me back to the fold, was in business – a generous, volatile man, who had commanded a parachute battalion at Arnhem. He gave me a number of photographs and papers (mainly Press cuttings) and told me something of the family background and what he remembered of my father. Unfortunately it wasn't much. My father had spent many summer holidays with them at Harlech, where the two brothers played golf together; but Derek was young – he was only twenty when my father died – and knew him simply as a favourite uncle. Uncles, favourite or wicked, tend to be taken at face value, especially when they are celebrities and unmarried. Derek certainly had no inkling of my existence until much later, and then by inadvertence. Nor had he any knowledge at the time of the extent of my father's debts. Though aware of a sharp retrenchment in his family's household expenses, he hadn't linked this with Dr McCardie's contribution towards baling his brother out.

The McCardies, I learned, were not fecund. In fact there was every likelihood that the name would disappear. Derek's brother Harry was a bachelor. His sister Jane was married and had two sons, but they of course bore her husband's surname. His own two children were girls and would themselves no doubt marry and assume other names – as indeed they have. I took my mother's name. Of my father's six siblings only Margaret, besides William, had children and they were both daughters – Ruth and Peggy, married but childless, in their mid-seventies when I met them.

For upwards of forty years Mrs Bindley, Derek's 'Aunt Maggie', and Ruth after her, had guarded my father's reputation. They were brought up when there was still a taint of social inferiority about 'trade', which affluence couldn't conceal, and Sir Henry McCardie, high in one of the most distinguished professions, was the jewel in the family crown. His suicide was distressing enough. When articles appeared which touched upon his private life and threatened to undermine his public standing, such as those written for *The People* by his confidential clerk and some later slapdash, speculative pieces by Edgar Lustgarten, they had been deeply upset. They wanted him to remain untarnished. As part of this process, Mrs Bindley must, I think, have destroyed the bulk of his private papers, for I cannot believe there were no more than the few that remain. The only document of value that came down to me was an annotated copy of the Statement he prepared (but did not publish) after the Amritsar trial, and some associated letters. Virtually all that was left of him otherwise, apart from a bundle of photographs and Press cuttings, was George Pollock's commemorative book, in which the author left out what he could not praise.

When Betty and I were invited to meet Ruth and her husband, Ronald Sherbrooke-Walker, at the United Services Club, I did not know this. I went there in the hope that she would have many of my father's papers. The Sherbrooke-Walkers were a prosperous, kindly, conventional couple, ardent members of the Sherlock Holmes Society and very devoted: he called her 'Midge'. Wide travel, especially to Kenya and South Africa, had made them accustomed to probing the social background of a new acquaintance, careful not to be too friendly in case it turned out to be the wrong one; I don't think either of them had come to terms with the brash, post-imperial, welfare-oriented consumer society ushered in after the War. Ronald had served in the old RFC and been shot down behind the German lines in 1916 – the year of McCardie's elevation to the Bench – so that we had some flying experience in common. For work with the Army Cadet Force, he had received the CBE. By profession he was a chartered accountant. He wasn't much interested in McCardie, but he was a stickler for the proprieties and, so far as the private life of his wife's uncle was concerned, in his opinion, the less said the better – once one starts to lift stones, heaven knows what may be running around underneath.

Ruth was in full agreement. Not only that, she strongly pressed me not to advertise for reminiscences or other material from people who might have known McCardie. And, if she knew any more herself, it was pretty obvious she wasn't going to let on. I was taken aback by her reluctance to contemplate anything from me but another encomium, Pollock Mark II. It wasn't simply a matter of social conformity, though like her mother she had an almost morbid addiction to respectability. She had made a heavy emotional investment in her splendid uncle. So, to a lesser extent, had her sister Peggie, who, I found later, still kept a little cache of letters he had sent her in her teens. The McCardie family were tremendous coverers-up, a trait my father fully shared. Even Derek had spoken of my 'taking up the cudgels' on his behalf. Certainly in Ruth's eyes, the purpose of any memoir would not be to uncover the truth, but to re-embellish my father's reputation. It did not occur to her that his memory could better be honoured by pulling up the blinds and letting in the light. Nor, I suspect, had she made any room in her private pantheon for Mayna and me. Kind as she was, she never enquired, and I doubt if she ever wondered, how we might have felt. She was a just woman, but her friendship was, as it were, precautionary. Her loyalty I respected, and of her abiding affection for her uncle there was no doubt. She remembered trips to the theatre with him – José Collins (the cold wash of the sea beneath that Norfolk pier still undreamed of) singing in *The Last Waltz* at the Gaiety – and she was the last of the family to speak to him before he died: he was ill in his flat and she took him a bunch of violets. She wanted others to see him as she saw him. A mistress and an illegitimate child may seem a small enough peccadillo in the perspective of half a century – after all, respectable (which is to say, propertied) men like Wilkie Collins and George Cruikshank and Alfred Ackerley kept mistresses just round the corner from their wives, not cocottes, but comfortable, workaday women with plenty of children. But Ruth took a more austere view. It is difficult to imagine that I could have written anything about her uncle which would be acceptable to her unless I'd omitted all mention of my mother and myself. We were dents in the image. I was not prepared to hammer them out; she would have been horrified if they'd been left in. Ronald didn't depart from the view that, when there was a skeleton in the cupboard, the right thing was to keep the door shut. So, though none of us said so and we continued to write to each other from time to time, resumption of the memoir was shelved once more. An honest account would have been deeply hurtful so long as Ruth and Peggie were alive.

Life jogged along, we and the McCardies slid into a comfortable cousinly relationship – not meeting often, but keeping in touch. In due course mortality took its toll. Derek died, then Ruth and Ronald and Peggie; only Harry and Jane McCardie of their generation now remained. The way was clear for the memoir, but I was slothful. Though my father's ghost had not been laid, he only occasionally troubled me – for instance, when I received a letter from my fey wartime night companion at Hunstanton Town Hall, to tell me that he had walked in his ermine out of a wardrobe in her home and spoken to her. She and Geoff now lived in a sad house in Essex where we went to see them; but McCardie didn't appear again. I had retired by now and my energy was depleted. I would have subsided into a final phase of gardening and week-end breaks and crossword puzzles, the memoir uncompleted, had not an extraordinary event occurred. Extraordinary for me, that is, for of itself it was the sort of thing that happens every day – the publication of a book.

The book, entitled *Jigsaw*, was by Sybille Bedford and came out in paperback in the autumn of 1990. It was described as a biographical novel – an uneasy genre because the reader can never be quite sure what in the book is fact and what is fiction. Certain characters, as the author explained, appear as themselves under their own names. Others, who appear under different names, 'are to a large extent themselves'. Yet others 'are a percentage of themselves'. The book was an absorbing evocation of the 1920s and was shortlisted for the Booker Prize.

One of my lately acquired second cousins, Amanda McCardie (now Amanda Parker), happened by chance to read the book and was astonished to find in it a character called the Judge, one of those who were 'to a large extent themselves' for he was quite obviously her great-uncle, Mr Justice McCardie. In the book he is generally referred to as 'Jack' (echo of 'Mac'?), but in one chapter the author lets out that 'Henry' was his real first name. There was no mistaking him – the short compact figure, the senatorial head, the witticisms regularly reported in the newspapers, the passion for social reform, the gambling, the suicide, the flat in Queen Anne's Mansions, all were there. A lot more was there as well: most notably, one of Sybille Bedford's friends, older than she was, of course, but a woman with whom she was on intimate terms, was the Judge's mistress! Her name in the book is Rosie Falkenheim. Her actual name was Kate, and I shall call her Kate from now on. Through her, Sybille met McCardie. When she was seventeen, she twice lunched with him at Sanary in the south of France; and came to learn later of his gambling and an attempted suicide which was hushed up. It was Kate who had found him slumped in his flat after he shot himself.

Amanda knew about Mayna, and Kate clearly wasn't she. There was no mention of Mayna or anyone like her in the book, or of a child. Had Kate known about us, she would have told Sybille, for she held nothing back; and Sybille would have said so. Her account of Kate would otherwise not have made sense. If therefore what was said in *Jigsaw* about her was fact, not fiction, my father must have had a secret life of which Mayna and I were entirely ignorant. Kate in her turn must have been entirely ignorant of us. So Amanda wrote to Sybille Bedford to ask if it *were* true. Sybille confirmed that it was. Amanda then told me, and together we came to see Sybille and talk to her. She was as interested in our story as we were in hers. Although McCardie's story played a minor part in her book, it was a significant one because of her friendship with Kate, because his relationship with Kate was so fascinating and because Sybille herself had written much about Judges. She was intrigued by them, the way their minds worked, the drama of the Courts. McCardie was the first one she'd met and he had left his mark.

What Sybille said about my father was so familiar, and her account of his association with Kate fitted so neatly in the matter of timing, that I could not fail to believe it. It might have been a piece cut out from my own jigsaw. The picture changed in front of my eyes like one of those optical illusions so beloved by psychologists. While I knew that circumstances for Mayna and me must in fact have been as I remembered them, they suddenly looked different. The warm, affectionate Mr Hardie whom I'd treasured in my heart turned into someone I hadn't really known at all. Had Mayna really known him either? Or Kate? Would either have behaved differently if each had known about the other? Mayna had little choice; but I'm sure that, already isolated, she would have been desolate. McCardie must have known that: he deceived her so lovingly. It would have been cruel to tell her as well as unintelligent. He hoped to get by undetected. I would have been deeply upset on Mayna's behalf, had I known then. Now, when I'd got over my astonishment, I found I didn't mind. It both hurt and made me laugh, like iodine in a cut. And in a curious way it brought my father closer. Something conspiratorial crept into the bed-time kiss, and Mr Hardie's piercing eyes had a new, sad twinkle in them.

Another thought strikes me. Among the items which came down to me from Mayna was a packet of German banknotes of enormously high denominations – 500,000 marks, one million marks, two million marks – clearly products of the post-war German inflation which had wiped out Kate's family's fortune. I came across these notes the other day. They seemed odd things for Mayna to possess and I used to wonder where they came from. Could it be that Kate gave them to my father and he gave them to Mayna? That would be an extraordinary link between the two women who knew nothing of each other!

What about Mrs Bindley and her daughters? How much did they know? I have a letter Derek McCardie sent to Peggie Bindley when her mother died in 1949 in which he refers to 'the secrets you are now discovering... Aunt Maggie was an extremely gallant and courageous lady [who] guarded and protected her family as very few people could or would have done.' He went on to speak of 'this fearful shock'. The secrets, the fearful shock, couldn't surely have been Mayna and me – we scarcely deserve such a roll of drums. Indeed, Derek told me that he did not know of my existence until some years later. Was it the attempted suicide? Was it the discovery of the liaison with Kate? Was it blackmail, which has more than once been suggested? Whatever it was, it may well have accounted for Ruth's circumspect talk at the United Services Club – an apparent frankness, but in reality a careful exercise in damage limitation.

The following extract is taken from Sybille Bedford's introduction to the second edition of Jigsaw, published in 1999. It was added by Elizabeth Archer after Henry Archer's death.

Within weeks of [the] publication [of *Jigsaw*], a very unexpected light was cast on a prominent player in the sub-plot, the Sisters' story. He was a judge, a real live High Court judge, well-known in his time as brilliant, eloquent, somewhat controversial: great fodder for the Press. What was heard off the bench on a morning could often be read in the evening papers. In fact, the Press knew nothing, but nothing, of his private life. Today it would have bloated the headlines. A few people *must* have known something; each would have come across one or another fragment of the truth. I, by the oddness of his circumstances, got to know a part of what seemed the core of it, 'the Judge's story', such as I told it in the present novel. There, I strictly stuck to what I knew at first hand, which was little enough, if enormous in terms of the Judge's position and career. These I saw as safe – he had died in the early 1930s, and indeed for the next fifty years nothing of my end of the story appeared to have surfaced. Not so after *Jigsaw*. A friend, a very sharp-minded QC, confronted me with a straight inquiry. I was summoned –

dinner at the Reform – cross-examined: the Judge in the novel *must* have been, could not have been other than, unadulterated Judge X. He, my QC friend, put a few data together; I conceded. He was right. (And not going to proclaim it from the roof tops. One may feel smug enough knowing something others don't.) We sat on, speculating on the wonders of the cover-up. However, this was far from being that was that. Within days I was approached by a young woman who baldly declared herself, name and all, to be our Judge's great-niece, professing affectionate memories of her uncle and no knowledge whatsoever of my facts about his life. She proposed to come and see me. We settled for a day and a time. She would bring a surprise, she said, a big surprise. I would be unprepared – she would not prepare me.

When the bell rang, there were two strangers on the doorstep, a young woman and a man, a pleasant, quiet man, he turned out to be, a retired civil servant, of nearer seventy, one guessed, than sixty. She introduced him as the Judge's natural son. And here we had the pivot of another story – one judge, two stories, parallel much of the time, two halves each ignorant of the other. No whiff of the son's existence ever reached the sisters, none of theirs ever reached the son. Now *he* had read *Jigsaw* and *I*, the sisters' surviving witness, soon read the typescript of the son's autobiography which tells, and tells it well, his half of the tale of what must have been quite a feat of double deception by an attractive and well-liked public man.

I got to like the son – he shares his father's first name (which will not be found in the book) – I talked to his wife. I still hope that his autobiography, which contains a good deal more than his parents' story, will be published. All of this has left me with a puzzled sense about the relativity of given truth.

Twenty-eight

The account of my father's relationship with Kate rests upon Sybille Bedford's story. Without her book I should have known nothing about it. She told the story from Kate's point of view; I shall try and tell it from McCardie's. As with all stories, its shadows change when seen in different lights.

In the years before the 1914 War, the years of high-waisted women and the ripple of top hats, the 'happy years' when McCardie reached the height of his success as a barrister, he was, as I've mentioned, accustomed to go abroad for some of the long vacation. He was unencumbered by any obligations. He relished the travel and a spree at the tables. He liked to spend part of his holiday at some fashionable resort, it might be Vevey between the mountains and the lake: Switzerland was a favourite place. The sense of affluence, the murmur of voices in many European tongues, the elegant women, and the social life with its powerful sexual undertow provided an ideal diversion before he returned to the unremitting slog of No. 2 The Cloisters.

On one such holiday in 1912, he met a family from Berlin – a doctor's widow, and her two daughters. He was staying, as always, at an expensive hotel, with balconied rooms overlooking the lake. The family had rooms on the same floor. They spoke English. The younger daughter was very pretty, the elder daughter was not; she was an animated and intelligent girl with an ungraceful figure. He attached himself to the pretty daughter and they made a handsome pair. In my childhood summers, I remember, he often wore an old panama hat of which he was extremely fond. He looked well in it: it may have dated from those days.

The mother was delighted and although he was a Goy (the family were Jewish) he was charming and amusing, and it was, after all, just a summer flirtation with her pretty daughter: tennis, trips on the lake, dancing in the evening. The elder daughter went her own way.

The family returned to the same resort next year, and so did McCardie. They took the same rooms, their friendship was resumed. Again he squired the younger daughter; he enjoyed her company and it was pleasant to be seen with a pretty girl. She liked him, she was charmed and flattered, but they were never intimate — her real affinity was with Jews; and music was her central interest. As her mother had foreseen, she did not take him seriously as a suitor. She was content to flirt and so was he. Which was prudent, because he was in fact her sister's lover. It was only a short journey along the balconies to Kate's room, where the window was left open for him. In the morning, as the mist was lifting from the lake, he returned the same way. The clandestine embraces and the danger of discovery added spice to the affair. (When, much later, Kate's sister discovered the deception, her pride was bitterly hurt; she did not have a forgiving nature and she never forgave McCardie. 'That man!' she would say.)

The following summer the women came again, but left early. McCardie did not come at all. It was 1914. But he didn't forget Kate. He wrote to her and she to him. They managed to correspond throughout the war, appropriately via Switzerland.

Meanwhile he wasn't left unconsoled. Mayna was still there. His liaison with her had been firmly established before the War and continued during it; the affair with Kate was, as it were, an agreeable supplement. When he was made a High Court Judge in 1916, he suddenly had more time on his hands and he arranged, as described earlier, for Mayna to come up to London and live in a service flat close to his own. Slipping down the corridor in Queen Anne's Mansions might not offer the same challenge as shinning over balconies in Switzerland, but he was getting less agile; and the zesty risk of exposure was no less, indeed rather greater now he was a Judge. It was a convenient arrangement which might have continued for longer had he not taken a risk too many and made Mayna pregnant. When her condition could no longer be hidden, she went down to Bournemouth to have the baby, having refused McCardie's offer of marriage with, I think, relief on both sides.

By now it was 1919. The War was over and longer-term plans had to be made. Manifestly Mayna could not come back to Queen Anne's Mansions with me; apart from the impropriety, my bawling would have destroyed the consolation my father was accustomed to receive after a hard day in Court and, more often than not, a demanding evening engagement. No, the proper place for Mayna and, the child was with her family in Norfolk. Stratton House was purchased as I've recounted, and she moved there with her parents, comfortably tucked away. He would make regular week-end visits down the familiar line from Liverpool Street and stay, as before, at the Sandringham Hotel. A little golf wouldn't come amiss. It would be a simulacrum of the old days.

But this left a gap in London. He had grown used to the comfort of warm arms and a sympathetic ear. With Mayna gone, he missed them more and more. There was a possible remedy: he turned to Kate. She was more than willing to provide them. She still loved him. No-one else had taken his place. She got on well with men, she was sexually attractive, she had other affairs; although her looks told against her. Sybille has described her as having, in her thirties, 'a long, sallow, vaguely simian face, some hard crinkly hair, small brown eyes that were humorous rather than sad, and a not very good figure. Clothes hung badly. If you stretched the definition you might just have called her a *jolie laide*'. Kate could see what would become of her if she allowed herself to go on loving McCardie but did nothing when he needed her. She wanted him; Berlin in the early 'twenties held nothing for her. He was making her a kind of proposal; she might never get another. The decision almost made itself: she left her family home and her job in an art gallery and came to England. As a Jewess and a German – so soon after the War, when feelings still ran high – a flat in the Mansions did not seem apt. She would have been a fish out of water and deplorably conspicuous. Nor would she have wanted it. She was a more independent woman than Mayna, a product of the liberal, materially indulgent upper bourgeoisie, who expected to have a place of her own. So she took one room in lodgings in Upper Gloucester Place, where she installed her own furniture. She ordered *The Times* and prepared to enjoy London and such freedom as her allegiance to my father allowed. When he wanted her, she would go to him. She came and went unobtrusively. In the evening she dressed formally, as Mayna had done: he liked that. Did he help her with money? Almost certainly. She brought practically nothing from Berlin and she only worked part-time in her brother-in-law's antiquarian bookshop in London. Though she lived modestly, she always seemed to Sybille to have enough to live in reasonable comfort. Before long, gambling and the 1929 New York stock market crash were to wipe out McCardie's assets, too. Heavily in debt, with a reduced salary and no capital, by a quirk of fortune he had in the end to look to her for money, as he did to Mayna. Neither, of course, had more than a tiny fraction of the resources needed to bale him out. They were helpless witnesses to a slide into bankruptcy they could do nothing to prevent.

McCardie's suicide left Kate, like Mayna, grief-stricken, shocked. It was *she* who first discovered him, his skull blown away, dead in his chair. She left unseen and, heroically, telephoned the Mansions from a public box, purporting to be a typist who had an appointment with him but could not get an answer. Strangely, no-one disputed her story and her association with McCardie never emerged. But life had lost its savour; there was nothing more for her except to live it out. She had to take a job again because she had to earn her keep. By this time she had moved in with her sister, who had followed her to England with her Scottish husband, from whom she was now divorced. There they were, two middle-aged Jewish ladies, speaking English with the delicate German accent that always suggests intellectual vigour and high culture, walking with their little wire-haired terrier near Parliament Hill. I've seen so many like them and wondered so often what tide of fortune had carried them there.

In the social circles in which McCardie moved by virtue of his achievements, affairs were generally winked at so long as you were not found out. Whether a man kept a mistress in St John's Wood or took a guardsman in the park was a matter for him. It was public scandal they could not forgive. Judges in particular were expected to be above reproach. McCardie's own family did not in principle share this permissive view, but they strongly endorsed it in practice, as Mayna discovered. And McCardie himself was well aware that he had to safeguard his reputation if he was to continue the work which meant so much to him, whether as a Judge or a reformer. Had he been occasionally promiscuous, there would have been no problem. But his affairs – or rather his intimate friendships – with Mayna and Kate were not like that. No doubt his first efforts had been bent towards achieving what most men want to do, to get them into bed; but he was after much more than physical satisfaction, he wanted companionship, the special, sexually permeated companionship which a woman can give. He wanted it on his own terms; he didn't want marriage. As a handsome and successful man, attractive to women, he knew himself to be a good marital catch, and he had made sure he wasn't caught. Only his sense of honour or shame (perhaps both) made him suggest marriage to Mayna when she became pregnant, and I'm certain he didn't press the matter with any enthusiasm. There is a passage in one of Chekhov's letters to Alexei Suvorin written on 23 March, 1895, which could well have found an echo in McCardie:

> I can't stand happiness that goes on day after day, from one morning to the next. When a person keeps on telling me the same thing every day, in exactly the same tone of voice, I begin to feel violent. That's how I feel, for example, when I'm with Sergeyenko [an old school friend]. He's very much like a woman ('intelligent and responsive') and when we're together I can't help thinking that I might get a wife who was like that... Give me a wife like the moon, who won't appear in my sky every day.

McCardie's long experience at the Bar and his stint in the Divorce Court had given him every reason to be wary – 'By binding himself in matrimony,' he once remarked, 'a man receives little or no benefit from the law. He incurs responsibilities so vast that no man could contemplate them without the rosy-tinted spectacles of love.' But I'm sure there were more deep-seated reasons which made him suspicious, possibly afraid, of marriage. He chose two women – a beautiful working-class girl (though with a middle-class polish) and a cultivated, unhandsome German Jewess – who were both plainly unsuitable to be his wife. They knew this. They knew that the virulent snobbery of the time in Mayna's case and, in Kate's, the anti-Semitism jokily disguised ('the tribe of Moses') made marriage to either unpropitious, to say the least. The beef-witted son of a viscount, snug in the complacent world of the hunt ball and the point-to-point, could marry a chorus girl and not give a damn; an Irish merchant's son who'd left school at sixteen was infinitely less secure. With Mayna and Kate he was safe against matrimonial attack. And he was shielded against it from more conventional directions by his established position as the 'Bachelor Judge'. Social status, and the impressive mummery of the law which helped to endow him with it, meant much to him. 'Henry would never *not* conform,' Kate's sister said, 'except in private.' Neither Mayna nor Kate – it might have been different with Kate's sister, as McCardie had sensed – wanted to compromise him or risk their peace of mind in a bid for a fragile respectability. They never expected to marry him, however much in their secret hearts they might sometimes wish things had been otherwise. They had no illusions about their place in his life. His work and his standing in the world came first and they came second. This, in his view, was as it should be.

Things worked out extraordinarily well for him. My arrival proved a godsend in fact, once there was no sign of the secret getting out. I would grow up, of course, which might require some tricky assimilation, but that was a long way off. Meanwhile, as a father he couldn't help but feel a certain pride when he went down to Bournemouth to see me gurgling in my pram. Pride, but also restlessness. He was fifty, less susceptible to the innocent charm of Mayna, whose youth had fluttered by and departed, and more attracted by the sophisticated Kate, whose letters, bridging the war years, revived carefree memories. Mayna was still pretty – hair bobbed now – but not cultured; Kate was cultured but not pretty. My father did not have to choose between them, he could have both – and without conditions. Dissimilar physically except for the same high cheek bones and narrow eyes, they were essentially alike in temperament. Both were quite undomesticated; Kate, like Mayna, never lifted an iron and rarely boiled an egg. Both demanded nothing from him except to fulfil his needs, dressing up for him in the evening (I suspect a certain fetishism –

witness his notorious pronouncements on women's clothes), prepared to live, so far as he was concerned, in virtual isolation, to be taken nowhere, to meet no-one. There was good reason for concealment, perhaps – but few women, despite his tenderness and affection, would have been so tame.

Thus a rough and ready routine was established which was to last until his death – town wife and country wife, but without the psychological investment that real wives would involve. The symmetry must have appealed to him, emotionally and intellectually; in some degree they represented two sides of his own character. Mayna had an advantage over Kate because of my existence, which strengthened a bond that might otherwise have weakened, and because of her status as the senior mistress. McCardie came to join us, operating of course from the best hotels, on the annual seaside holidays I have described. After Switzerland Kate had only one holiday with him, described by Sybille in her book, at Sanary, where he loved to watch the pretty girls on the beach and where she was invited to lunch with them and they drank burgundy together. Afterwards Kate said to her, as near as maybe: 'This is the first time – since all those years ago in Switzerland when he was a young man – that we have ever *not* been alone together. I never see him with anyone, I never hear him talk to anyone, other than a waiter or a jury, I didn't know what he was like in company ... you are the only human being I have seen him sitting at a table with, this is the only time I heard him talk to someone *I* know. You cannot understand what this means to me.' Mayna would have understood. And so would I.

Twenty-nine

On the face of it my father's behaviour towards Mayna and Kate was insensitive, to say the least, and marked by uncharacteristic duplicity. Philandering abroad whilst Mayna stood by in England; sleeping with Kate whilst paying court to her sister; sending love letters to Kate whilst sleeping with Mayna; packing off Mayna when she was pregnant and summoning Kate in her place; carefully concealing from each the existence of the other; introducing neither to any of his friends or acquaintances; playing the part meanwhile of moralist from the Bench and of paragon to his family. A deplorable catalogue. But I don't suppose he saw it this way. I expect he regarded it rather as a sensible response to how things were – endowed, given his temperament, with added appeal by the hazard of possible discovery and the pleasure of keeping a number of balls spinning in the air at the same time. He may have enjoyed secrecy for its own sake. Some people do. He was middle-aged now, when we all have something to hide. Why make everyone unhappy in order to ease his conscience, or rather to ease the conscience that others felt he ought to have? He was a clear-minded man who saw no point in trying to reconcile irreconcilable things. Far better to deal with each set of circumstances on its merits and fend off any awkward explanations with a few fibs. The longer explanations are put off, the less indispensable they seem.

In fact I'm not sure that the arrangements he entered into, for all their apparent oddity, did not satisfy the deeper instincts of all parties. They certainly satisfied his own. His family were well content to bask in his achievement and proved resolute to protect his reputation when it was threatened. Mayna loved him. He took for granted too easily the sacrifices she made for him – he kept her virtually in purdah; her capacity to make an alternative life in London was negligible, her life in Norfolk circumscribed and friendless. Nevertheless I can testify to his constant kindness and tenderness. His relationship with her remained warm and loving. – He continued to spend much time with her. He brought her gifts. His surviving letter to her (albeit asking for money) was written in terms which presuppose a long intimacy. I cannot speak for Kate, whose position was less extreme. Although she did not know many people, she was able to make use of London, its galleries, theatres and restaurants, and her sister and husband came to live nearby. Everything suggests, however, that her relationship with McCardie, apart from one brief questionable episode which I shall come to, remained as warm and easy as Mayna's. He dictated to them both how they should live and they obeyed, each knowing that she had a corner of his heart, a place exclusively her own.

To keep one's life in separate boxes works all right so long as things are going well. But in my father's case there was the fatal destructive urge which threatened increasingly to blow the lid off and expose everything. He had always been a gambler, like his father. Even at the Bar, he had gambled, sometimes heavily. But the burden of work he supported and the nature of the job, in which each case is charged with risk, and the knowledge that he could pick up fees virtually for the asking, allowed him to indulge his craving for play without much danger. It was not yet compulsive. The danger came after his ascent to the Bench. All achievements bring some measure of disillusion and judicial life proved perilously peaceful after a decade and more of almost unendurable strain. It left a disturbing vacuum. McCardie had no domestic security to cushion or protect him against the sudden loss of pressure; he was, as it were, left homeless in his tiny flat, deprived of the daily tourneys, one of whose prime attractions was the excitement inherent in their pursuit. Not many cases, at least after his spell in the Divorce Court, made intellectual demands or seriously taxed his knowledge of the law. When they did, he made a meal of them, loading down his judgements with precedent – a tendency, as C.P. Harvey said, sometimes encouraged by Counsel who, knowing his propensities, sought to arouse a favourable interest by citing a number of authorities not easily reconcilable and inviting him to sort them out, which he was only too glad to do. Sometimes, in passing, he would be deliberately provocative. Though he had no objection to stirring up trouble, it wasn't provocation for its own sake – he espoused the causes he believed in with a passion that did not extend to his women – but coming from the Bench it was provocation just the same.

 He did his best in other ways to stave off the urge to gamble by filling his time up to the brim; the earlier account of his routine after the day in Court was over would suggest that this would be more than enough for most men! But it was not enough for him. Like Trollope, he was afraid of two things above all – loneliness and boredom. Mayna and Kate helped him to fend off loneliness, but the consolation they could offer was not conjugal and did not go deep enough. Boredom was always waiting in the wings, a metaphysical torment which animals in captivity can die of and which could drive him relentlessly towards his addiction. His depressive temperament, which spurred him to achievement, also made him dangerously dependent on success and vulnerable to criticism, however much he might pretend otherwise. A 'flight into work' is the classic means to keep encroaching fears at bay. Hence his insensate industry. But when that failed, there was only one sure way of blotting them out – to gamble deep, more than he could afford to lose, to enter another secret life which made the daily treadmill silly and dull and brought that marvellous buzz.

Once embarked upon, the desire to gamble became intense and impossible to control. The size and frequency of bets had to be constantly increased to achieve the necessary level of excitement; the more money lost, the more acute the need to try to win it back – the fatal 'chasing' syndrome. By now he could not stop; to win was not the point: winning meant only there was more to risk. There is only one end to such a cycle: to hit rock bottom. The compulsive gambler is playing to lose; it is a kind of death wish. The realisation at last that everything has gone brings a suicidal depression. McCardie must have been fully aware of the folly of what he was doing. The laws of probability offered no precedent to support him. He was laying on the line not only his private fortune, but his whole career and reputation, a lifetime of achievement. It seems absurd that such a rational man could have behaved so. But what is irrational isn't subject to rational control. He only knew that he had to gamble with all he had to feel emotionally alive, to recapture some lost intensity of experience.

Kate, if not Mayna, knew how far he was a risk-taker. It had added to his charm, given an edge to it, brought him to her bed. What she didn't know, until she came to London, was the scale of risk he was prepared to take, the power of the genie once it got out of the bottle. Then it frightened her, but by then neither he nor she had any power to control it. After they came back from their holiday in France, she was having tea with Sybille one winter afternoon when she started to talk about his gambling, lulled perhaps by an illusion that the holiday had muted the restlessness which plagued him and that other holidays together might lay it by the heels. Sybille describes in her book the gist of what Kate (alias Rosie) said:

> 'I knew he had worries but he wouldn't tell me what they were. Then one day he did: he was owing a large sum of money, more, far more than he could pay.'

For some months he had been losing, and losing again:

horses and cards. (He gambled in private houses, never at a club, though abroad he played in casinos at whatever was going, chemin de fer, roulette.) He was owing his bookmaker, he was owing friends, people who trusted him. But now he thought he could see a way out, there was a race coming up, he had been told of a horse... He would scrape together such credit as he still had. Rosie pressed her savings on him, he took them – they weren't much, every hundred counted, he told her, with that horse: if it won, he'd re-coup himself.

It didn't. The week after, he told Rosie he was going away for a few days to sort things out in his mind. He left her thinking he was going to stay with some cronies in Gloucestershire. Instead he went to a country hotel and took an overdose. By a miracle he was discovered in time, rushed to a nursing home and eventually revived; another miracle, the whole thing, suicide attempt, gambling debts and all, was kept out of the press, hushed up with the help of colleagues, connections, friends. Other friends stumped up the money. The whole of it. He was alive, he was free; rumours there had been, yet his career was intact.

They made him give his word never to bet on a horse again, never to touch a card.

'He hasn't, of course. He can't. At first he was so relieved. The awful threat gone. Everything again before him... That did not last. Now he misses it most of the time. It is very hard.'

Against this account of attempted suicide there must be some question mark. Although Sybille testifies to its essential truth, it was a long time ago and it is hearsay. Stories get embroidered and some of the emphasis here is wrong – the word 'cronies', for instance, seems inapt and McCardie never to my knowledge showed an interest in card games (though baccarat may have been different). He never played cards with me, nor did he play bridge. I have found no evidence of the episode elsewhere. But then, if it was all hushed up, I wouldn't. If Ruth Sherbrooke-Walker knew, she did not tell. So far as I can ascertain, McCardie was only once in hospital – when on circuit in February 1928 he was admitted urgently to the Clifton Nursing Home, Bristol, for a gall-stone operation. Had he been taken into such a prestigious institution after an overdose, it is hard to imagine that the story would not have got out. A small private home, probably now defunct, is more plausible. The background fits in with my own memory of going with him to a greyhound stadium. My father was certainly gambling at that time, uninhibited by any promises. I must have been at least ten, which would make it 1929 – a boom year just before the bubble burst. No word of anything untoward reached me then. Mr Hardie appeared as generous as ever, his visits and our holidays with him apparently untroubled; and Mayna showed no overt signs of anxiety – very different from her concern in November, 1930, when he wrote the letter quoted earlier, and her dismay in the following years when he touched the palm of insolvency and borrowed (or borrowed back, I should say) more and more from her. Perhaps, if a first steep plunge into debt and an attempted suicide occurred, Mayna might not have known. It seems unlikely; but she was unsophisticated, in less frequent touch with him than Kate, and it is possible. He wasn't a man to burden her with unnecessary information.

Sybille mentioned another story about my father – one which does not appear in her book and against which a larger question mark must remain. Kate told her that a year or so before his death, he had fallen in love with a woman, half French, half Irish, who attempted to blackmail him; had indeed been set up for the purpose. His salary of £5,000 a year was wealth in the thirties. When he learned the truth, he was devastated, not only emotionally, but in his self-esteem, already wobbly.

If there *was* such a third woman, clever and sexually attractive – and there seems no reason for Kate (or Sybille) to invent her – it would have gone hard with my father. A man who falls in love in his sixties gets the disease badly: shingles instead of chicken pox. For a gambler on the downslope of his years it would be like a draught of youth, an ardent counter-claim seeming to offer a miraculous escape from his addiction. If she let him down, the blow would have been devastating; he no longer had the resilience to recover from the hurt. If she tried to blackmail him, it would have been a knife turned in the wound. He was all too vulnerable to blackmail which, if not acceded to, could have swiftly destroyed the reputation that meant everything to him. He had by now little enough to pay over, but she could have taken what little he still had. Whether she did, Sybille wasn't told. In the last months of his life he turned again to Kate and, in desperation, to more reckless gambling. It was all the Stock Exchange now. He had never promised to give that up. That was not betting, but investment – as Ambrose Bierce observed: 'The gambling known as business looks with austere disfavour on the business known as gambling.' The distinction was clearly defensible in my father's mind: he wasn't a lawyer for nothing. But the effect was equally disastrous – it was the Hatry crash all over again, this time without reserves. Kate nursed the illusion that, if he went bankrupt, they could retire together to Australia or some such place and he could continue his reforming work. He had floated the idea to console her. It was a pipe dream, and he knew it.

Mayna, remote from the centre, knew nothing of any other woman, and Sybille, as I say, did not include this further revelation in her book. It would, she said, have upset the balance. There may have been another reason – it seems hard to believe. Her book was half a novel, and one of the problems of a novelist is to endow with credibility the astonishing things which happen in real life. This story is implausible, so implausible that it could well be true. Elderly men do fall for younger women, especially those who set out to catch them, and captivating women of part French and part Irish extraction do exist, however romantic it may sound. There were constant rumours at the time of McCardie's death that he was being blackmailed. This may be because men, like Sir Gervais Rentoul, were casting about for more persuasive explanations of his suicide than those publicly offered at the time. Such rumours are often artificially bolstered up because people quote each other, but Montgomery Hyde refers in his biography of Birkett to 'the subsequent confession of two notorious blackmailers that they had obtained money from him [McCardie] by this vile means'. Unfortunately he gives no details. Interestingly, Pollock mentions in his book that

> McCardie tried a gang of three blackmailers at the Old Bailey, consisting of an attractive young woman of twenty-five and two men... Her counsel tried hard to establish that she was simply the dupe of her two male confederates, but McCardie by his analysis of the evidence showed pretty clearly that she was anything but a passive partner and, when all three were found guilty by the jury, he sentenced them all to penal servitude.

Again no details. But there is a suspicious echo here. Probably we shall never know the truth.

As I write of these last years, I am even more acutely conscious of the want of sufficient information. I've hazarded too many conjectures about his private life as it is; there's a danger of attaching more importance to that than to his work. But I make no apology. His life was robust enough, interesting enough, quirky enough and, at the end, tragic enough, to deserve an account much more than merely complimentary.

VII
SUMMING UP

I listened to the doctor and, according to my habit, applied my usual measures to him – materialist, idealist, money-grubber, herd instincts and so forth, but not a single one of my measures would fit, even approximately; and, curiously, while I only listened to him and looked at him, he was, as a man, perfectly clear to me, but the moment I began applying my measures to him he became, despite all his sincerity and simplicity, an extraordinarily complex, confused and inexplicable nature.

Anton Chekhov, *The Wife*

Anyone who tries to draw a portrait finds himself drawing more than one person. My father was hard to pin down, possessing to a singular degree the art of disguising reticence by apparent confidence and a companionable charm. Most of the friendships with which people nourish their lives are probably more superficial than their reminiscences lead us to suppose, and, for all his wide acquaintance, my father was a lonely man. Mayna and Kate and his clerk, Philip McCann, and his sister Maggie and his cousin James McCardie Martin were as close to him as anyone; he still must have concealed a great deal from them. One so adept at covering up his tracks must also, I'm sure, have concealed a great deal from me. But, as I've slowly both discovered him and found him out, I seem almost to have come upon the place where he really was, behind his masks. (According to Lord Radcliffe, the Judge, like a Greek actor should always speak from behind a mask. The mask my father wore on the Bench was only one of many; but it was the one which, unfortunately for his *réclame* in the part, he was most often tempted to drop.)

I like to think of him in his less guarded moments – the schoolboy playing in the Victorian sunshine at his grandfather's house in Wirksworth; the youthful versifier on the beach at Aberystwyth; the fledgeling barrister on the Midland Circuit fiddling with his wig; the driven advocate working until the early hours at 2 The Cloisters, watching a mouse come out to eat the crumbs he'd spread for it; the spry escort in his panama by the lakeside; the secret lover slipping along the balconies to claim from Kate 'midnight's kind admittance';

the gambler lured to the tables to play for stakes too high; the war-time romance with Mayna and that May night when they embraced without thinking what they were about, and produced me; the newly dubbed Sir Henry (face fresh lathered in Erasmic soap with a silver shaving brush I still have) walking briskly, bowler-hatted, across St James's Park on a summer morning to the Courts; McCardie, J., presiding over a tedious case in Kings Bench IV, sucking sweets and twitching his ermine cuffs; my longed-for Mr Hardie travelling down to Norfolk on the Friday evening train in his old tweeds, his mackintosh stuffed with sweets and magazines; the golfer thin-lipped on the tee as his topped drive scuttles into the rough; the principal speaker rising at the Horatian Society three months before his death to propose the toast of Quintus Horatius Flaccus; the tired guest climbing into bed after he'd rolled up his clothes like the Georgians did and stuffed them in a drawer...

One by one the painted slides go by: a magic lantern, but who planned the show? I'm sure that the powerful character of his mother – the grandmother I never met – played a significant part. Mrs McCardie was an able woman, but she was painfully shy as a girl and emotionally insecure. By Victorian standards she married late, socially below her station and not, it would seem, for love. Her husband, never very 'respectable', was prosperous when she married him, much less so when he died. But she soon learned to come to terms with misfortune and, faced with the task of bringing up seven young children as a widow, to assume the dominance generally asserted by a father. Ambitious for her sons, she looked to them to restore and surpass the social standing of her own family, the Hunts. 'I think a position in society is a legitimate object of ambition,' Henry James blandly observed. Carlyle had been harsher in 1843: 'What is the hell of the modern English soul? With hesitation, with astonishment, I announce it to be the terror of "Not Succeeding".' An almost frantic search for acceptability in the right quarters was no less strong twenty years later, and Mrs McCardie, more even than her husband, was acutely conscious of it. Call it snobbery if you like.

Two of her sons lacked the calibre she looked for – indeed, Arthur proved a positive nuisance; two had it, William, the eldest, and Harry, her favourite. There was only enough money to send one son to university: William went to Cambridge and became a doctor. Harry was as clever as William, but a late developer, wayward, engaging, a bit feckless, disappointing at school, uncertain what course to take, a boy on whom her ambition was waiting to settle. Like all children, he could sense his mother's unspoken expectations, her need that he should make his mark. The Victorian ethic of striving and attainment had been dinned into him, as his early notebooks show. When after some messing about, he discovered a profession – the law – for which he was ideally suited, his latent talents were lit up. He applied himself with astonishing industry and self-denial. His mother encouraged and financially supported him in the early days when briefs were few. He only left home when she died, the last to go. He secured her love absolutely, but at a price. It was no hindrance, rather the reverse, to the development of his intellectual powers or, indeed, of his social graces, but it impoverished his emotional development. What had given him courage as a boy threatened to smother him as a man. The rebellious self he had suppressed was never assimilated. In his long climb to the Bench he was acting in line with its pressures and it fuelled his indefatigable industry and steady success. But it also fuelled alien compulsions which emerged, increasingly, in forms he had no rational control over: moods of depression, impetuous acts, reckless gambling (and a moneyed man must gamble deep before he feels the thrill of losing), the terrifying tedium always lying in wait, hidden anger against the Establishment and in the end, suicidally, against himself. He was wary of intimacy, at his best in company to which he was largely indifferent, careful to dodge emotional commitment. Marriage, for instance. Women of parts set off alarm signals, threatening to provoke a situation which mimicked the early experience of his mother's implacable love. He idealised that love in his conscious mind – to her, he said, he owed more than he could ever tell. But his judgements tell a different story. He speaks there constantly of women as inferiors; and he chose for himself only those women whom he could dominate and so feel secure with.

Mayna was one such. The wide gulf in their backgrounds cemented their attraction for each other. His affection and concern for her is not in doubt, but he wanted the comforts of marriage without its responsibilities. A formal acknowledgement of her as his wife would have wreaked havoc with the secret self he had built up, socially and psychologically. And why, he thought, hook love and marriage together? To unhook parenthood from marriage proved more awkward, but matters could surely be satisfactorily arranged. He did his best to see they were – to shoehorn me into the respectable middle class, to ensure that I had a reasonable education and so to protect me from the scandal of his own action. But he failed. I never made it. I never lost the consciousness of being 'different'. I was as unwilling as he was, but for other reasons, to get too close to my friends; I was marked with an invisible brand. If I seemed to succeed, it was because (if the tautology may be permitted) I was successful. If I hadn't been, I would soon have slipped back, because I had no ambition to go forward. I'd no wish to climb the ladders I was expected to climb – at school, at university, in the RAF, in the Civil Service. It was simply that, having been pushed on them, I was desperate to avoid the humiliation of falling off. In giving me the privilege of life but withholding the privilege of legitimacy, my father thus left me the worse for wear. He did his best not to – I did not realise what comfort I derived from his presence until he was no longer there – and I don't blame him. I just record it as a fact. With Mayna, while I can see clearly how it all happened, I can't absolve him from blame. He took what he wanted and she found herself alone, her emotional life sadly centred round someone she could never possess and perhaps never really knew: she loved the man she took him for.

With Kate it was much the same. Having avoided marriage with Mayna, he had no thought of entering into it with Kate. The social and personal consequences, given his position and his reputation, would have been no less unwelcome. Besides, there wasn't a child – he didn't intend to make the same mistake twice. Kate, moreover, was tougher. She was closer to the women of today in valuing independence and exhibiting a certain freedom of behaviour and sexual tolerance. She had few scruples in that regard, as the lakeside deception of her sister showed. Had she been prettier, she might well have deployed her attributes in a ruthless way. I didn't know her, of course, and I may have misjudged her. She was equally devastated by his death. In thinking about the bond between them, I'm reminded of Dr Johnson with his adamantine common sense:

> 'Marriage, Sir, is much more necessary to a man than to a woman: for he is much less able to supply himself with domestic comforts. You will recollect my saying to some ladies the other day that I had often wondered why young women should marry, as they have so much more freedom, and so much more attention paid to them while unmarried, than when married. I did not mention the *strong* reason for their marrying – the *mechanical* reason.' BOSWELL. 'Why that *is* a strong one. But does not imagination make it much more important than it is in reality? Is it not, to a certain degree, a delusion in us as well as in women?' JOHNSON. 'Why yes, Sir; but it is a delusion that is always beginning again.'

My father may have died for want of a wife; but Kate did not suffer, I'm sure, for want of a husband, however much her sister, divorce notwithstanding, sought to persuade her otherwise.

For good reasons my father kept his public and private lives entirely separate. His public life fulfilled, or nearly did, his worldly ambitions, gave him status and money and intellectual satisfaction. The law fascinated him and its rewards were necessary to him. He liked to be among those whose opinion mattered. He was not conceited, but he was proud of his standing in the world and jealous to keep it safe. His private life, on the other hand, satisfied an almost contradictory set of expectations – a desire for mechanical satisfaction in the Johnsonian sense, without commitment and emotional demands, a craving for secrecy and risk, a need to fend off an inexplicable sense of loss as he grew older – a kind of grief for what had not been. Whilst seeming so accessible, he was always moving out of reach. He was free with all he had, except himself. This was true of his dealings with men as well as women. Charming and friendly, ready to listen and generous with help, he was not a clubbable man. The Athenaeum and the Reform didn't see much of him. The kind of life he led was not such as to foster abiding friendships. His relationships were warm, but made in the knowledge that he could walk out when he wanted to and shut the door.

All this seems to fit. But I'm left with an uneasy feeling that it comes out too pat and a little askew. Generations of psychiatrists, as Rebecca West said, have laid the blame for all our unhappiness at the mother's tired feet. My father would have called for documentary evidence, of which I have little or none, and pointed out that his private life and its springs were nobody else's business, even his mistresses'; and that anyway how could I possibly know what went on in his mind, or in Mayna's, or in Kate's for that matter? Curiosity is a dangerous guide and it might be safer, he would have advised had he been in my place, to settle for the simplest explanation – the disposition he was born with. His giant power of work was more than some freak of his bringing-up. He was dealt a marvellous hand, but there were hereditary jokers in the pack. A history of melancholy and instability – his aunt Marie Theresa, his sister Carrie – and of gambling existed in his family, and one does not have to look to his upbringing to account for them. It was his misfortune to inherit great talents yoked to a courageous, humane but suspect temperament.

In any event his private affairs, fascinating as they are to me, were not central to his life. Idealisation of personal relations may be one of the reasons why marriage has become so shaky and my father, in preferring lesser bonds with lesser expectations (and being immune from the problems encountered by men of property in attending to their dynastic needs), may have been ahead of his time in this as in other ways. He was certainly one of those for whom their work is the chief part of life and gives most meaning to it. His love of the law was abiding and fulfilled his deepest needs. It would be wrong to say that personal relations were peripheral, but they were less important. His heart was where his talent blossomed.

He was not a great advocate, but his long stint as a junior, combined with his exceptional memory, his acute tactical sense, his discretion, his industry and his total reliability, attracted a volume of business which was unexampled in his time – or probably since. He was popular at the Bar by reason not only of his easy camaraderie, but also his scrupulous fairness to opponents. He was equally successful with Judges as with juries. He seemed to have just the sort of central mind which the Judiciary required. When he was elevated to the Bench the expectation was that he would be a lawyer's Judge, not a Judge who would interest the general public.

That expectation proved wrong. He *was* a Judge of interest to the general public; he made sure of that himself. As a Judge in the legal sense, his promise was not fulfilled. He never got into the premier league. He hadn't the questing mind of a Devlin or a Scarman; and his learning, though wide and deep, wasn't expanded by the historical perspectives of someone like Pollock. Nor in the field of common law, which is essentially Judge-made, was he prepared, as Denning was, to move the law forward and take exposed positions. This despite his reiteration of the need for adapting the common law to changing mores and his extolling of its merits – 'If this country were to sink tomorrow beneath the waves, the record of the Common Law of England would stand for ever on the noblest pages of history.' Perhaps he was made costive by his vast knowledge of precedents; perhaps he prized the need for certainty above the just result; perhaps he thought that legal tinkering on the margin in relation to the scale of reform he looked for would be like pissing in the sea. It wasn't for lack of courage that he seemed to draw back from judicial creativity. Divergence from the consensus is of course more difficult for trial Judges than for those higher up the hierarchy, but rumblings in the form of *obiter* can, as Devlin has said, give warning of unsettled weather ahead. That wasn't enough for McCardie. He made his personal views known loudly and unambiguously from the Bench. The tight control he exercised over his private affairs prevailed not at all in his public statements. He thus provoked a double criticism – first, that he didn't always do all he legitimately could to do justice between the parties before him, as in the case of the soldier seeking divorce mentioned in Chapter 16 (though, in fairness, this was early in his career as a Judge when he would be reluctant to invite rebuke and the Judicial climate was very different from today's); second, that his public championing of controversial causes put the impartiality of the Bench in jeopardy. I suppose he must have realised after the row about his judgement in the O'Dwyer libel case that he'd spiked his chances of promotion. After that he no longer felt inhibited. He was prepared to burn his boats. It spoke for his mettle and enthusiasm, but these weren't the qualities he was put there for. 'The disinterested application of the law,' Devlin said, calls for many virtues, such as balance, patience, courtesy and detachment, which leave little room for the ardour of a creative reformer... Enthusiasm is not and cannot be a judicial virtue. It means taking sides and, if a judge takes sides on such issues as homosexuality and capital punishment, he loses the appearance of impartiality and quite possibly impartiality itself.

In one assessment of his career mention is made of the verdict of Tacitus on the Emperor Tiberius: *Omnium consensu capax imperii nisi imperasset.* The parallel is apt. If he'd never held judicial office, McCardie would have been classed as an ideal candidate for the Bench. And at first he seemed to show himself to be exactly that. He brought to the job a clear, fresh mind, impulsive perhaps, but steeped in legal history. His mastery of the common law was unequalled (though he took rather too romantic a view of it). At the same time he was intensely curious about contemporary life in all its aspects. But, while holding opinions on the desirability of flogging and the sanctity of Empire which would have done credit to the heavy brigade at the Athenaeum, he showed himself in other areas to be radical to his boot-straps. He developed a habit of putting his finger on the roots of attitudes and institutions which were most sensitive to criticism and most unaccustomed to being touched. His zeal for change and his taste for rebellion caused him to make pronouncements both on the Bench and off it in terms designed to attract the attention of the sensational Press, whose darling he duly became. He never played safe. The views he canvassed, at least most of them, may seem sound enough today, even commonplace, but they didn't then; and anyway the Bench was not the place to promote them. As a consequence he acquired the reputation for partisanship which did neither him nor his office any good. Even sympathetic colleagues felt he was going too far and privately told him so; some less sympathetic, like Lord

Justice Scrutton, could not refrain from administering a public rebuke.

These criticisms hurt. He cared deeply what other people thought about him. Yet he often chose deliberately to provoke criticism – partly just in order to make things happen. A strong vein of rebelliousness, long repressed, was always struggling to get out and made him reckless, even on his own showing. Rebelliousness can fill a void, but it creates one too; and if, as in my father's case, it flouts the professional ethos in which the rebel's self-esteem is rooted, the emptiness created can be deeper than before. Judges notoriously represent 'the opinions of the day before yesterday'; McCardie was advancing the opinions of the day after tomorrow. This was a tribute to his percipience and magnanimity, but by stripping himself of the rules, he stripped himself of the support of the rules. Prudence and practical wisdom and, in the last resort, self-preservation, should have told him to go easy. It was absence of the latter qualities that precluded the further advancement which Gordon Hewart had forecast for him and for which his unusual talents otherwise fitted him. Had he been clubbable, he might have been more cautious.

A willingness to override convention in favour of duty is a fine sentiment. The difficulty for McCardie was how to tell where his duty really lay and act accordingly. He lacked the spirit of moderation: he was either saying something indiscreet or doing something indiscreet. The sensible thing would have been to retire and expound his views as a private individual. He more than once intended to retire and to break the shackles which his judicial status imposed on him. He rattled the chains, but he couldn't shake them off. The time was never right. Either he liked the law – and its trappings – too much, or he could not afford to lose the money. Latterly both. Naturally he seized any chance of putting his views across in public lectures and meetings, for which he was in constant demand. But he was aware that expressing them from the

Bench gave them a 'bite' which they wouldn't have had otherwise. Some of his apparently impulsive utterances from the Bench were, I'm certain, less impulsive than they seemed. He knew very well that unless you go overboard you don't make a splash. Besides, it was exhilarating. No doubt he also wanted to bring together in one synthesis his love of the law as a guardian of stability and his intense desire to see reform of some of the satellite systems that circulate round it – the problems of marriage, sexual relations and the like. His Court was his stamping ground. That's where he wanted to say what he had to say.

Being profoundly unconventional, though wedded to a deeply conventional profession, the conflict in his mind between the deference for authority fostered by case law, 'the codeless myriad of precedent, the wilderness of single instances' where he prowled about with such relish, and the free play of a critical intellect and a sympathetic heart became evident from the start of his judicial career. He was not religious, but he was a man who, but for the grace of God, might have been a renegade bishop. He became increasingly troubled by the problems of social deprivation, obscurantism and plain prejudice which came before him every day and which he made it his business in his systematic way to find out more about. He brought to bear a simple calculus: are they defensible by reason? Do they contribute to human happiness? Are they consistent with individual dignity?

'Most judges,' said Laski, 'are vaccinated against speculation by their careers at the Bar.' Against the sort of speculation Laski was talking about (but unfortunately not the other sort), McCardie's vaccination simply didn't take; instead he caught the disease badly and exhibited the most florid of symptoms. God knows, his years of repetitive toil at the Bar should have given him a lethal dose of professional deformation; yet it didn't. Out of it emerged a caring, free-thinking individual. Never having been a KC, he had none of 'the barnacles of singularity' which too often become attached to the successful silk. But more than that, he had left King Edward's at sixteen and was self-taught. Neither school nor university had given him the conventional going-over, so that he brought to the Bench, besides immense physical resilience and plenty of brains, an unusual combination of personal qualities. There's always a danger in talking about other people that you end up by attributing to them bits of yourself; but I sense that, like me, he never quite fitted in. He used society and its little hierarchies as a stairway to success, and he enjoyed the challenge of climbing up, but deep down he held no brief for it. He was subtly 'out of sync', an outsider wanting to be an insider, but staying an outsider still. His grossly excessive tipping may have been symptomatic. In part it was a reflection of the way he was made, but in part it was a reaction to his experience.

In an acutely status-conscious society, he was excluded from his colleagues' shared ethos of public school and university. Invitations to country house parties and shooting partridges in season couldn't make up for it. He did become a Freemason (like his brother William), but half-heartedly; its curious boy-scout rituals did not appeal to him. The comradeship of the Bar Mess he literally had no time for in his busy years and when he became a Judge that potential consolation was also taken away. A Judge is cut off, victim of a strange condition. An element of remoteness is an inescapable feature of the job. He can't go to a pub and jug it up with the boys. He can't have rows in shops. He has to watch his invitations. He suddenly becomes a member of a very small circle – much smaller then than now – with a strong esprit de corps which he transgresses at his peril, as McCardie learned. He was pressing for social reforms among colleagues who showed no relish for the change. Lawyers are not naturally interested in such reforms any more than policemen are. McCardie, always telling people what they didn't want to hear, must have been a constant irritant. The more celebrated and influential he became outside this little society, the more insecure he grew within it; and the more preoccupied with his inner conflicts. He was gambling heavily. Every human being has things which in the long run he can neither assimilate or forgo. Having achieved so much, my father could look to achieve no more. The fairy-tale castle he built had brought loneliness and despair; it was getting dark; he could hear the black dog sniffing about its walls; all he could do at the end was to pull the whole thing down about his ears.

One can't, perhaps fortunately, choose a father, but, if I had to choose one, I don't think I would have chosen a different one. Starting from nowhere, his achievements in a demanding profession were remarkable, even if his industry sometimes got in the way of his talent. His sympathies were wide, his intellectual curiosity irrepressible. He had a marvellous sense of fun. He blew away the cobwebs; it was nice to know he was around. Above all, he had courage, without which other qualities are no good at all. Extravagant he may have been, and impulsive, moody, addicted to wearing spats, in personal relations selfish and sometimes less than honest, with a liking for personal publicity which didn't do him any good. But he spoke up for the poor – there haven't been many on the Bench who did. He was never cold, he was never mean and he made two women reasonably happy.

His ephemeral reputation in the Press is not a fair measure of his stature. The 'tiny niche in legal history' that he hoped might be reserved for him is secure; to be described by a former Lord Chancellor as 'the greatest master of case law in our time' isn't a compliment easily earned. To read his judgements is like seeing a galleon in full sail, canvas spread, catching each breath of wind. To the rest of the fleet he might sometimes look to be carrying too much top-hamper and heading off station: a touch Nelsonian perhaps. But his faults were the mirror image of his virtues – his passion for gambling, for instance, was so entwined with what was admirable in his character that one can hardly separate them. Whatever his failings, at least respectability wasn't one of them; and he had the kind of enemies a man ought to have. He may have seemed more disingenuous than he was because the English look to truth as the basis of personal morality; whereas he, like the Italians and perhaps the Irish – his father's people – consider that charity and generosity are at least as important. It is tragic that a life which promised so much should end as it did. But, though I am left with a terrible feeling of waste, it wasn't a life wasted. He only took a short cut near the end. He started with nothing and ended with nothing, and that, in essence, is what we all do.

His niece Ruth would not have approved of this book. Let my uncle's achievements speak for him, she would have said; he should be judged by his best, keep quiet about the worst. I don't agree. Judged by his best, yes – leave out the worst, no. Athenians grew weary of hearing Aristides called 'The Just'. Truth has a cleansing power – we can't assess the weight of any man's achievement if we leave out of account his flaws and weaknesses. Rather, they help to point his achievement up. They're as much a part of the *thereness* of him as his virtues and help to make him dear to us. People sometimes conjure up an after-life where bodiless spirits, purged of their transgressions, chant for ever the praises of the Creator. Such an arrangement would surely cause both Him and us acute embarrassment. Sons want to know what their fathers have been up to and, if I were to meet my father again, I would want to meet him as he was, amusing, testy, obstinate, formidable sometimes, singing the songs he used to sing. A man's merits don't move us. It's when we remember one of his infuriating habits, or come across a tie he's worn or a line of his familiar handwriting, that our hearts melt.

* * *

Having come to the end, I find myself stranded in a kind of time-warp. On one side, an elderly man seems to be approaching out of the future, not the past: is he really me? On the other side, receding, small and clear as through the wrong end of a telescope, a young – well, not so young – barrister is walking arm in arm with his girl on the cliff top. Fields stretch back from the lighthouse, full of harebells and scabious and wild daisies, and scores of larks nest in the long grass and burst out skywards in little fountains of song. They were busy at it in my boyhood and I remember mornings bathed in the sad promise of summer when I would lie in the grass where lovers used to lie and listen to their music sprinkle on its whispering blades – chest high to me then – and watch the daisies wave like miniature trees above my head. Barrister and boy, linked so strangely together, had more in common than they knew. One thing for sure: they wouldn't recognise the place now – street lamps, double glazing, fitted kitchens, neatly parked cars. But the waves still roll towards the shore in exemplary formation, the unrespectable wind still sings its dirge in the dipping telephone wires. I feel once again the old, fierce loneliness; but also, I wonder why, a curious consolation.